the study of deviance:
perspectives and problems

DON C. GIBBONS
JOSEPH F. JONES

PORTLAND STATE UNIVERSITY

Prentice-Hall, Inc., Englewood Cliffs, New Jersey

Library of Congress Cataloging in Publication Data

GIBBONS, DON C
    The study of deviance.

    (Prentice-Hall sociology series)
    Includes bibliographical references.
    1. Deviant behavior. 2. Social problems.
I. Jones, Joseph F., 1933–   joint author.
II. Title.
HM291.G49   301.6'2   74-12363
ISBN 0-13-858936-4

To Carmen and Suzanne

10 9 8 7 6 5 4 3

Printed in the United States of America

The quotation on pages 98 and 99 is reprinted by permission of Indiana University Press from *The Sutherland Papers*, edited by Albert Cohen, Alfred Lindesmith, and Karl Schuessler, © 1956 by Indiana University Press, Bloomington. Now available from the University of Chicago Press in a revised edition entitled *Edwin H. Sutherland: On Analyzing Crime*, © 1973.

The quotation on pages 156 and 157 is reprinted from Stanton Wheeler, "Socialization in Correctional Institutions," in David A. Goslin (Ed.), *Handbook of Socialization Theory and Research*, © 1969 by Rand McNally and Company, Chicago, pp. 1019–1021. Reprinted by permission of Rand McNally College Publishing Company.

Prentice-Hall International, Inc., *London*
Prentice-Hall of Australia, Pty. Ltd., *Sydney*
Prentice-Hall of Canada, Ltd., *Toronto*
Prentice-Hall of India Private Limited, *New Delhi*
Prentice-Hall of Japan, Inc., *Tokyo*

contents

preface

There has been a large outpouring of works on the sociology of deviant behavior in recent years, ranging from relatively low-level, conceptually unsophisticated books full of descriptive materials on various forms of deviant conduct, through collections of observations on specific types of deviance, as well as several sophisticated theoretical treatises, and finally, to some relatively murky expositions upon the processes of becoming deviant. However, this book is different from any of the works described above. To begin with, it is addressed to a student audience rather than to professional sociologists. Its title highlights our emphasis on the activities that are engaged in by those sociologists who examine, probe, and scrutinize deviance. Our intent is to show the student what those who claim to study deviant behavior actually do in the way of intellectual pursuits. The book explicates the major explanatory problems within the field of deviance analysis, identifies many of the theories and hypotheses that have been offered in response to the questions posed, and takes note of various still unresolved conceptual issues in deviance analysis. The commentary centers on the major theoretical queries that need to be addressed whether the researcher intends to study criminality, suicide, mental disorder, or some other form of deviance. Thus, we note that certain core questions need to be asked about social-structural factors in all of these patterns of deviance. In much the same way, basic processes such as stigmatizing experiences can be examined across all of the specific forms of norm-violating conduct.

But *The Study of Deviance* is more than a primer on deviance analysis. The study of deviance is an area in which some of the most exciting contemporary sociology is being carried on. At the same time, the emerging perspectives on deviance are characterized by a good deal of ambiguity, fuzziness, and conceptual muddiness. We have endeavored to draw attention to a number of these places where repair work on the theoretical structure is in order.

This book is fairly devoid of various facts about how prostitutes learn their trade, social class variations among the mentally disordered, the social structure of armed robbery gangs, juvenile backgrounds of predatory criminals, or other material of that kind usually found in deviance textbooks. Even so, the book is directed primarily to a student audience. We hope that this work will be used in undergraduate courses where students are introduced to theoretical concerns regarding deviance as well as to a collection of titillating facts about social misconduct.

We received a good deal of help from Professors R. Kelly Hancock and Dennis D. Brissett in the development of this book. Also, the anonymous Prentice-Hall reviewers offered a number of important suggestions for additions and revisions in the manuscript, many of which have been incorporated into the final draft of the book. We wish to acknowledge the contributions of those reviewers. Mrs. Roslyn MacDonald, Ms. Marjie Lundell, and Ms. Kathy Grove carried the burden of typing various drafts of this material. We would also like to acknowledge the assistance given us by the Kaiser Foundation Health Services Research Center, Portland, Oregon. In the event that deviations from scholarly or editorial norms turn up in the book, each of us wishes to announce that the stigma belongs to the other author.

introduction

W hat is sociology? How does the sociologist study social deviance? What makes the sociological enterprise different from the psychological, legal, and journalistic attempts to understand human behavior? A broad answer is that the sociologist views these matters from a unique perspective, and thus he asks questions that are not entertained by the others. He also employs a particular set of terms and concepts in his work that are not part of the everyday vocabulary of nonsociologists.

The behavioral area of social deviance is one that has caught the attention of many sociologists in recent years, and a large specialized terminology has been developed to describe norm-violating conduct. Terms and concepts such as *anomie, primary deviance* and *secondary deviation, stigma, career contingency, putative deviation, stigma management, opportunity structures,* and *deviance disavowal* are among those words which sociologists find useful to communicate the results of their studies of deviance. This book introduces the terminology and concepts employed in the study of deviance so that the student can learn to talk and think like a sociologist. Then, it explicates the major questions posed and theoretical perspectives taken by those scholars who study deviant behavior. Thus, we aim to provide some answers to the questions raised at the beginning of this chapter and to help students understand social deviance from the sociological perspective.

THE STUDY OF DEVIANCE

It is fairly difficult to define the words *deviance* and *deviant* in terms that everyone will accept. On the one hand, many sociologists agree on specific kinds of social conduct which can be classified as deviant. Also, in practice "deviants" are often persons who are beyond the pale, caught up in various forms of socially condemned conduct. Thus, "deviance" is frequently equated with crime, drug addiction, juvenile delinquency, prostitution, homosexuality, and mental disorder. Although some theorists have suggested that deviance also ought to encompass persons who engage in malingering, skullduggery, chiseling, and other such peccadilloes, this conception has not yet become popular. For the most part, the study of deviance has been heavily concentrated upon "nuts, sluts, and preverts."[1]

Although most sociologists usually include crime, mental disorder, and other forms of conduct listed above in their inventories of "deviance," some have also included extramarital sexual behavior, birth control practices, militant students, married virgins, and flying saucer observers as examples of deviance. Accordingly, it would be difficult to develop a single short list of deviant conduct on which all sociologists would agree. Instead, the sociological literature is filled with idiosyncracies in which various instances of conduct are identified as deviant in one essay and not in others.

Consensus on the nature and scope of deviance is lacking among laymen as well. Citizens often exhibit a good deal of concern about many of the kinds of conduct studied by sociologists, although laymen are more likely to speak of hoods, junkies, queers, hookers, and crazies, than to use the more neutral language of the sociologist. Many people, however, also consider such disparate sorts as liars, career women, bearded men, divorcées, and motorcycle gang members as deviants or nonconformists.[2] In short, it would be a serious error to assume that terms such as *deviance* and *deviant behavior* have the same meaning among sociologists or among nonsociologists.

Sociologists usually offer a definition of deviance as behavior that violates institutionalized expectations or behavior that represents departure from societal norms, while the deviant is defined as one who does those things. There is a good deal of confusion, however, about the meaning of such words as *institutionalized expectations.* Similarly, sociological unanimity is lacking on the notion of a norm, and there are some who would argue that few, if any, societal norms actually exist. This contention goes beyond the observation about terminological ambiguity and claims that some of the elements included in theoretical definitions of deviance do not actually exist. We shall have more to say about these issues in chapter four.

Lack of clear key terms and concepts thus characterizes the field of deviance study. New and rapidly growing subject areas in sociology and other social sciences have usually arisen from broad perspectives and rough conceptual notions that define the boundaries of the phenomena to be examined and that direct attention to some of the important questions to be answered regarding the behavior. Fields of study grow by increments, and theories and hypotheses are refined as investigators accumulate empirical evidence; this evolution of an area of study from creation to maturity takes a good deal of time.

The study of deviance is at a relatively early stage of development, as shown by the large number of conceptual quarrels among social analysts. Many of these arguments center around the meaning of unclear terminology rather than the adequacy of empirical evidence concerning some clearly delineated hypothesis regarding deviant behavior. On this point, Paul Rock has noted that: "The sociology of deviance is emerging as a distinctive perspective on problems of rule-breaking and social control. Among its integral features is an antipathy toward the systematization of its ideas. This antipathy has allowed the developing perspective to maintain contradictory positions on important issues."[3]

Three main lines of work have been conducted by students of deviance. First, as we have already noted, there has been much *conceptual elaboration* in which sociologists have concentrated on new concepts such as "putative deviation" to be used in the study of deviance. Second, a relatively large number of *particularistic insights and gross hypotheses* about deviant behavior have been offered in the sociological literature. For example, much has been heard about the alleged harmful effects of social labeling on identified deviants. A number of theorists have argued that singling individuals out as criminal or mentally ill, particularly when this labeling is accompanied by incarceration in an institution, ineluctably drives them further into a career in nonconformity. The problem with such claims is not that they are wrong, but that they are too broad and imprecise. As we shall see in chapter eight, empirical events are much more complex than suggested in these contentions. In turn, the existing evidence on the consequences of being labeled and processed as a deviant indicates that they are far from uniform. The impact of labeling depends on such things as the nature of the nonconformist behavior, the identity of the labelers, and countless other factors.

The third feature of this area of interest involves inordinate attention to *empirical observations* about behavioral activities among certain deviant groups. In recent years we have been besieged with reports on how teen-age prostitutes "turn out," the learning of sexual techniques such as fellatio by prostitutes, data on how homosexuals conduct themselves in their fleeting episodes of sexual behavior in public rest rooms, the activities of middle-class "swingers," or the social division of labor among participants in armed robberies or among alcoholic drinking gangs.

Descriptions of how deviants go about their business are often useful in revealing to the uninitiated the activities of social worlds with which they are unfamiliar. Then too, these reports frequently serve to "normalize" the deviant by showing him to be involved in fairly mundane and ordinary conduct. For example, empirical reports on the social bonds and activities among homosexuals suggest that homosexuals are almost like heterosexuals because members of both categories are better described in terms of their employment activities, friendship ties, and recreational activities than in terms of their sexual preferences. Like the heterosexual, the homosexual is a person who spends most of his time doing things that have little or no relationship to his sexual orientation.

Although we do not wish to belittle the importance of rich empirical descriptions of deviant performance, in our view, more attention ought to be given in deviance books to explication of the major dimensions of the field, that is, to identification of the larger themes and contentions to which these descriptive details should be tied. Furthermore, the student ought to be introduced to the conceptual and empirical issues that perplex those who are engaged in the serious probing of the dynamics of deviance.[4]

The pages to follow certainly are not entirely devoid of empirical observations about the real world of deviance. On the contrary, chapter five discusses studies of social perceptions and attitudes toward nonconformity, and chapter eight covers a very large collection of investigations on the effects of social labeling experiences. Other observational reports on rule-breaking behavior can be found throughout the remainder of the book. Even so, this volume differs from many others that have appeared in recent years in that it contains relatively few of the descriptive details found in other texts.

DEVIANTS AND SOCIOLOGISTS

In a provocative essay some years ago, Howard S. Becker posed the question, "Whose Side are We On?"[5] He took pains to argue that in the study of social behavior generally, and in the examination of deviant activity in particular, a value-neutral or objective, detached stance cannot be maintained. For example, if we study a prison setting or a mental hospital, we can look at matters from the point of view of the guards and keepers *or* from the perspective of the inmates, but we cannot avoid taking sides with one group or another. If we assign credibility to the picture of the patients or convicts maintained by the keepers we shall be accused of bias by the former, while if we tell the story from the inmates' standpoint, giving credence to their claims and complaints, we shall be charged by the officials with distortion. Similarly, if we present a portrayal of parolees that stresses the difficulties they encounter from pressures by their parole officers, someone is likely to berate us for a soft-headed and unwarranted sympathy for lawbreakers.[6] Even so, there is no way that we can take sides simultaneously with both parolees and parole agents. Although Becker does not explicitly advise us to do so, the sense of his thesis is that we ought to line up with the underdogs (deviants), for they need our attention and concern much more than do the overdogs (the agents of social control).[7] Further, when we portray the world of the underdogs as they experience it, we are likely to create sympathy and compassion for them and reduce the severity of social condemnation and rejection inflicted on them.

Examination of the recent sociological literature shows that most researchers on deviant behavior have in fact taken the underdogs' side and have presented accounts of life styles of prostitutes, homosexuals, criminals, and other nonconformists that are sympathetic to the deviants. The student of deviance usually shows liberal preferences in tolerance and sympathy for criminals, the mentally disordered, and other nonconformists.

Alvin W. Gouldner has criticized Becker severely in a witty but slightly unfair article in which he contends that Becker's position on taking sides is essentially conservative rather than radical.[8] Gouldner concedes that the underdog's position merits an airing when he argues: "The underdog's standpoint therefore deserves to be heard in sociology not because he alone lives in a world of suffering. A sociology of the underdog is justified because, and to the extent, that this suffering is less likely to be known and because—by the very reasons of his being underdog—the extent and character of his suffering are likely to contain much that is avoidable."[9]

At the same time, Gouldner claims that Becker and others are solicitous of deviants, not because of their suffering, but because of their quaint and exotic character. According to Gouldner, contemporary students of deviant behavior are often "zookeepers of deviance" who take pride in showing off the rare specimens they have uncovered in the urban zoo.[10] Further, he charges that much current discussion views deviants as victims of society who are neither responsible for their suffering nor for its alleviation. Instead, nonconformists are seen as social unfortunates who need to be managed by bureaucratic caretakers. Insofar as sides are taken, it is for the deviant and against the callous or incompetent agency bureaucrat. The social control structures themselves are not attacked; instead, the posture is an ameliorative one calling for improvements in these organizations. According to Gouldner, this posture is consistent with the ideology of the welfare state which fails to "see deviance as deriving from specified master institutions of this larger society, or as expressing an active opposition to them."[11] A more radical analysis of the kind encouraged by Gouldner would direct more attention to basic defects in the structure of modern society and would devote much less concern to the activities of individual deviants.

These themes have been voiced even more stridently by Alexander Liazos.[12] He charges that, although theorists express as one of their main concerns the humanization and normalization of the deviant, the emphasis on the social category of deviant may actually have the opposite effect. Persistent use of the label and concentrating attention only on certain deviants tends to reinforce our feelings that nonconformists are truly different from the rest of us.

Liazos has much to say about one-sided attention to a restricted segment of the deviant population. He notes that analysis continues to center upon garden-variety deviants who are relatively powerless. Thus, he contends: "As a result of the fascination with 'nuts, sluts, and preverts' and their identities and subcultures, little attention has been paid to the unethical, illegal, and destructive actions of powerful individuals, groups, and institutions in our society."[13] Liazos also argues that sociological discussions of violence in American society are defective, for they portray it as restricted to slum dwellers, certain minority groups, street gangs, and "motorcycle beasts." He maintains that the proper study of violence would focus upon *covert institutional violence* in the form of oppression, consumer exploitation through the sale of defective and dangerous products, mass destruction of people and the landscape in Viet Nam, the Watergate affair, and various other kinds of violence and exploitation which are central to this political and social order.[14] Liazos would have us banish "deviance" from sociological inquiry in favor of the phenomena of oppression, persecution, and suffering, for by failing to do so "we neglect conditions of inequality, powerlessness, institutional violence, and so on, which lie at the basis of our tortured society.."[15]

Parallel claims have been advanced by Alex Thio, who charges that the sociology of deviance both past and present is strongly class biased.[16] In his view:

> The class bias reveals itself through either one, or, more frequently, both of the following modi operandi: (1) In research strategy, students of deviance tend to follow the conventional, stereotyped lead in tracking down deviance, focusing on the deviance of the powerless class but relatively neglecting the deviance of the powerful. As a result, they either explicitly or implicitly suggest that the powerless are generally more

deviant than the powerful. (2) In explaining the etiology of deviance, they tend to concentrate on the individual deviant or his immediate milieu and thus avoid analysis of the established power structure in their society. The sociologists of deviance may be said to tacitly support the power elite because both their research and analysis imply that the powerful are not only morally superior but should not be held responsible for *causing* deviance within their society. (emphasis in the original)[17]

Thio is not content merely to hurl the charge of class bias, because he also calls for inquiry into the deviance of overdogs and into the causal processes through which the power structure creates deviant underdogs. Similar themes are now voiced by some criminologists who call for a shift of attention toward the crimes of the powerful.[18] According to these writers, we need to abandon conventional liberal perspectives in favor of criminological radicalism. We are urged to inquire into racism, sexism, capitalistic exploitation of the oppressed at home and in other lands, and other phenomena which cause criminality. Some radical criminologists would even advocate creating a new society based on socialist principles as the solution to the crime problem.[19]

Our own views on these issues can be stated fairly briefly. First, we agree that much sociological discussion of deviants presents a relatively sympathetic view of the tribulations of the norm violator. Second, as Liazos suggests, the recent emphasis on deviance as a field of inquiry has probably inadvertently contributed to the portrayal of deviants as behaviorally quite distinct from nondeviants. Stereotypical thinking which characterizes deviants as engaged in bizarre acts and which divides the world into the "good guys" and "bad guys" or "deviants" and "normals" has probably been encouraged by sociological writings, in spite of frequent admonitions by the theorist that deviance is mundane and commonplace, marked off from conformity only by degrees rather than in absolute terms. For example, even though the writer or lecturer strives to communicate a sense that homosexuals differ little from those who exhibit other sexual preferences, an opposite impression may sometimes unwittingly be conveyed by his observations. Similarly, criminological discussions may well lead many to imagine that criminals are a separate and dangerous class of citizens, in spite of research findings to the contrary. In much the same way, sociological analyses of drug addicts may often encourage among laymen "drug fiend" beliefs about narcotics users, even though contrary evidence is offered in these analyses. In all likelihood, students frequently emerge from college courses on deviance with their stereotyped notions reinforced rather than undermined by class discussions. At the very least, we need to guard against tendencies to be zookeepers of deviance, dragging out bizarre specimens for social audiences to examine. The sociological task is to enlighten and inform rather than to entertain.

We also concede that Liazos, Thio, and others are correct in their claims that deviant acts on the part of those in power have received little attention by sociologists and that theorizing has been fairly silent regarding racism, sexism, or capitalistic exploitation as sources of deviance. Our explanatory theories have stopped far short of implicating the master institutions of society in the production of mundane forms of deviance or in the violations of the social elites or overdogs.

We agree that more attention to racism, sexism, and domestic and international oppression is in order; but, we would point out that those who have urged a more radical posture upon us and who have argued for the study of racism and other forms of oppression have not managed to move very far beyond polemical expressions regarding the need for new directions of inquiry.[20] No radical theory of deviance has been produced to date. Much more hard intellectual work is in order if we are to trace in detail the interrelationships between the forms of deviant conduct and such phenomena as racism and oppression.[21] We will return to this matter in chapter six, where we will consider a number of the sociological theories that have been offered regarding social-structural patterns and deviance. Several of the social conflict or radical arguments about deviance and criminality that have been put forth will be examined in that chapter.

SUMMARY

This chapter has noted the relatively inchoate form of the study of deviance along with some of the major lines of endeavor that have been pursued. We have examined several recent arguments which have encouraged us to focus on phenomena that have not heretofore been given much scrutiny by sociologists. Let us now turn in chapter two to a brief summary of the major intellectual currents that have preceded the modern study of deviance.

NOTES

[1] Alexander Liazos, "The Poverty of the Sociology of Deviance: Nuts, Sluts, and Preverts," *Social Problems* 20 (Summer 1972): 103–20.

[2] Jerry L. Simmons, *Deviants* (Berkeley: Glendessary Press, 1969), p. 3.

[3] Paul Rock, "Phenomenalism and Essentialism in the Sociology of Deviance," *Sociology* 7 (January 1973): 17–29.

⁴ Although we intend to comment on a number of the conceptual and logical difficulties that plague the field of deviance, we do not pretend to offer rigorous solutions to those problems. Articulation of a formal theory or theories of deviance goes well beyond the purposes of this text. On these matters, see Charles W. Lachenmeyer, *The Language of Sociology* (New York: Columbia University Press, 1971); Jack Gibbs, *Sociological Theory Construction* (Hinsdale, Ill.: Dryden Press, 1972); a witty essay on these matters is Clifford D. Shearing, "How to Make Theories Untestable: A Guide to Theorists," *The American Sociologist* 8 (February 1973): 33–37.

⁵ Howard S. Becker, "Whose Side Are We On?" *Social Problems* 14 (Winter 1967): 239–47.

⁶ For an example of such a report, see John Irwin, *The Felon* (Englewood Cliffs, N.J.: Prentice-Hall, 1970).

⁷ Although Becker pays most attention to the agents of social control as overdogs, he also includes exponents of "the popular morality" from the broader community in the community of overdogs.

⁸ Alvin W. Gouldner,"The Sociologist as Partisan: Sociology and the Welfare State," *The American Sociologist* 3 (May 1968): 103–16. Gouldner's critique is not entirely fair or well reasoned. For example, he argues that because Becker stresses labeling processes as central to the deviance-defining processes, he should take the side of the labelers and social control personnel, but he appears to side with those who are labeled, the underdogs. But, one could just as logically argue that Becker's theory and sentiments dispose him to side with the deviants.

⁹ Ibid., p. 106.

¹⁰ Ibid.

¹¹ Ibid., p. 107.

¹² Liazos, "The Poverty of the Sociology of Deviance."

¹³ Ibid., p. 111.

¹⁴ Ibid.

¹⁵ Ibid., p. 119.

¹⁶ Alex Thio, "Class Bias in the Sociology of Deviance," *The American Sociologist* 8 (February 1973): 1–12.

¹⁷ Ibid., p. 1.

¹⁸ See, for example: Richard Quinney, "The Ideology of Law: Notes for a Radical Alternative to Repression," *Issues in Criminology* 7 (Winter 1972): 1–35; Quinney, "Crime Control in Capitalistic Society: A Critical Philosophy of Legal Order," *Issues in Criminology* 8 (Spring 1973): 75–99; David M. Gordon, "Class and the Economics of Crime," *Review of Radical Political Economics* 3 (Summer 1971): 51–75; Ian Taylor, Paul Walton, and Jock Young, *The New Criminology* (London: Routledge and Kegan Paul, 1973). The historical shifts from conservative to liberal-cynical to radical criminology have been discussed in Don C.

Gibbons and Peter G. Garabedian, "Conservative, Liberal, and Radical Criminology: Some Trends and Observations," in Charles E. Reasons, ed., *The Criminologist: Crime and the Criminal* (Pacific Palisades, Calif.: Goodyear Publishing Co., 1974).

[19] Quinney, "Crime Control in Capitalistic Society," p. 95; this solution is also implied strongly in Gordon, "Class and the Economics of Crime."

[20] However, some hints as to the directions that radical sociology might take can be found in Albert Szymanski, "Toward a Radical Sociology," *Sociological Inquiry* 40 (Winter 1970): 3–11; J. David Colfax and Jack L. Roach, eds., *Radical Sociology* (New York: Basic Books, 1971).

[21] For some beginning stabs at this problem, see Gordon, "Class and the Economics of Crime"; Charles Perrow, *The Radical Attack on Business* (New York: Harcourt Brace Jovanovich, 1972); William J. Chambliss and Robert B. Seidman, *Law, Order, and Power* (Reading, Mass.: Addison-Wesley Publishing Co., 1971); Stuart L. Hills, *Crime, Power, and Morality* (Scranton, Pa.: Chandler Publishing Co., 1971).

social pathology,
social problems,
social disorganization,
and deviance

Those matters which sociologists examine under such labels as *social problems, social pathology, social disorganization,* and *deviance* arise from their observations of human behavior. These sociological labels are used to describe problems which concern many laymen as well, although the nonprofessional might use words such as *bad people, crazy persons, queers, radicals,* or *hoodlums* to describe similar problems. The particular forms of deviance which provoke public concern may change, but the process of singling out some activities as beyond the pale is a basic social process. Public identification of aberrant, unusual, or nonconformist conduct often grows out of the laymen's concern that these activities pose some threat to social order, that they constitute a social problem or manifestation of social disorganization.[1]

Many sociological treatises dealing with collections of variously defined social ills have been written since the beginning of modern sociology in the United States. In addition, college courses on the topic have been among the most popular of sociology department offerings. Examination of a sample of books on the topic shows that many of them pay detailed attention to crime and juvenile delinquency, suicide, mental disorder, alcoholism, sexual misconduct, and drug addiction. In more recent books, concern has also been voiced regarding warfare, civil disorder and urban rioting, unemployment, racial discrimination, and other problems of complex urban societies.[2]

It would be a mistake, however, to suppose that an unbroken historical pattern of analysis can be discerned in these books, or that sociologists have consistently addressed themselves to these phenomena from a traditional and shared conceptual perspective. Instead, these matters of public concern were at one time examined as instances of social problems or social disorganization, while recently a set of views stressing social deviance and deviant behavior has been applied to them. As we shall see in the passages to follow, these orientations represent different ways of looking at crime, vice, and mental disorder. The level of sophistication of sociological analysis has also varied. Modern perspectives on nonconforming behavior are a good deal richer, more detailed, and more sociological than were earlier formulations. This introductory section traces some of the major stages which preceded the development of deviant behavior theories and includes some remarks about the sociological study of deviance.[3]

SOCIAL PATHOLOGY

The social pathologists of the early 1900s were sociologists concerned with various forms of behavior which they considered morally outrageous and worthy of condemnation. These early pathologists talked in terms of medical metaphors, and their harangues likened societal conditions to diseases and defects in physical organisms. When these early observers railed against crime or prostitution, it was as though they were directing attention to social abscesses or lesions within an otherwise healthy social organism.

Several critics of the early social pathology viewpoint have noted that this perspective was one in which pathological conditions were defined in terms of the private moral standards of the sociologist.[4] Pathological conditions were those patterns and activities which "everyone knows" are "bad." Also, the social pathology viewpoint was characterized by a very low level of conceptualization, both with regard to its identification of pathological conditions and to its analysis of the etiology of these conditions. Explanations of pathological conditions were often *ad hoc* in character, rather than applications of some overarching theory regarding the genesis of social pathology. These explanations usually stressed bad home situations, idleness, or other social conditions bordering on "sinfulness" or "wickedness." Rarely did any observers entertain the hypothesis that at least some of the forms of pathology might be useful or functional within the society in which they were found.[5] For example, few of them saw any link between prostitution and societal conditions which generate a demand for purchasable sexual intercourse.

Edwin M. Lemert has provided an illuminating description of these early social pathologists:

> Generally speaking, these late nineteenth and early twentieth century sociologists grouped together under the heading of "social pathology," those human actions which ran counter to ideals of residential stability, property ownership, sobriety, thrift, habituation to work, small business enterprise, sexual discretion, family solidarity, neighborliness, and discipline of the will. In effect, social problems were considered to be any forms of behavior violating the mores from which these ideals were

projected. The mores behind the ideals, for the most part, were those of rural, small-town, and middle-class America, translated into public policy through the rural domination of county boards of supervisors and state legislatures and through the reform activities of humanitarian social workers and Protestant religious federations. In this connection, we note with special interest that many of the early writers on social pathology lived their more formative years in rural communities and small towns; often, too, they had had theological training and experience, so that it was only natural that they should look upon many forms of behavior associated with urban life and industrial society as destructive of moral values they cherished as universally good and true.[6]

Sociological texts dealing with social pathology abounded in the early 1900s, as did allied works such as criminology books with a social pathology perspective.[7] The last work to receive the title *Social Pathology* was Lemert's classic volume written in 1951. But the only point of similarity between that book and earlier works on social pathology was the title, for Lemert's book is a pioneering statement of many viewpoints which have been incorporated into contemporary thought on deviance. The social pathology orientation has long been obsolete.

THE STUDY OF SOCIAL PROBLEMS

Whereas the social pathologists took their topics for study from their own moral views, students of social problems concentrate on the general citizenry. Thus, both early investigators and contemporary students define social problems as conditions which a significant segment of citizens believe should be ameliorated.[8] But we see a shift of the sociologist from diagnostician of social ills or pathology to social reporter and critic. In the latter role, he identifies social problems as any conditions which trouble citizens. Conversely, if a situation which the sociologist regards as undesirable is not so defined by the public (or some powerful segment of it), then it is not a social problem.[9] The sociologist's own views of morality are not to intrude into his study of social problems.

There are two central tasks for those who study social problems. The first is the problem-defining process in which sociologists try to discover the conditions under which a social situation is likely to become identified as a problem by the public. In one of the clearest expositions of a social problems perspective, John I. Kitsuse and Malcolm Spector have recently argued that the problem-defining process is *the* distinctive subject matter for social problems analysis. They aver that:

. . . the explanation of the "subjective element" of social problems—the process by which members of groups or societies define a putative condition as a problem—is the distinctive subject matter of the sociology of social problems. Thus, we define social problems as *the activities of groups making assertions of grievances and claims with respect to some putative conditions.* The *emergence* of a social problem, then, is contingent on the organization of group activities with reference to defining some putative condition as a problem, and asserting the need for eradicating, ameliorating, or otherwise changing the condition. The central problem for a theory of social problems, so defined, is to account for the *emergence and maintenance of claim-making and responding activities.* Such a theory should comprehend the activities of any group making claims on others for ameliorative action, material remuneration, alleviation of social, political, legal, economic disadvantage or other consideration. (emphasis in the original)[10]

Objective social conditions are not always perceived in the same way by different observers. Prostitution, for example, may be a matter of lively concern in one community but may provoke no attention in another, even though the amount of prostitution is about the same in both communities. Or consider the findings of Maurice D. Van Arsdol, Jr., Georges Sabagh, and Francesca Alexander, who report that some citizens in Los Angeles who live in high smog areas perceive smog as a problem while others do not, and that some who do *not* live in areas of excessive smog nonetheless perceive smog to be a major annoyance in their neighborhood.[11] Students of social problems have devoted much effort in trying to discover the basic stages and elements operative in the problem-defining process and to define what has been termed by some "the natural history of social problems."[12]

In the second assignment, the investigator attempts to explain the genesis of various social problems. This chore also faces those who study deviant behavior, because their inquiry is directed at various aspects of social organization which are thought to cause, or to relate to the cause, of different social problems. Indeed, modern books on social problems or deviant behavior show such agreement on causal analysis that the contents of these texts are almost interchangeable. In short, whether the sociologist studies crime, alcoholism, or mental disorder as *social problems* or as *deviant behavior,* he is likely to use many of the same concepts. In either case, analysis rests heavily on the influence of social class factors, differentials in opportunities to achieve cultural goals, rapid social change, and the growing complexity and anonymity of urban life.

But the study of social problems and the analysis of deviant behavior are not entirely identical. We noted in chapter one that deviant behavior is usually identified as action which violates some identifiable conduct standard or norm. Since social problems are defined as conditions about which a large number of persons are concerned, social problems are not restricted to matters of norm violation. Indeed, the commonsense meaning of social problem is one which often draws attention to matters of technological complexity, such as smog or traffic congestion, rather than to breaches of social rules. Thus, some social problems, such as crime, are at the same time matters of norm violation and deviant behavior, and some social problems do not involve breaches of conduct rules so they are not considered cases of deviant behavior. Finally, there are some kinds of deviance which are not matters of general public concern, such as widespread employee pilferage or marital infidelity, and hence are not social problems. These relationships are shown in table 1.

table 1   Deviant Behavior and Social Problems

	DEVIANT BEHAVIOR	NONDEVIANT BEHAVIOR
SOCIAL PROBLEM	crime, mental disorder, alcoholism	smog, traffic congestion, air pollution
NONSOCIAL PROBLEM	employee pilferage, "swinging" and marital infidelity	socially acceptable behavior

SOCIAL DISORGANIZATION

The various social ills of modern society such as crime, mental disorder, suicide, and alcoholism, have also been approached from a "social disorganization" framework. In this perspective, a set of processes or patterns labeled as social disorganization has been used to explain certain undesirable forms of behavior. According to this argument, those societies which exhibit a high degree of social disorganization will also be found to contain much crime, alcoholism, and mental disorder. Conversely, however, these same social disorders have also sometimes been viewed as indicators or manifestations of social disorganization. Indeed, one problem with the social disorganization perspective in application has been that it has often been tautological or circular; it becomes impossible to distinguish the cause of social disorganization from the manifestation of it. Unless independent measures of social disorganization can be devised, the condition cannot be used to explain crime, mental disorder, or other problems.

Robert E. L. Faris has written one of the clearest expositions of social disorganization theory.[13] There is a curious logic in the way Faris (as well as many others) identifies the basic features of social disorganization. He begins by listing the characteristics of successful social organizations and uses simple, agrarian folk societies as a model. According to Faris:

> A successful society is one which constitutes a relatively stable system of coordinated activity among its members, which achieves a satisfactory adaptation to the physical surroundings in which the people live, and which enables the members to survive, propagate their kind, and carry on the generally accepted tasks of the group, whatever the members conceive these to be.[14]

In Faris's view, successful social organizations involve integration of customs, rich folk knowledge, effective teamwork and morale, and harmonious social relationships.[15] He points to folk societies as examples of social organizations with these characteristics. Anthropologist Robert Redfield describes these societies as small in size, isolated from surrounding cultures, having nonliterate populations, and depending on folk knowledge for solving problems.[16] In addition, they show strong group solidarity, little unconventional behavior, homogenous personality types, complex kinship relations, dependence upon folkways, and use of informal social controls rather than formal codes of law to control personal behavior. Existing societies approximate the folk society model, but both Faris and Redfield see the world's underdeveloped, agrarian nations as the closest fit to the model.

The syllogism followed by Faris is: successful social organizations possess certain specified characteristics; folk societies share these traits; the United States is not a folk society; therefore, the United States is characterized by social *dis*organization. No logician would honor that pattern of argument.

One empirical objection raised to the social disorganization theory is that simple folk societies are not as devoid of deviant and problem behavior as Faris and others assume. On this point, Nicholas J. Demerath has noted that mental disorders do not appear to be completely nonexistent in relatively primitive societies.[17] A similar conclusion flows out of the research of Joseph W. Eaton and Robert J. Weil, whose studies deal with mental disorder among the Hutterites, an Anabaptist religious group with a relatively simple social order.[18]

The fundamental difficulty with the social disorganization viewpoint, however, is that, while masquerading as an objective conceptual framework, it is subjective and judgmental. Faris defines disorganization as the breakdown of order or system, the disunion or disruption of constituent parts, as well as the condition of being so disrupted. Is American society disorganized according to this definition? Perhaps, since many people are concerned about certain behavior they would like to see eradicated. Still, it seems questionable that American society is about to disintegrate so the disorganization must be partial. Then to what degree is America disorganized? The answer is not self-evident. Finally, even if we agree that the United States has a large number of difficulties such as crime, air pollution, traffic congestion, and alcoholism, it is not at all clear that a more organized system producing fewer of these phenomena could be evolved without fundamentally altering the nature of this society. In short, American society is surely organized differently than a folk society, but the decision that it is disorganized is one which does not flow out of any objective comparison with the folk society.

This same judgmental problem is found in Robert K. Merton's definition of social disorganization:

> Social disorganization refers to inadequacies or failures in a social system of interrelated statuses and roles such that the collective purposes and individual objectives of its members are less fully realized than they could be in an alternative workable system.[19]

Merton's definition is clear enough, but whether or not it lends itself to the objective study of social conditions is an open question. Let us agree that the collective purposes and individual objectives of American society and American citizens are sometimes not fully met. But, it is that state of affairs properly designated as social disorganization? How can we be sure that there is some alternative workable system which would more adequately fulfill these purposes and objectives? Since we cannot be sure, some kind of subjective judgment is necessary if societies are to be designated as disorganized.[20] Compare Merton's definition of social disorganization with his view of deviant behavior, in which he tells us that: "Whereas social disorganization refers to faults in the arrangement and working of social statuses and roles, deviant behavior refers to conduct that departs significantly from the norms set for people in their social statuses."[21] We deem the latter definition the clearer and more objective of the two.

It is for such reasons that the social disorganization viewpoint has declined in importance in modern sociology. In the few recent versions of it, the meaning of the viewpoint has been drastically altered from the traditional one. Thus Albert K. Cohen has tried to reduce the flabbiness of the perspective by restricting it to situations in which the procedural rules that order some ongoing pattern of social activity have been breached, and an abrupt and unanticipated halt to the social process occurs.[22] Following Cohen, we might speak of social disorganization when a sociology faculty meeting is abruptly terminated before the business of the department has been concluded because a fist fight broke out among several departmental colleagues. Or, social disorganization ensues if the leader of an infantry platoon is killed in combat, no one steps forward to assume command, and the members of the platoon flee in several directions. Cohen's revision of the social disorganization notion limits its application to a description of a social state of affairs; social disorganization thus becomes a condition to be explained, rather than an explanatory framework for social problems.

In another novel use of the social disorganization notion, Reece McGee offers a set of arguments based on the proposition that people do pretty much what is expected of them by others most of the time.[23] When an individual or group fails to behave as others expect, that condition is labeled by McGee as social disorganization. It ought to be recognized that McGee is not talking about social disorganization in its traditional meaning, for he uses the term synonymously with "deviant behavior."

We should not leave the reader with the impression that the decline of the social disorganization perspective has also resulted in the total demise of propositions within that orientation which stress the role of societal imperfections in the etiology of deviance and social problems. The intellectual shift has been more a matter of terminology than one of drastic changes in thoughtways about these phenomena; that is, many sociologists have abandoned the term social disorganization but have continued to hold hypotheses about the influences of rents, tears, and imperfections in the social fabric as lying behind various kinds of socially condemned activities. For example, Edwin H. Sutherland and Donald R. Cressey have put forth the notion of *differential social organization* to describe the social-structural conditions that lead to criminality.[24] Differential social organization is their term for heterogeneity of norms thought to characterize modern, complex, industrialized societies. Regarding the similarity between social disorganization and differential social organization, they observe that:

> This condition of normative conflict is ordinarily considered social "disorganization" or "unorganization" because the social pressures for conformity on the part of the person are not uniform or harmonious. In this condition, the society does not possess consensus with respect to societal goals or else does not possess consensus regarding means of achieving agreed-upon societal goals. Consequently, the individual is confronted with alternative goals or means, or he exists under conditions in which the norms of many members of the society are unknown to other members. . . . Actually, the social conditions in which the influences on the

person are relatively inharmonious and inconsistent are themselves a kind of social organization. Such social organization is characteristic of all except the earliest societies and the most isolated contemporary societies, although there are wide variations in the degree of heterogeneity and in the pervasiveness of normative inconsistencies.[25]

Chapter six provides a detailed examination of a number of theoretical statements about the social-structural sources of deviance that parallel the views of Sutherland and Cressey. In particular, that chapter will take a close look at the anomie formulation of Robert K. Merton, the most well-known exposition produced by an American sociologist on the social sources of deviance.[26] The reader will see that social disorganization arguments have much in common with many of these currently favored perspectives on social structure and nonconformity.

DEVIANCE

This book deals with theoretical perspectives on deviance and deviant behavior rather than social problems or social disorganization. There is little question that interest in social disorganization is waning, although concern for analysis of social problems remains a lively tradition in sociology. At the same time, the rise of various sociological perspectives on deviance in the past decade is clearly one of the most prominent trends in modern sociology. Doubtless there is a variety of reasons for the growing popularity of the study of deviant behavior. One important factor is the scientific pretensions of modern sociology; that is, scientifically oriented sociologists have been forced to acknowledge that such notions as social disorganization carry a heavy judgmental burden. Deviance, on the other hand, appears to refer to phenomena which are objective and amenable to scrutiny by methods of social science. At any rate, books on deviant behavior, sociology courses on deviance, and journal articles reporting various facets of deviant conduct have become numerous.

Nearly all contemporary concepts of deviance center about *norm violation* as its identifying mark. For example, Marshall B. Clinard offers the definition: "Deviant behavior is essentially violation of certain types of group norms; a deviant act is behavior which is proscribed in a certain way."[27] Albert K. Cohen has offered a similar idea: "We define deviant behavior as behavior which violates institutionalized expectations—

that is, expectations which are shared and recognized as legitimate within a social system."[28] Or, examine Robert K. Merton's definition: "Deviant behavior refers to conduct that departs significantly from the norms set for people in their social statuses."[29]

Students of deviance differ, however, both in terms of their specific views about the proper subject of study and in terms of the explanatory hypotheses which they prefer. Some sociologists focus on the deviant actor and the norms he violates, while another group of investigators emphasizes the social audiences who observe and react to instances of rule-violation. The latter, often known as "labelers," insist that deviance is the product of social interaction between those who engage in acts *and* those who label the behaviors as deviant. They also say that discrediting labels are not automatically conferred upon persons who violate norms, and some norm violators escape public attention while others are saddled with stigmatizing tags such as "embezzlers," "hoods," or "fairies."

There is some ambiguity in the arguments of labelers, for they sometimes appear to claim that a person is not a deviant unless *his own specific actions* have been singled out and identified by some social audience. At other times these theories appear to argue that some *category* of behavior becomes deviant only when it has become a matter of concern to some social audience; thus, for example, sexual acts between members of the same sex are only deviant insofar as some social group has decided to regard such actions as "bad," "evil," or in some other way "reprehensible." In this view of things, an individual engaged in homosexual acts would be regarded as a deviant if homosexuality is subject to social condemnation, even though that specific person might not have been singled out by others as a homosexual. When discussing various facets of deviance, labelers as well as others usually proceed from this latter "rule-breaking" or "norm violation" position and concern themselves both with deviant endeavors and consequences of being apprehended in these activities. Those who assert that deviance is a social label and that deviants are persons to whom the label has been applied also speak of hidden deviants, secret deviants, or deviant acts.

There is thus considerable convergence on the view that deviance involves negative social labels; hence we should study persons to whom such labels have been applied or *who run some risk* of having a discrediting tag fixed upon them. By implication, then, the sociologist has no business identifying persons as deviant if their behavior cannot be shown to offend or violate the normative standards of some specific group.

SUMMARY

This brief chapter has traced some origins of the field of deviance analysis. We have seen that social pathology arguments, social disorganization theories, and social problems perspectives have been popular, but much attention now centers about the study of deviance. Chapter three turns to an explication of the major foci and dimensions involved in current theorizing and research on deviance.

NOTES

[1] Laymen do not usually speak of "social disorganization," of course, but they do verbalize disquiet about perceived breakdowns or flaws in the social order. The sociological notion of social disorganization bears a good deal of similarity to these public views about societal breakdown.

[2] But, recall our comments in the preceding chapter, where we noted the fact of considerable confusion and disagreement among sociological and lay conceptions of deviance. Individual sociologists have also exhibited considerable variability regarding matters collected under the rubrics of social pathology, social disorganization, or social problems. Thus, although certain topics such as criminality and mental disorder are discussed by nearly all, idiosyncratic enumerations of deviance or problems are also common. Chapter four deals in detail with the conceptual confusion regarding definitions of deviance.

[3] For other summaries of these trends in the development of deviance analysis, see Edwin M. Lemert, *Human Deviance, Social Problems, and Social Control,* 2nd ed. (Englewood Cliffs, N.J.: Prentice-Hall, 1972). pp. 3–25; Jack D. Douglas, "Deviance and Order in a Pluralistic Society," in John C. McKinney and Edward A. Tiryakian, eds., *Theoretical Sociology* (New York: Appleton-Century-Crofts, 1970), pp. 367–401; Nanette J. Davis, "Labeling Theory in Deviance Research: A Critique and Reconsideration," *Sociological Quarterly* 13 (Autumn 1972): 447–74; David Matza, *Becoming Deviant* (Englewood Cliffs, N.J.: Prentice-Hall, 1969).

[4] C. Wright Mills, "The Professional Ideology of Social Pathologists," *American Journal of Sociology* 49 (September 1943): 165–80.

[5] An illustrative case of social pathology arguments is Stuart Alfred Queen and Delbert Martin Mann, *Social Pathology* (New York: Thomas Y. Crowell Co., 1925).

[6] Edwin M. Lemert, *Social Pathology* (New York: McGraw-Hill Book Co., 1951), p. 1.

[7] For example, see the first American criminology text by a sociologist: Maurice Parmelee, *Criminology* (New York: Macmillan Co., 1918); see also Don C. Gibbons, "Say, Whatever Became of Maurice Parmelee, Anyway?" *Sociological Quarterly* 15 (Autumn 1974).

⁸ Some recent social problems texts are: Howard S. Becker, ed., *Social Problems* (New York: John Wiley and Sons, 1966); Howard C. Freeman and Wyatt C. Jones, *Social Problems* (Chicago: Rand McNally and Co., 1970); Robert K. Merton and Robert S. Nisbet, eds., *Contemporary Social Problems*, 3rd ed. (New York: Harcourt Brace Jovanovich, 1971); S. Kirson Weinberg, *Social Problems in Modern Urban Society* (Englewood Cliffs, N.J.: Prentice-Hall, 1970); an inclusive statement regarding the core ingredients of social problems analysis is John I. Kitsuse and Malcolm Spector, "Toward a Sociology of Social Problems: Social Conditions, Value-Judgments, and Social Problems," *Social Problems* 20 (Spring 1973): 407–19.

⁹ As with nearly all general claims in sociology texts, these claims regarding social problems analysis admit certain exceptions. Not all who have expounded upon social problems have taken their subject matter from public views about problematic conditions. Instead, some have argued that sociologists are equipped to identify social problems that are not recognized as such by the citizenry. On this point, see Kitsuse and Spector, "Toward a Sociology of Social Problems."

¹⁰ Ibid, p. 415.

¹¹ Maurice D. Van Arsdol, Jr., Georges Sabagh, and Francesca Alexander, "Reality and the Perception of Environmental Hazards," *Journal of Health and Human Behavior* 5 (Winter 1964): 144–53.

¹² The argument that there is a "natural history" or identifiable set of stages in the problem-defining process is attributed to Fuller and Myers. See: Richard C. Fuller and Richard R. Myers, "Some Aspects of a Theory of Social Problems," *American Sociological Review* 6 (February 1941): 24–34. One piece of evidence indicating that social problems do not always emerge in the fashion described by Fuller and Myers is: Edwin M. Lemert, "Is There a Natural History of Social Problems?" *American Sociological Review* 16 (April 1951): 217–23. Becker is in general agreement with Fuller and Myers on the argument that the study of the problem-defining process is a basic task, but he also points out that in a pluralistic society, one group's "problem" may not be seen in the same light by another group. See: Becker, *Social Problems*, pp. 1–31. Another recent statement of this kind is Malcolm Spector and John I. Kitsuse, "Social Problems: A Re-Formulation," *Social Problems* 21 (Fall 1973): 145–59.

¹³ Robert E. L. Faris, *Social Disorganization* (New York: Ronald Press Co., 1955).

¹⁴ Ibid., p. 6.

¹⁵ Ibid., pp. 6–31.

¹⁶ Robert Redfield, "The Folk Society," *American Journal of Sociology* 52 (January 1947): 293–308.

¹⁷ Nicholas J. Demerath, "Schizophrenia Among Primitives," *American Journal of Psychiatry* 98 (March 1942): 703–7. Also see Lemert's discussion of drinking behavior in Polynesian societies. Lemert, *Human Deviance, Social Problems, and Social Control*, pp. 218–45.

[18] Joseph W. Eaton and Robert J. Weil, *Culture and Mental Disorders* (New York: Free Press of Glencoe, 1955).

[19] Merton and Nisbet, *Contemporary Social Problems,* pp. 819–20.

[20] Kitsuse and Spector have offered a similar evaluation of Merton's views on social disorganization. Kitsuse and Spector, "Toward a Sociology of Social Problems," pp. 408–9.

[21] Merton and Nisbet, *Contemporary Social Problems,* p. 805.

[22] Albert K. Cohen, "The Study of Social Disorganization and Deviant Behavior," in Robert K. Merton, Leonard Broom, and Leonard S. Cottrell, Jr., eds., *Sociology Today* (New York: Basic Books, 1959), pp. 474–81.

[23] Reece McGee, *Social Disorganization in America* (San Francisco: Chandler Publishing Co., 1962), p. ix.

[24] Edwin H. Sutherland and Donald R. Cressey, *Principles of Criminology,* 8th ed. (Philadelphia: J. B. Lippincott Co., 1970), pp. 93–112.

[25] Ibid., p. 95. A parallel orientation to that of Sutherland and Cressey's regarding crime can be seen in Don C. Gibbons, *Society, Crime, and Criminal Careers,* 2nd ed. (Englewood Cliffs, N.J.: Prentice-Hall, 1973).

[26] Robert K. Merton, *Social Theory and Social Structure,* revised and enlarged ed. (New York: Free Press of Glencoe, 1957), pp. 131–94.

[27] Marshall B. Clinard, *Sociology of Deviant Behavior,* 3rd ed. (New York: Holt, Rinehart and Winston, 1968), p. 28.

[28] Cohen, "The Study of Social Disorganization," p. 462; see also Cohen, *Deviance and Control* (Englewood Cliffs, N.J.: Prentice-Hall, 1966), p. 1.

[29] Merton, *Social Theory and Social Structure,* p. 824.

SELECTED READINGS

BECKER, HOWARD S. *Outsiders.* New York: Free Press of Glencoe, 1963. A collection of essays developing some of the major themes of the labeling view of deviance. Discussion of social reactions to deviance, careers in deviant behavior, and other social processes in deviance.

CLINARD, MARSHALL B. *Sociology of Deviant Behavior* (4th ed.). New York: Holt, Rinehart and Winston, 1974. General textbook containing a large amount of empirical evidence on deviance.

COHEN, ALBERT K. *Deviance and Control.* Englewood Cliffs, N.J.: Prentice-Hall, 1966. A relatively brief explication of the major dimensions involved in the analysis of deviance.

GLASER, DANIEL. *Social Deviance.* Chicago: Markham Publishing Co., 1971. A brief exploration of deviance, including a typology of nonconformity.

LEMERT, EDWIN M. *Human Deviance, Social Problems, and Social Control* (2d ed.). Englewood Cliffs, N.J.: Prentice-Hall, 1972. Collection of essays by a major figure in the development of modern viewpoints on deviance. Some of the essays amplify many of the themes first presented in *Social Pathology*.

———. *Social Pathology*. New York: McGraw-Hill Book Co., 1951. A sociological classic, outlining many of the basic arguments and propositions that are incorporated in modern labeling views on deviance.

LOFLAND, JOHN. *Deviance and Identity*. Englewood Cliffs, N.J.: Prentice-Hall, 1969. A detailed and thoughtful discussion of deviance and social processes in deviant behavior from a symbolic interactionist perspective.

MATZA, DAVID. *Becoming Deviant*. Englewood Cliffs, N.J.: Prentice-Hall, 1969. An occasionally difficult explication of some of the main images of man held by students of deviance in the past and present. Also discusses in considerable detail some aspects of the process of becoming a deviant.

SCOTT, ROBERT A., AND JACK D. DOUGLAS, eds. *Theoretical Perspectives on Deviance*. New York: Basic Books, 1972. Contains a number of essays on various conceptual problems and issues in the study of deviance.

dimensions of deviance: problems for study

W hat is the study of deviance about? What are the major questions raised by deviance analysts? Some categorization of the large outpouring of speculative and theoretical contentions and the sizeable research literature that has accumulated is needed. Without such a classification, an exposition on deviance risks producing more bewilderment than enlightenment.

A classification dealing with the substantive interests of criminologists offered by Don C. Gibbons can be modified slightly and used to sort out the dimensions of deviance study.[1] That classification includes: definition of deviance and deviants, epidemiology of deviance, the sociology of deviance, the social-psychology of deviant acts and deviant careers, and societal reactions to deviance. Chapter three offers a brief discussion of the central elements involved in each of these interrelated concerns; the remainder of this book provides detailed commentary regarding the study of deviance within this framework.

DEFINITION OF DEVIANCE AND DEVIANTS

The first order of business in any field of study is to define clearly the phenomenon to be studied, for until we agree on the parameters of the activity to be investigated, we cannot begin collecting basic facts about the phenomena (epidemiology), nor can we progress toward an explanation of the activities or behavior. Regarding this definitional issue, Albert K. Cohen declared: "The most pressing problem in the field of social disorganization and deviant behavior is to define these terms. If we cannot agree on what we are talking about, we cannot agree on what is relevant, much less on what is important."[2] Unfortunately, sociologists have yet to agree upon a precise conception of the phenomena to be studied within the category of deviance.[3]

Chapter four will deal with these problems of definition in detail. But for now, let us agree that we shall study behavior which violates societal norms; deviants are thus the people who engage in such activity. Using this working definition, we can proceed to explain issues regarding the nature of deviance. One important issue centers around the epidemiology of deviance and specific patterns of deviance.[4]

THE EPIDEMIOLOGY OF DEVIANCE

The term *epidemiology* is usually associated with public health studies of the extent, distribution, and characteristics of various forms of physical illness or disease; hence, the epidemiology of tuberculosis concerns facts about the number of tubercular persons in the population, their social characteristics, and so forth. In a similar fashion, one can speak of the epidemiology of mental disorder or some other form of deviance and can ask questions about the number, spatial location, socioeconomic characteristics, and other parameters of the behavior to be explained.

Epidemiological data are necessary to explain deviance, for a clear and detailed picture of the phenomenon to be studied is basic to causal inquiry. For example, consider the claim made some years ago by the noted San Francisco newspaper columnist, Herb Caen, who alleged that there were 50,000 male homosexuals in that city. We suggest that this estimate is virtually meaningless. To begin with, what is a "homosexual"? Does the figure provided by Caen include male hustlers who engage in homosexual acts but who do not define themselves as "gay"? Does it encompass those persons who do not perform homosexual acts but regard themselves as homosexuals? Clearly, markedly different counts of "homosexuals" would result from each of these definitions. Then too, even if we knew what conception of homosexuality was employed by Caen, what reason is there to suppose that he was able to make an accurate count of such persons, given the concern of many people for concealing their socially condemned sexual preferences? In short, this statistic seems to be a mere intuitive estimate. Although it has been widely quoted as a definitive statement on the epidemiology of homosexuality in San Francisco, no one really knows how many homosexuals do inhabit that city.[5]

Another illustration of the epidemiological question can be found in current assertions of the mass media that there has been in recent years an alarming increase in juvenile drinking. These claims are largely conjectural, because no firm evidence to support them is available. It would be quite premature for us to start offering explanations for this alleged trend before we have determined that there has been, in fact, a marked upsurge of alcohol consumption by adolescents.

Although much more research is needed, a large part of the existing data on deviance is epidemiological in character. Several studies have been conducted on the issue of social class linkages to mental disorder, with results that are somewhat confusing.[6] Definitional variations regarding the notion of "mental illness," along with methodological problems, have resulted in some confusion as to precisely what these studies show regarding the extent and social class distribution of mental disorder.

Epidemiological investigations regarding crime and delinquency have also been conducted, but again, their cumulative results are not entirely clear.[7] In particular, many inquiries into hidden delinquency have been made. Some people have concluded that nearly all youngsters commit delinquent acts and these researchers argue that officially identified delinquents do not differ significantly from other youths in their misbehavior; instead, they are simply unlucky because the juvenile social control machinery is biased against working-class youngsters and blacks, and official action is most likely to be taken against these juveniles. Other students of delinquency have argued, on the basis of the same epidemiological data, that youths who have been processed through the juvenile justice machinery (official delinquents) are generally involved in more serious and repetitive acts of deviance than are hidden or unofficial delinquents.[8]

The thrust of this commentary indicates that the issue of the distribution of deviance is by no means a settled one. Instead, much more work is needed before we can be confident that we have interpreted the basic facts about deviance correctly.

THE SOCIOLOGY OF DEVIANCE

Let us assume that we have gathered enough epidemiological data about some pattern of deviant conduct and can be fairly confident that we have apprehended at least the general contours of the phenomenon. The sociologist must then identify the *causes* of this behavior and outline a body of generalizations or propositions which account for these phenomena. Although this explanatory task is many-faceted, it has two main parts which are closely related but analytically separate problems. The first involves developing social-structure explanations for the kinds of deviance observed in a society; the second concerns discovering the process of how specific individuals acquire patterns of deviant conduct.[9] We use the term *sociology of deviance* to identify the first problem because inquiries into the nature and effects of social structure are at the heart of sociological investigation. The second matter, the development of deviant careers by specific individuals, is identified as the *social-psychology of deviant acts and deviant careers.*

Investigators have not always kept the distinction between these two queries clear. As Albert K. Cohen has indicated:

> Much that travels under the name of sociology of deviant behavior or of social disorganization is psychology—some of it very good psychology, but psychology. For example, Sutherland's theory of differential association, which is widely regarded as preëminently sociological, is not the less psychological because it makes much of the cultural milieu. It is psychological because it addresses itself to the question: How do people become the kinds of individuals who commit criminal acts? A sociological question would be: What is it about the structure of social systems that determines the kinds of criminal acts that occur in these systems and the way in which such acts are distributed within the systems? In general, a sociological field is concerned with the structure of interactional systems, not with personalities, and the distribution and articulation of events within these systems.[10]

Edwin H. Sutherland's theory of differential association to which Cohen alludes holds that persons become criminals through associations with carriers of criminal norms.[11] Now, if Sutherland's claims are not addressed to the sociology of crime (and deviance), what would such a theory be like? One illustrative case would be a theory designed to account for crime rate variations between the United States and certain European nations which seem to indicate that American society is more criminalistic or criminogenic than other societies because of the inordinate stress on material success and endemic disrespect for law and order in American values and beliefs. Although these claims have not been adequately tested, and such research would be difficult to carry out, the kinds of evidence called for are relatively clear. Crime rates would have to be assembled to rank societies in terms of criminality, whereas indices of cultural values, attitudes toward materialism, law enforcement, and so on would be required to test causal propositions.[12]

Chapter six reviews a number of theories directed at social-structural explanations of rates of deviance. These formulations include the pioneering arguments of Emile Durkheim regarding a condition he termed "anomie" which he saw as centrally implicated in patterns of suicide. A more contemporary theory dealing with rates is Robert K. Merton's version of anomie, based loosely on Durkheim's theory. We shall also note some other recent formulations centering around value-pluralism and social conflict in modern societies. These theories challenge arguments, such as the one by Merton, which emphasize hypothesized core values and social-structural features of American society.

Several commentators have noted the lack of coordinated effort between those who focus upon rates questions and those who are interested in the study of deviant acts and careers. David J. Bordua has called the latter "The West Coast School" and has commented that:

> In some ways there is a West Coast School (many of whose members were trained elsewhere) and an East Coast School in the analysis of deviance and control. The Eastern approach, centering on people like Parsons, Merton, and Homans, tends to begin with a model of social order and poses the problem of why there is violation of norms and to be mainly concerned with the problem of social control as a part of the interest in the conditions of persistence or equilibrium of social systems. . . . The differences between these two schools are not large, and indeed, except for Lemert, the "labeling" theorists seem to have decided to honor what we have called the Easterners almost by ignoring them.[13]

Although Bordua's general point is well taken, some theorists have endeavored to deal jointly with rates questions and deviant career issues. Edwin M. Lemert's work, noted by Bordua, is one case in point,[14] as are some of Albert K. Cohen's writings.[15]

THE SOCIAL-PSYCHOLOGY
OF DEVIANT ACTS AND CAREERS

The analysis of deviance involves both explanation of differentials in rates of deviance and exploration of the processes by which specific individuals come to engage in deviant acts and how some of them acquire deviant attitudes, self-conceptions, and behavior patterns. Cohen identifies the latter in the passage cited above as a psychological issue. Our preference is for the term *social-psychology of deviant acts and careers,* because social psychology is that discipline most concerned with *socialization*—the processes through which individuals learn to behave in human fashion. While socialization is most often used with respect to the learning experiences of infants and young children, the term is also employed in connection with learning experiences by which mature individuals acquire new behavior patterns, such as the socialization of the medical student, the worker, the criminal, or the homosexual; these are all learned patterns of behavior.[16]

The social-psychological rubric refers to both deviant acts and deviant careers in order to acknowledge that involvement in deviance in individual cases ranges from single, isolated instances of norm-violation; to more repetitive but casual, sporadic patterns of activity; and finally, to systematic "careers" in which those involved have become engaged repeatedly in norm violations.

Sociologists who focus on the activities of individuals are usually interested in observing people involved in various degrees of deviance. Thus we want to identify those factors which account for initial acts of norm violation as well as those contingent events occurring after the first encounters with nonconformity that push individuals toward or away from further involvement in deviant conduct. Accordingly, we shall examine hypotheses regarding the genesis of initial acts of norm violation in succeeding pages of this book, as well as pay attention to various contingencies that facilitate career patterns in deviance.

Albert K. Cohen points out that several different approaches have been taken to the question: "Why do they do it?"[17] Those of a psychiatric persuasion have stressed "kinds of people" theories to account for criminals, delinquents, homosexuals, or other deviants. These popular and frequently encountered arguments aver that deviants are psychologically "sick" and that their deviant conduct is a product of psychological impairment and is evidence of the "sickness." Sociological observers, on the other hand, are much more likely to emphasize "kinds of situations" formulations.[18]

Our attention in chapter seven will concentrate on the recent outpouring of contentions which has been termed the *labeling perspective.* Those commentaries stress value pluralism and value conflicts out of which initial acts of deviance flow, along with risk-taking activities in which persons get involved in tentative flirtations with norm-violating activities. Additionally, labeling formulations emphasize such matters as career contingencies, arguing that initial acts of deviance may result in various career outcomes depending on the subsequent experiences of the deviant actors. In particular, social responses or labeling events are regarded as particularly crucial in propelling persons down deviant paths. These stigmatizing experiences are said to foreclose the possibilities for withdrawing from deviance. The person who acquires a spoiled identity, it is said, is unlikely to abandon it, for in the eyes of persons around him, "once a thief, (homosexual, crazy person, etc.), always a thief."

SOCIETAL REACTIONS TO DEVIANCE

Societal reactions are thus accorded heavy emphasis in the writings of labeling theorists. We are told, for example, that being identified as a delinquent by a juvenile court may be a powerfully negative career contingency and may push the stigmatized youth into further lawbreaking conduct. Similarly, some argue that involuntary commitment of an individual to a mental hospital exaggerates the person's difficulties and increases the likelihood that he will become chronically mentally ill. Along the same line, the individual who becomes labeled as a homosexual may well find that his life experiences become markedly altered by that fact.

There can be little doubt that labeling experiences and "degradation ceremonies" often have markedly deleterious effects on the deviant actor. We ought to recognize, however, that the labeling phenomenon is extremely complex, with varied outcomes in particular cases of deviance. We shall take up this subject in greater detail in chapter eight. At this point, let us note that it is possible to find cases such as amateur shoplifters in which the labeled deviant is driven *out* of aberrant behavior by the experience. Other instances can be identified in which labeling events have a benign or neutral effect on the deviant, while still other cases are observed in which labeling does have the assumed negative impact on the person. In summary, current assertions about labeling experiences sometimes oversimplify and exaggerate certain aspects of what turns out to be a host of very subtle and complex processes.

We often ask questions about the effects of social labels on specific persons; however, there are other aspects to the question of social reactions to deviance. It must be remembered that deviance is a concept derived from observations of real life and not simply imposed on the world by the sociologist. For example, sociological interest in homosexuals as deviants is warranted since laymen hold hostile sentiments toward "queers" or members of the "gay community." Accordingly, we ought to inquire into social definitions of deviance as a basic focus of attention, in addition to our interest in the impact of social sentiments upon deviant actors.[19] Chapter five reviews a collection of studies which have dealt with social reactions to deviance and also directs attention to certain aspects of social definitions that need more research scrutiny.

ETHICAL ISSUES
IN THE STUDY OF DEVIANCE

We have been concerned thus far with *what* to study regarding deviance; however, a brief aside is in order regarding the issue of *how* to engage in sociological inquiry. Do sociological researchers have a special mandate to pry into the private affairs of others? Are we free to deceive policemen into believing we wish to study the behavior of citizens when we really want to uncover facts about deviant acts on the part of the officers? Does freedom of sociological inquiry give us license to play with the rights of deviant or nondeviant citizens in other ways? We think not. But questions of this kind have received relatively little attention by social investigators in the past, and we believe that queries about the ethical limitations of research are equally important as those conceptual issues that dominate the pages of this book. Accordingly, our concluding chapter is a relatively detailed excursion into the terrain of ethical obligations to research subjects.

SUMMARY

Chapter three has sketched out the nature of deviance analysis by identifying the central issues that occupy the attention of theorists and researchers. We noted that the definitional problem is the first order of business and that some answer to the question: "What is deviance?" must be agreed on before we can deal with causal arguments or other concerns. Chapter four takes up the varied definitions of deviance that have been proposed by scholars, and presents the conception of deviance that we regard as the most fruitful of the alternatives.

NOTES

[1] Don C. Gibbons, *Society, Crime, and Criminal Careers,* 2nd ed. (Englewood Cliffs, N.J.: Prentice-Hall, 1973), pp. 4–13; see also Albert K. Cohen, *Deviance and Control* (Englewood Cliffs, N.J.: Prentice-Hall, 1966), pp. 41–47.

[2] Albert K. Cohen, "The Study of Social Disorganization and Deviant Behavior," in Robert K. Merton, Leonard Broom, and Leonard S. Cottrell, Jr. eds., *Sociology Today* (New York: Basic Books, 1959), p. 461.

[3] It should also be noted that sociological discussions often treat such terms as *deviance* and *deviants* as interchangeable. This practice slurs over the point that norm-violating acts are extremely commonplace, often carried on by persons who do not see themselves as nonconformists and who are not seen as deviants by others, but recurrent involvement in deviant acts by persons who exhibit role-definitions of themselves as nonconformists is much less frequent. Stated differently, not all deviance is the work of incumbents of deviant roles.

[4] Resolution of the definitional question is of extreme importance in the study of deviance, particularly with respect to epidemiological undertakings. The use of different definitions of the problems for study leads to varied and contradictory epidemiological findings. For example, there are several definitions of criminality which could be utilized by a researcher, each of which would direct attention to different facts about crime. For a discussion of definitional problems as they influence epidemiological studies in medical care utiliza-

tion, see Herman A. Tyroler, "The Classification of Disease," in Merwyn R. Greenlick, ed., *Conceptual Issues in the Analysis of Medical Care Utilization Behavior* (Washington, D.C.: U.S. Department of Health, Education, and Welfare, 1970), pp. 35–52.

[5] This same point could be made about Jess Stearn, *The Sixth Man* (New York: Macfadden Books, 1962), which asserts that one out of every six American males is homosexual. The accuracy of such judgments is surely open to question.

[6] See, for example: August B. Hollingshead and Frederic C. Redlich, *Social Class and Mental Illness* (New York: John Wiley and Sons, 1958); Leo Srole, Thomas Langner, Stanley T. Michael, Marvin K. Opler, and Thomas A. C. Rennie, *Mental Health in the Metropolis: The Midtown Manhattan Study* (New York: McGraw-Hill Book Co., 1962).

[7] Epidemiological data on crime and delinquency are presented in detail in Gibbons, *Society, Crime, and Criminal Careers*, pp. 99–123; and in Gibbons, *Delinquent Behavior* (Englewood Cliffs, N.J.: Prentice-Hall, 1970), pp. 13–32.

[8] That is the conclusion in Gibbons, *Delinquent Behavior*.

[9] These two explanatory problems are also discussed in Ronald L. Akers, "Problems in the Sociology of Deviance: Social Definitions and Behavior," *Social Forces* 46 (June 1968):: 455–65.

[10] Cohen, "The Study of Social Disorganization," p. 462.

[11] Edwin H. Sutherland and Donald R. Cressey, *Principles of Criminology*, 8th ed. (Philadelphia: J. B. Lippincott Co., 1970), pp. 75–91.

[12] We ought to note that there are some extremely thorny problems which would have to be faced in any meaningful analysis of crime rates and social structure across different societies. Some discussions of this question imply that there are universal definitions of crime such that the same behavior is recognized as beyond the pale in all societies; but, criminal laws and concepts of criminality in a particular society mirror the basic values of that society. In contemporary United States, private property is highly valued, so that legislatures have created a vast number of criminal laws to protect private property. [For a discussion of the origins of these laws, see Jerome Hall, *Theft, Law and Society* (Indianapolis: Bobbs-Merrill Co., 1952)]. Crimes against property are thus identified in great numbers in this society. By contrast, Erikson has shown that Puritan society in early America centered about spiritual values; hence the offenders who were recognized in that society were witches and other persons who violated spiritual values, rather than robbers and thieves. See Kai T. Erikson, *Wayward Puritans* (New York: John Wiley and Sons, 1969). On this same general point, Bohannan has commented upon the discrepancies between British and African conceptions of culpable homicide. See Paul Bohannan, ed., *African Homicide and Suicide* (Princeton, N.J.: Princeton University Press, 1960). The researcher who would make meaningful comparisons of levels of crime from one society to another will have to find some way to identify criminality without introducing ethnocentric biases into his research.

[13] David J. Bordua, "Recent Trends: Deviant Behavior and Social Control," *Annals of the American Academy of Political and Social Science* 369 (January 1967): 154.

[14] Edwin M. Lemert, *Social Pathology* (New York: McGraw-Hill Book Co., 1951); Lemert, *Human Deviance, Social Problems, and Social Control,* 2d ed. (Englewood Cliffs, N.J.: Prentice-Hall, 1972).

[15] Albert K. Cohen, "The Sociology of the Deviant Act: Anomie Theory and Beyond," *American Sociological Review* 30 (February 1965): 5–14.

[16] See Orville G. Brim, Jr., and Stanton Wheeler, *Socialization After Childhood* (New York: John Wiley & Sons, 1966).

[17] Cohen, *Deviance and Control,* pp. 41–47.

[18] For a discussion of situational factors in criminality, see Don C. Gibbons, "Observations on the Study of Crime Causation," *American Journal of Sociology,* 77 (September 1971): 262–78.

[19] Some of the facets of these two are discussed in Akers, "Problems in the Sociology of Deviance."

CHAPTER FOUR

what is ``deviance''?

Some years ago, J. L. Simmons conducted research in which he asked laymen to indicate activities they considered to be cases of deviance.[1] He reports that 180 persons listed over one thousand items of behavior as deviant, a fact which suggests that there is considerable confusion among the citizenry as to the nature and extent of these phenomena. One might suppose, however, that sociologists who inquire into these matters operate with a shared, explicit definition of deviance, in contrast to the confused laymen. In fact, the sociological literature shows considerable divergence on the basic question of what we intend to mean by terms such as *deviance* and *deviant behavior*. Briefly stated, there are two markedly different basic definitions of deviance found in the sociological literature, so that depending upon which definition we follow we are directed to pay attention to widely different matters.

One commonly encountered notion restricts attention to behavioral transgressions against major "societal" norms, and in this conception, deviance refers to violations of culturally widespread conduct standards. The other definition is an omnibus one, holding that deviance consists of violations of major and minor rules alike, and occurs in social systems of all sizes, from dyads and small groups to societal collectivities.

We will examine a sample of these two definitions below. But first, we need to take a quick look at the notion of "norms" as employed by sociologists. What do we mean by norms, conduct rules, or standards of behavior?

Norms are nearly always defined by sociologists as guides to action

A large part of this chapter is adapted from "Some Critical Notes on Current Definitions of Deviance," by Don C. Gibbons and Joseph F. Jones, from *Pacific Sociological Review* Vol. 14, No. 1 (January 1971) pp. 20–37, by permission of the Publisher, Sage Publications, Inc.

that presumably produce behavioral regularity on the part of individuals and parallel lines of conduct on the part of collectivities of persons. Indeed, the existence of a social norm is often inferred from observations about behavioral regularities. We observe that the members of some group behave in relatively uniform ways, leading to the conclusion: "There must be a social rule governing those people's behavior." The problem with this practice is, of course, that we sometimes go no further than the inference from behavioral regularities, and we fail to obtain independent evidence about the norm itself. While we are free to entertain such surmises about the existence of norms, we ought not to suppose that the concept is anything more than tautological when used in this way.

Whether inferred from behavior, or directly observed in some way, norms are thought of as rules or guides to behavior that are internal. The observer who wishes to obtain direct evidence of norms questions people about the behavioral rules which they give allegiance to or follow in their own activities. Some rules or norms are codified, that is, written down in rule books, sets of criminal statutes, and the like, but even so, common sociological practice is to regard these as norms for specific persons only insofar as those individuals have at least some general psychic awareness of the written rule.

These remarks about norms are deceptively straightforward, because they imply that when persons verbalize some personal rule or norm, their actual behavior can be predicted on the basis of that internalized standard. But a moment's reflection tells us that individuals frequently give verbal allegiance to such conduct rules as "Thou shall not steal" at the same time that they are involved in stealing from their employer, from a retail store, or from some other business concern. Since the deeds of persons do not always match their words, can a verbalized standard be called a norm when it is not accompanied by congruent behavior?

Sociological quarrels regarding norms have also questioned whether any broad societal norms can be identified in complex societies, or whether norms exist only within subcultures or other smaller collectivities. Then too, there is the issue of whether norms are best visualized as relatively rigid rules or categorical imperatives that require specific behavior on the part of persons or as flexible and relatively elastic standards to which strict conformity is not demanded.

Much sociological literature deals with norms and reflects the difficulties that sociologists have encountered with this core concept. The remainder of this chapter is devoted to an examination of some of this dialogue, particularly as it relates to deviance. Let us begin with the distinction between "societal" norms and other kinds of social rules.

DEVIANCE AS VIOLATION
OF MAJOR "SOCIETAL" NORMS

A number of conceptions define deviance as violations of "societal" norms. For example, Simon Dinitz, Russell B. Dynes, and Alfred C. Clark are editors of a reader in which it is asserted that: ". . . the essential nature of deviance lies in the departure of certain types of behavior from the norms of a particular society at a particular time."[2] Similarly, Eliot Freidson avers that deviance is: ". . . conduct which violates sufficiently valued norms, that, if it is persistent, is assigned a special negatively deviant role, and 'is generally thought to require the attention of social control agencies.' These are the forms of deviance that are often called 'social problems.' "[3] In a similar vein, Marshall B. Clinard speaks of deviance as behavioral transgressions exceeding the tolerance limits of the community, while the forms of deviance which he analyzes are those which violate major "social" norms.[4] John Lofland has written extensively about deviance and explicitly rules out attention to forms of norm violation that occur in formal organizations or face-to-face groups and opts instead for behavior that breaches "societal" norms.[5] John De Lamater restricts his attention to transgressions on a "societal" level.[6] Close examination of other essays on deviance shows that many are also oriented toward similar conceptions of deviance as violation of "societal" norms.

Nearly all those who define deviance in this way pay most attention to deviants such as criminals, delinquents, mentally disordered persons, homosexuals, and prostitutes. Those who favor a "societal" definition of deviance apparently do not intend the term to cover all violations of behavioral rules that can be observed in different quarters within society. Note that Freidson's definition directs attention to criminals, mentally disordered individuals, and the like. Similarly, Lofland restricts the term to behavior which violates important social rules and which is strongly disapproved of, such as homosexuality, prostitution, alcoholism, suicide, and mental illness.[7] Most of these activities are prohibited in the criminal law, the police are charged with ferreting out instances of these behaviors whenever they occur; and formal organizations have been invented to deal with apprehended deviants of these kinds.[8] Persons who violate these norms often get caught up in "secondary deviation" in which they assume the identity of "hood," "lush," "gay," etc., and restructure their other social roles around their deviant role.[9]

OMNIBUS DEFINITIONS OF DEVIANCE

There are other norms, usually uncodified, which are commonly accepted within a society, to which attention could also be paid. For example, those who noisily eat food in a theater often provoke mildly hostile responses from other patrons, as do persons who utter obscenities at cocktail parties or adults who eat mashed potatoes with their fingers. But in such cases, social control efforts to deal with these transgressions are usually informal ones undertaken by those few persons who directly observe the behavior, and the controls are not carried on in the name of society. Furthermore, these transgressions do not often grow into deviant roles. Some deviance theorists would have us study rule breaking of this kind, along with rule violations within narrowly circumscribed collectivities; this persuasion might be called an omnibus conception of deviance.

Omnibus definitions hold that deviance consists of breaches of any rule in any social system from dyads to societal organizations. William A. Rushing, for example, asserts that deviant behavior is conduct which violates group standards, including such things as norms among industrial workers which restrict worker output.[10] However, it is significant that nearly all of the anthology edited by Rushing deals with such forms of deviance as criminality, alcoholism, suicide, and drug addiction, rather than "rate-busting," gossip, and kindred activities.

Albert K. Cohen is another exponent of an omnibus definition of deviance. In one place, he tells us that: ". . . deviance, as I use the term, is just as much concerned with the violation of the normative rules or understandings of households, business firms, fraternities, ball teams, committees, and so on, as with 'social-problem' deviance, and that all such violations are as much testing grounds for the ideas ventured in this book as are armed robbery and drug addiction."[11] In the same book he reports that the subject of that work is: ". . . knavery, skulduggery, cheating, unfairness, crime, sneakiness, malingering, cutting corners, immorality, dishonesty, betrayal, graft, corruption, wickedness, and sin —in short, deviance."[12] But as in Rushing's book, few cases of knavery, unfairness, and malingering are systematically examined; most of the analysis is directed at juvenile delinquency, mental disorder, and criminality. Sociologists have yet to develop a body of theoretical notions which can subsume the myriad forms of deviance included in Cohen's definition. The anomie notions and other social-structural conceptions which Cohen employs appear to be difficult if not impossible to apply to petty kinds of deviance.

Robert K. Merton's definition holds that: ". . . deviant behavior is conduct that departs significantly from the norms set for people in their social statuses."[13] There is nothing in that statement which would restrict it to departures from major "societal" rules and behavioral standards.

Stanton Wheeler's writings on deviance are somewhat ambiguous on the choice between a "societal" view of deviance and an omnibus one.[14] On the one hand, he indicates that: "We define deviant behavior as conduct that the people of a society generally regard as aberrant, disturbing, improper, or immoral, and for which specific social control efforts are likely to be found."[15] On the other hand, he discusses deviation in varying levels of social units, such as married pairs and small groups of friends, saying that much can be learned about "societal" forms of deviance from these smaller unit forms. We have suggested above that this is a dubious contention.

Another somewhat ambiguous statement on deviance is that of Howard S. Becker's which says that social groups create deviance through the rules they invent and apply to others.[16] Becker does not specify the size of the group that must be involved for behavior to be deviant; but if deviance is defined as infractions which are reacted to and unfounded allegations of infractions, there is nothing in that conception which should restrict our attention to major "societal" rules.

In a lengthy essay, David Matza defines deviance as straying from a path or standard. [17] Although this essay is relatively devoid of specific linkages to the everyday world of deviant conduct, there is nothing in the notion of straying from paths which would confine attention to major "societal" norms. Another recent contribution to this study is an anthology by Jack D. Douglas in which most of the essays are silent on definitions of deviance.[18] However, the chapter in that book by Marvin B. Scott and Stanford M. Lyman defines deviance as failures in mutual expectations of various kinds held by actors in collectivities of varied sizes.[19]

Norman K. Denzin has presented one of the most detailed and sophisticated statements of broad conceptions of deviance.[20] He maintains that sociologists have devoted too much attention to public forms of deviance and have failed to give adequate heed to more ephemeral forms of misconduct in daily life. According to Denzin: "We must return to the mundane and routine forms of behavior to establish a solidly grounded theory of deviance. In short, a complete theory of deviance must account for misconduct that does not come to the attention of broader agencies of social control."[21]

Denzin's analysis begins by noting rules of conduct as guides for interaction in daily life.[22] These rules specify standards for interaction, defining what we may expect of others and also what expectations they may have regarding our behavior. For example, the rules of conduct governing teacher-student interaction in universities specify the deference relationship and other appropriate action patterns. According to Denzin, it is possible to distinguish several basic types of rules of conduct. First, there are those rules that are formalized into laws and enforced by specialized bodies such as the police. Denzin terms these rules of the civil-legal order. The reader will note the similarity of this type to what we have called "societal" norms. Also, as Denzin notes, violations of the rules of the civil-legal order have received most of the attention of deviance theorists, and interest has centered on violations of these rules and the activities of the rule-enforcers who are responsible for dealing with nonconformists.

A second set of rules identified by Denzin are ceremonial rules or rules of civil propriety, commonly designated as standards of etiquette. These conduct guides govern face-to-face interaction among persons in public and private settings. One example would be the norm specifying that persons should maintain a degree of physical distance from each other while in conversation, while another would be the conduct rule requiring individuals to verbalize standardized opening salutations when beginning a conversation. According to Denzin, rules of etiquette operate most frequently in situations involving strangers who have come together in some interactional setting.

In Denzin's view, a third category of rules has received less attention by sociologists: rules of relationships or relational properties. These rules are extremely commonplace, for they consist of all those behavioral standards that evolve within specific, relatively enduring interactional relationships, such as between the members in a particular family. Many of these relationally specific rules of conduct permit the members of the interactional network to behave in ways that violate the ceremonial rules of civil propriety. For example, many marital partners evolve shared rules of sexual intimacy that depart from standards of civil etiquette. In short, persons who are involved in sustained, meaningful interpersonal relationships develop rules of conduct that differ in important ways from the standards governing the activities of strangers in relatively transitory contact with each other.

Denzin's major recommendation is that we devote more attention to social relationships and violations of rules of conduct in those relationships. His proposal calls for a very broad, all-encompassing analysis based on an omnibus conception of deviance. He would have us examine closely the feelings of embarrassment, irritation, and annoyance that arise when the relational specific rules within particular interactional networks have been violated. He defines these breaches of rules as instances of deviance, while embarrassment and so forth are the social reactions to these actions. Relational deviance is misconduct that is not formally treated or recognized by the broader society or its social control agencies.[23] In Denzin's words: "Few persons ever come in contact with the courts and legal institutions, but many persons are defined by some set of others as deviant; and it is my position that it is persons of this order that any theory of deviant behavior must be held accountable for. In short, a shift in focus of attention has been proposed."[24]

Several studies which have examined violations of norms in relatively small, circumscribed groups stand as examples of the work that will be required if the omnibus definition of deviance, including behavior in small social systems and relational networks, is taken seriously. For example, Dean Harper and Frederick Emmert studied the violation of work rules among postal delivery employees, finding that many of these acts took the form of standardized or patterned evasions.[25] Joseph Bensman and Israel Gerver examined violations of work rules dealing with the use of taps to enlarge holes illegally in aircraft assemblies in order to facilitate the assembly of misaligned parts.[26] Among other things, they found that deviance truly is in the eyes of the beholder, for tapping behavior was regarded as wrongful by some groups in the aircraft industry but not by others, and at the same time temporal fluctuations existed in the extent to which tapping was held to be deviant. Ellwyn R. Stoddard gathered some observations dealing with deviant behavior among policemen ("blue-coat crime").[27] He offered the contention that many illegal practices of police officers are upheld as acceptable conduct in the informal code among policemen. The forms of conduct analyzed by Stoddard are all versions of being "on the take," in which policemen supplement their regular pay with the proceeds from shakedowns, bribery, and stealing.

These illustrations of postmen, aircraft workers, and police officers indicate the vast number of social positions and social groups which we should attend to if we follow the omnibus definition of deviant behavior. Violations of colleague standards and university rules among members of sociology departments quickly come to mind, as do cheating among students, bad manners at the dinner table, acts of philandering on the part of married persons, masturbation, breaches of social etiquette by members of social fraternities, and belching—an almost unlimited number of deviant practices.

DISCUSSION

We have noted that two conceptions of deviance are found in the sociological literature. The "societal" definition restricts attention to behavior which (1) presumably violates culturally widespread conduct rules, (2) arouses strong societal reactions, (3) results in formal social control activities directed at it by the police, correctional bureaucracies, and the like, and (4) often leads into "secondary deviation," that is, a deviant role-career. Secondary deviation arises out of the efforts of the deviant to cope with the stigma attached to his deviant label, his experiences at the hands of the social control agents, and other such contingencies.

The omnibus conception of deviance covers the forms of misconduct subsumed in "societal" definitions, but it also includes violations of relatively widespread but only mildly condemned forms of behavior, such as the failure of a male to yield his seat to a woman on a bus or failure to leave an appropriate tip in a restaurant. Additionally, the omnibus position holds that breaches of norms within small, severely circumscribed social systems should be included within the ambit of deviance analysis, so that violations of work rules and group norms constitute forms of deviance. Implicit in the omnibus conception is the belief that general, underlying principles can be discovered to account for these myriad forms of misbehavior. Thus as we have already noted, some have argued that we can learn much about societal forms of deviance from the study of rule breaking in small social systems.

Which of these definitions should we adopt? On what basis should we choose one conception over the other? Are there important consequences from opting for a certain definition?

The choice of a definition ultimately rests on some assumption that the behaviors it covers share enough ingredients in common to warrant being investigated as a package. Advocates of an omnibus definition of deviance apparently believe that all rule-breaking acts are alike in some important ways, such that some general explanatory principles account for them. Clearly, violations of understandings and expectations in dyads and friendship cliques occur daily throughout society. Flatulence, belches, social errors, rate busting, and chiseling are part of social interaction. Perhaps someone will ultimately show that violation of an understanding between marital partners belongs in the same conceptual category as cheating at pinochle, a breach of table etiquette in a sorority, or a transgression against the criminal law, but the connections between these activities are not now apparent to everyone.

Stated differently, it would be difficult to discover any explanatory theory which can satisfactorily explain the *occurrence* of these various forms cf norm violation. Belching, for example, may arise out of defective socialization or involuntary physiological events. Whatever its origins, they are not likely to have much in common with the social sources of rate busting, cheating in a college classroom, or defective driving skills.

It might be argued by some that the omnibus conception of deviance deals with triviality, because it directs attention to much behavior which is of little consequence and which perhaps does not need sociological scrutiny.[28] Perhaps we do not need sociological inquiry into belching and other relatively innocuous forms of misconduct. But whatever one's view, it appears that any search for explanatory principles covering all activities included within omnibus conceptions of deviance is likely to be unfruitful.

Nor can we find social responses to unite the many forms of behavior included under omnibus definitions, except that many of these responses are informal ones. Stepping on the toes of a dancing partner may provoke a variety of responses, so that the action is sometimes ignored, sometimes becomes the occasion for termination of the dancing episode, and sometimes brings about hostile comments from the offended party or derision from those who witness it. Whatever the response, it is likely to be different from the actions of work partners toward the fellow employee who dawdles too long at a coffee break or of a waitress who mumbles *sotto voce* "stiff sonofabitch" at a nontipping customer.

The charge of triviality might be directed also at the omnibus conception of deviance as far as the consequences of nonconformity are concerned. Although these responses may be significant as social control mechanisms, they are qualitatively different from a sentence of fifteen years in the state penitentiary or involuntary commitment to a mental hospital. Whatever the social responses to petty forms of norm violation, or to rule breaking in small social systems, they probably do not often have major consequences regarding the self-orientation of the actor, nor do they fundamentally alter the social interaction networks within which these breaches occur. Emile Durkheim captured this difference in the following words:

> Robbery and simple bad taste injure the same altruistic sentiment, the respect for that which is another's. However, this same sentiment is less grievously offended by bad taste than by robbery, and since, in addition, the average consciousness has not sufficient intensity to react keenly to bad taste, it is treated with greater tolerance. That is why the person guilty of bad taste is merely blamed, whereas the thief is punished.[29]

The labeling view of deviance focuses on societal reactions, primary and secondary deviation, deviant role-careers, career contingencies, and kindred notions, and this view appears to have little or no applicability to much of the rule breaking included under the omnibus conception. These seminal ideas expressed by such writers as Edwin M. Lemert,[30]

Howard S. Becker,[31] Kai T. Erikson,[32] and Thomas J. Scheff[33] have, in fact, been applied almost exclusively to criminals, drug addicts, and mentally disordered persons. Bad manners, violations of colleague rules, and peccadilloes lie outside the purview of these notions.

The thrust of this commentary on omnibus definitions of deviance is that common principles and explanations are not likely to be uncovered to account for the origins of these activities or to determine reaction experiences directed at these breaches of rules. In short, we feel that the attempt to develop a substantive field of deviance analysis dealing with all the conduct included under an omnibus definition is an illusory goal.

Furthermore, the study of social relationships and rules of relationship of which Denzin speaks would be a truly heroic task, as would the investigation of rule violations within these social networks. We are in complete agreement with Denzin's assertion that: "the range and types of social relationships that characterize human interaction have remained largely unconceptualized by the sociologist. We have as yet not adequately described the effects of such relationships, nor have we sufficiently come to grips with the ways in which these ranges of experience are created, stabilized, and dismissed by persons themselves."[34] Thus those who propose that the study of deviance should inquire into rule violations wherever they occur and in social relationships of all sizes are in effect urging us to *create* a field of inquiry, rather than to build on work that has already been accomplished. Finally, the investigation of social relationships of all kinds and violations of rules within them would seem to us to convert deviance analysis into an amorphous undertaking encompassing nearly the whole of sociological analysis.

For these reasons, our choice is for the "societal" definition of deviance. However, a number of problems with this conception also need attention. If we adopt the "societal" position on deviance and agree to study behavior which departs from major "societal" norms and values, relatively few kinds of conduct can be identified which are universally condemned throughout society. Perhaps the assassination of the president, incest, violent rape, kidnapping, and treason qualify as cases of behavior approved by virtually no one in a given society, but few other examples come readily to mind.

One way to avoid the problem of "societal" norms is to argue that behavior is deviant if it violates norms shared by some significant number in the general population. But what degree of support must be reached for it to be regarded as significant? There are many activities which violate legal norms that clearly apply to all members of the society, but which are supported by only small numbers of citizens. Marijuana statutes stand as one example, for it might be argued that marijuana use is tacitly supported by very large numbers in the general population at the same time that it is heavily punishable under the criminal law. Other norms such as those dealing with sexual activities or pornography are also germane to this argument. The principal difficulty with the notion of "societal" norms is that it is often a social fiction rather than a characteristic of the empirical world.

Much of the behavior discussed in books such as those by Marshall B. Clinard,[35] Edwin M. Lemert,[36] or John Lofland[37] represents conduct approved by those who engage in it and also by many who refrain from it, but which is the target of hostility from other subcultures within society and from social control agencies. Then, too, there are various regional facets to deviance, such as interracial dating or interracial marriage which are found throughout society, but which provoke social condemnation in only some areas, regions, or community segments. Similarly, homosexuality occurs everywhere but results in violent responses mainly within certain subcultures. None of these cases seems entirely congruent with notions of "societal" norms involving rules that are shared by most members of a society.

A substantive field of deviance study can be based on the violation of criminal statutes, civil regulations, other codified conduct rules, and other identifiable behavior standards that apply to persons throughout American society, whether these rules are applauded by citizens or not. Indeed, students of deviant behavior currently focus attention on various transgressions of major rules, particularly of criminal statutes, many of which involve standards that run counter to widely shared attitudes of citizen groups. Major rules in this context refer to norms which are enforced by formal social control agencies. In this approach, deviants are persons who violate those rules which may be dealt with by formal agencies of social control, so that the person may be tried in court, or incarcerated in jail, prison, or a mental hospital.

In sum, in common usage a norm is typically said to be "societal" if violation of it risks provoking a general negative, formalized response. The question of the degree to which the rule or norm is buttressed by social sentiments is a separate empirical issue which needs to be addressed in sociological research. This kind of inquiry would examine: (1) the social process out of which various rules develop, including interest group conflicts and pressures, (2) the degrees of social support for certain rules and norms, and (3) changes over time in public sentiment concerning various behavioral standards. If this inquiry is to be a major focus of deviance analysis, much more work of the kind represented by studies discussed in chapter five is certainly in order, so that the empirical facts regarding social support for rules can be clarified.

The argument that societal norms exist, even in the restricted sense enunciated here, is certainly controversial. Many sociologists argue that it is almost meaningless to speak of norms as categorical imperatives or relatively fixed rules, violations of which are likely to provoke fairly predictable social control responses when they are observed by others. Persons of this persuasion argue that social reactions to violations of norms are highly unpredictable and are influenced heavily by local variations in community attitudes, enforcement policies, and interagency differences regarding responses to deviant acts, as well as the ethnic, marital, sexual, or socioeconomic characteristics of the deviant actors. Accordingly, it is not permissible to speak of societal norms but only of interpretations of conduct in specific situations.

As in many other sociological quarrels, adequate data to decide the argument are lacking. For example, some have interpreted the large research literature on "hidden delinquency" as supporting the view that deviant acts are ubiquitous on the part of American juveniles, that legally tagged juvenile delinquents are little different in behavior from nondelinquents, and that acquisition of the legal status of delinquent hinges on variations in community standards and agency policies rather than behavioral differences.

Another interpretation of the data on "hidden delinquency" would concede that situationally specific factors and agency policies often influence the actions taken against juveniles. At the same time, this second line of argument holds that those who are most markedly involved in violating the conduct standards of the criminal and juvenile codes run the greatest risk of acquiring the legal tag of adjudicated delinquent. In this view, social reactions are not capricious; legal rules and other conduct standards are frequently interpreted in similar ways in different communities and by different agencies, so that we can justifiably speak of "societal" norms in the restricted sense outlined above.[38]

Our preference is for this latter position. We hold that there are many social rules that are interpreted in relatively uniform ways in most communities, and that one can speak meaningfully of societal norms. It is possible to compare the activities of persons against these rules and to make some assessment of the degree to which their behavior deviates from these norms. But we readily concede the importance of studying those characteristics of individuals, communities, and social control agencies that also operate to influence the processes by which some are singled out for public attention as deviants. Ours is a middle-ground position that we think best mirrors the real world. We contend that social norms, behavioral acts of individuals, and responses of social audiences, including social control agencies, must all be examined in order to comprehend the complexities of deviance.

Is it then possible to devise a unified explanatory theory of deviance to account for most of the deviance occurring within society? In our opinion, even if inquiry is limited to violations of major "societal" norms, the likelihood for developing such a theory, however complex, is slim. Even the forms of misbehavior included in the "societal" conception of deviance are so varied, however, that any single explanation of them is impossible; and when we examine a more restricted range of deviance, such as juvenile delinquency, separate explanations are also required for the different forms which the activity takes.[39]

However, although general theories to account for *initial* involvement of actors in various forms of deviance may elude us, a coherent area of analysis is still possible if we restrict attention to "societal" norms. The rich concepts and insights of the labeling orientation, which focuses upon social reactions to deviants and the unfolding of deviant careers, can be developed further to provide valuable contributions to the already abundant empirical findings dealing with these matters.

SOME FURTHER OBSERVATIONS ON NORMS

As we have already noted, nearly all who speak of norms offer some kind of brief definition involving rules or standards that govern social interaction. Although Kingsley Davis offers no explicit definition of norms in his classic sociology text, he does talk about rules or standards that specify the behavior patterns that *ought* to be followed.[40] Davis also points out that the norms within a society are numerous and complex, and some kind of taxonomy is needed to bring order to this diversity. He makes some traditional sociological distinctions between folkways, mores, customary law, enacted law, and institutions. Institutions are sets of interrelated folkways, mores, and laws that have become organized around one or more societal function. Thus we speak of the marriage and family institution as a collection of rules and standards that guide marital and parent-child interaction patterns. Some but not all of these rules are embodied in codified family law in modern societies.

Some parallel remarks about norms are offered by Paul Mott.[41] He identifies norms as rules or standards that govern social interaction. Mott also observes that normative complexity characterizes modern societies, and he offers some rudimentary distinctions among norms, for instance between formal and informal standards. Along a similar line, James B. McKee identifies norms as rules of conduct that specify the "should" of behavior in social situations.[42] He, too, finds it necessary to distinguish between different kinds of norms, including folkways, mores, and laws (codified norms).

A larger survey of discussions of norms within the sociological literature would doubtless turn up many similar notions. Writers also often include some remarks about the complex and sometimes ephemeral character of norms, and it is commonly conceded that norms and rules are often more difficult to observe in the real world than is implied in sociological treatises. Stanton Wheeler has put the matter well:

> The term "norm" is a short and perhaps an oversimplified designation for something that cannot be seen or touched or even described very accurately, but something that every student of society knows exists because he can observe its effects on human behavior. The problem, however, is that norms are very difficult to portray as separate threads in the fabric of culture. The moment we lift a norm out of its context to see how it works as a guide to behavior, we are apt to discover that we have detached it from that shared body of experience which gives it whatever meaning it has to the persons whose lives are touched by it. Actually, the authority of any particular norm is hedged in by so many conditions and qualifications that it would be easier (and probably a good deal more accurate) simply to say that the social setting in which people act is governed by a moral climate, a normative temper, which cannot be broken up into its constituent parts.[43]

One of the most comprehensive discussions of norms has been offered by Jack P. Gibbs.[44] He begins his analysis by noting the difference between definitional and contingent attributes and points out that the former are those ingredients contained in the explicit definition of norms, while the latter refer to attributes that are present in the case of some norms and absent in others. Gibbs identifies the definitional attributes of norms as involving: "(1) a collective evaluation of behavior in terms of what it *ought* to be; (2) a collective expectation as to what behavior *will* be; and/or (3) particular *reactions* to behavior, including attempts to apply sanctions or otherwise induce a particular kind of conduct."[45] Virtually all of the conceptions of norms that have been offered by other scholars can be placed within this generic definition— that is, the definitional attributes of norms that are enumerated by Gibbs are usually central to the definitions offered by others who have analyzed social norms. Contingent attributes of norms, on the other hand, would include such variables as the specificity or severity of sanctions that are applied to violations of particular norms.

Gibbs's discussion then explicates some of the ways that particular normative patterns vary in terms of the definitional attributes identified above. For example, shared values among members of a group underpin some norms, such as the mores, while in other cases, particular norms may not be supported by shared values on the part of those to whom the norms apply, as in the case of rules imposed on a group by an external authority. Thus, legal codes in many African societies have been made up, in large part, of conduct norms imposed on these societies by colonial powers. We might expect little support for many of these laws among the African natives against whom they are enforced. Another illustration would be found in the instance of American laws forbidding private manufacture of whiskey. Those statutes receive little support from bootleggers or from their customers.

In other cases, the members of a social group may expect conformity to one norm and anticipate widespread evasions of another norm, even though they persist in the belief that neither normative prescription ought to be violated. For example, it is probably the case that most Americans believe that car salesmen ought to deal honestly and forthrightly with customers, at the same time that they express considerable distrust of car salesmen. Witness the hoary joke: "Would you buy a used car from this man?" Why should the joke always refer to car salesmen, rather than to refrigerator salesman, haberdashers, or other entrepreneurs?

We may also observe that sanctions are usually applied to some norm violations but infrequently to others. The contrast between white collar crime, which rarely is heavily punished, and ordinary felonies, which are the target of very marked punitive sanctions is one example of such discrimination. Finally, the sanctions levied against deviants may be applied by social audiences generally, or a special group such as the police or courts may be responsible for levying penalties against nonconformists. These distinctions in terms of definitional attributes generate a typology of norms, shown in table 2.

The sociologically informed reader will see that Gibbs has captured the essence of many of the distinctions among norms that are contained in other commentaries and has identified a larger number of norm-types than has been enumerated by others. For example, his forms of laws, types P, Q, R, and S, revolve around differences that others have noted, such as few collective values and sentiments to support some laws and strong social support for others. The Volstead Act, which existed during Prohibition illustrates the former, while laws against incest might be offered as a case of the latter type of law.

Gibbs acknowledges that extensive research is necessary before particular norms can be placed within his typology.[46] That is, empirical evidence is currently lacking on the extent to which specific rules and standards, including criminal laws, are backed up by collective evalu-

table 2 A Typology of Norms*

		[when the act occurs] Low probability that an attempt will be made to apply a sanction	[when the act occurs] High probability that an attempt will be made to apply a sanction:			
			By anyone (i.e., without regard to status)		Only by a person or persons in a particular status or statuses	
			By means that exclude the use of force	By means that may include the use of force	By means that exclude the use of force	By means that may include the use of force
Collective evaluation of the act	Collective expectation concerning the act	Type A: Collective conventions	Type D: Collective morals	Type H: Collective mores	Type L: Collective rules	Type P: Collective laws
	No collective expectation concerning the act	Type B: Problematic conventions	Type E: Problematic morals	Type I: Problematic mores	Type M: Problematic rules	Type Q: Problematic laws
No collective evaluation of the act	Collective expectation concerning the act	Type C: Customs	Type F: Possible empirical null class	Type J: Possible empirical null class	Type N: Exogenous rules	Type R: Exogenous laws
	No collective expectation concerning the act	Logical null class, i.e., non-normative	Type G: Possible empirical null class	Type K: Possible empirical null class	Type O: Coercive rules	Type S: Coercive laws

*Reprinted by permission from Jack P. Gibbs, "Norms: The Problem of Definition and Classification," American Journal of Sociology 70 (March 1965), p. 591. © 1970 by The University of Chicago.

ations or expectations. In short, we simply do not know very much about the degree of social support for prohibitions against various forms of behavior, nor do we have much evidence on societal expectations regarding conformity to these standards, so that Gibbs' essay can be read as a call for more research. Chapter five marshals some of the available data on social perceptions of normative rules.

Robin M. Williams, Jr., has also written incisively regarding normative variation in in complex societies, evasions of normative patterns, deviance, and related matters.[47] As he points out: "The institutionalized norms of social conduct never fully define concrete action. A norm is a standard (not necessarily explicit) for the course that action *should* follow, not a description of the action that actually occurs." (emphasis in the original)[48]

Behavior varies from normative prescriptions, in part, because of the generalized nature of norms and the specific situations of action. Many conduct norms are ambiguous, and allow for considerable behavioral diversity around the standard. Then too, modern societies consist of a mosaic of different subcultures, such that a major share of the deviation from allegedly universal norms actually centers about the clash of subcultural norms.[49]

Williams also devotes much space to analysis of *patterned evasions;* that is, instances of large-scale deviation from nominally supported social or legal norms. The conditions underlying patterned evasions are these:

1. For "reasons" functionally important to the social structure and the main value-systems, a certain activity, thing, or belief is prohibited and widely condemned.
2. But a large proportion of the socially powerful, and otherwise functionally essential, members of the relevant adult population demand the prohibited element.
3. Normative consensus is insufficient to prevent this demand from arising or to deter considerable numbers of individuals from catering to it.
4. But consensus is a great enough to prevent a public repudiation of the norm itself. [This fact derives from (1) above.]
5. Many of those who violate or evade the norm hold "essential" status in the social system; there is accordingly a strong resistance to wholesale punishment. [See (2) above.]
6. Hence, the situation is handled by: (a) public affirmation of the norm; (b) covert acceptance of widespread violation and evasion; (c) periodic token or "ritualistic" punishment, or punishment of those whose arrears unavoidably become public.[50]

It is clear from these remarks that Williams is not one who subscribes to a view of the social norms as dictating conformity. His analysis reflects a fundamental concern of modern deviance analysts: behavior generally, and conforming behavior specifically, is problematic. The intellectual challenge is to specify the conditions under which some behavior will be identified as conformist and other behavior as nonconformist or deviant.

The labeling school of thought on deviance has directed attention to normative variability and to the operation of various contingencies that influence the social reactions to norm violation. As we shall see in chapter seven, a central thrust of this perspective is that "deviance is in the eye of the beholder," that acts of norm violation do not automatically result in negative social responses being directed at the suspect. Accordingly, we shall have more to say about the subject of normative regulation of behavior and about responses to norm violations.

SUMMARY

This chapter has been concerned with the definitional task. We have observed two viewpoints on the proper study of deviance: the orientation that would have us center attention upon "societal" definitions of deviance and the perspective that would have us adopt an all-encompassing omnibus approach. We have opted for the "societal" definition. Further, this chapter has examined some aspects of norms and normative phenomena. We noted that relatively little is known about the social views of citizens regarding behavioral activities thought to be "deviant" or "conformist." In chapter five, we turn to a more detailed discussion of the empirical data that are available on that topic.

NOTES

[1] J. L. Simmons, "Public Stereotypes of Deviants," *Social Problems* 13 (Fall 1965): 223–32.

[2] Simon Dinitz, Russell B. Dynes, and Alfred C. Clark, eds., *Deviance* (New York: Oxford University Press, 1969), p. 4.

[3] Eliot Freidson, "Disability as Social Deviance," in Marvin B. Sussman, ed., *Sociology and Rehabilitation* (Washington, D.C.: American Sociological Association, 1965), p. 73.

[4] Marshall B. Clinard, *Sociology of Deviant Behavior,* 3d ed. (New York: Holt, Rinehart and Winston, 1968), p. 28.

[5] John Lofland, *Deviance and Identity* (Englewood Cliffs, N.J.: Prentice-Hall, 1969).

[6] John De Lamater, "On the Nature of Deviance," *Social Forces* 46 (June 1968): 445–55.

[7] Lofland, *Deviance and Identity.*, p. 1.

[8] Homosexuality, prostitution, alcoholism, crime, suicide, and juvenile delinquency are all cases of behavior which violate fairly specific, codified norms, and to which organized social control efforts are directed. The matter of "mental illness' is somewhat different, in that the "residual rules" which are broken by persons who have been formally designated as "mentally ill" are a good deal less clear. Becoming an identified "mentally ill" person seems to hinge upon contingencies of personal biography to a greater extent that in these other forms of deviance. See Thomas J. Scheff, *Being Mentally Ill* (Chicago: Aldine Publishing Co., 1966), pp. 31–54, for a discussion of "residual rule breaking" and mental illness. Attention is also currently being given to the attempt to define illness in general as deviance, and organized medicine as a response to this deviance. For a recent example of this attempt see Eliot Freidson, *Profession of Medicine* (New York: Dodd, Mead and Co., 1970), Part III.

[9] Edwin M. Lemert, *Human Deviance, Social Problems, and Social Control,* 2nd ed. (Englewood Cliffs, N.J.: Prentice-Hall, 1972), pp. 62–92.

[10] William A. Rushing (ed.), *Deviant Behavior and Social Process* (Chicago: Rand McNally & Co., 1969).

[11] Albert K. Cohen, *Deviance and Control* (Englewood Cliffs, N.J.: Prentice-Hall, 1966), pp. v–vi.

[12] Ibid., p. 1.

[13] Robert K. Merton, "Social Problems and Social Theory," in Merton and Robert A. Nisbet, eds., *Contemporary Social Problems,* 3d ed. (New York: Harcourt Brace Jovanovich, 1966), p. 824.

[14] Stanton Wheeler, "Deviant Behavior," in Neil J. Smelser, ed., *Sociology: An Introduction* (New York: John Wiley and Sons, 1967), pp. 604–66.

[15] Ibid., p. 608.

[16] Howard S. Becker, *Outsiders* (New York: Free Press of Glencoe, 1963). It is not entirely clear whether, in Becker's view, a specific person who engages in breaking a group-created rule is a deviant unless he becomes the target of a specific reaction. At one point (p. 14) rule-breaking behavior is separated from the term *deviant,* which is reserved for those labeled as deviant by some segment of society. At another point (p. 20), the category of "secret deviants"—who are not perceived as deviant—is identified, as well as "falsely accused," who are perceived as deviant when they have not actually broken a rule. Apparently, Becker's intent is close to that of Akers, who proposes that rule breaking be studied separately from reactions to specific rule breakers. See Ronald L. Akers, "Problems in the Sociology of Deviance: Social Definitions and Behavior," *Social Forces* 46 (June 1968): 455–65. A central issue then becomes one of identifying the circumstances under which specific rule breakers become identified and

labeled as deviant or avoid this tag. A reading of much of the current deviance literature would show that many students of deviance attend to both groups of rule breakers, those who have been labeled and those who have not.

[17] David Matza, *Becoming Deviant* (Englewood Cliffs, N.J.: Prentice-Hall, 1969), p. 10.

[18] Jack D. Douglas, ed., *Deviance and Respectability* (New York: Basic Books, 1970).

[19] Marvin B. Scott and Stanford M. Lyman, "Accounts, Deviance, and Social Order," in Douglas, *Deviance and Respectability,* pp. 89–119.

[20] Norman K. Denzin, "Rules of Conduct and the Study of Deviant Behavior: Some Notes on the Social Relationship," in Douglas, *Deviance and Respectability,* pp. 120–59.

[21] Ibid. p. 121.

[22] Ibid., pp. 122–26.

[23] Ibid. p. 138.

[24] Ibid., p. 151.

[25] Dean Harper and Frederick Emmert, "Work Behavior in a Service Industry," *Social Forces* 42 (December 1963): 216–25.

[26] Joseph Bensman and Israel Gerver, "Crime and Punishment in the Factory: The Function of Deviancy in Maintaining the Social System," *American Sociological Review* 28 (August 1963): 588–98.

[27] Ellwyn R. Stoddard, "The 'Informal Code' of Police Deviance: A Group Approach to 'Blue-Coat Crime,' " *Journal of Criminal Law, Criminology, and Police Science* 59 (June 1968): 201–13.

[28] The judgment that some behavior is trivial does not arise directly from observations about that activity. Stated differently, "triviality" is not a property of behavior which we observe through research scrutiny. When we observe behavior, we see particular lines of conduct, not "significance" or "triviality." Thus, the contention that some bit of activity is trivial is an opinion by the person who volunteers the claim. We would argue that observations about specific instances of social activity border on the trivial if they seem to lead only to the question: "So what?" Non-trivial social facts are those thought by the investigator or theorist to be linked to other important facts of human behavior. Non-trivial facts have sound theoretical consequences.

The view expressed here is that some behavior can be observed that seems to have no important links to anything else. It is of no particular importance except insofar as the sociologist wants to observe everything. A case in point might be a recent research report in one of the sociology journals by an investigator who spent some time in a Nevada bordello. He commented at length upon the situational discomfort he perceived while being fellated by a prostitute and regarding other features of the prostitute—"John" encounter. The "So what?" question comes to mind here. What significance does this report have for anything else? Does it tell us anything generally about prostitute-client relationships? Or does it tell us only about the discomfort experienced by a fairly naive customer? Whatever the significance of this report, its importance is not immediately self-evident.

Obviously, different observers are probably going to disagree about the "triviality" or "non-triviality" of many kinds of social acts, depending upon their perspectives, theoretical orientations, and so on. Thus some would claim that the observations of Erving Goffman are of profound importance, while others are less impressed with his detailed comments on social encounters. [Erving Goffman, *Relations in Public* (New York: Harper and Row, Publishers, 1972)].

However, we suspect that there are relatively few persons who would argue that acts of belching, flatulence, and bad table manners are of profound significance for what they tell us about anything else. In short, there may be some fair amount of agreement that the sociological need to know does not encompass the entire range of human behavior, that instead, it is possible to observe more than anyone really needs to know about fleeting bits and scraps of social encounters.

Our own view is that acts of criminality, sexual deviance, bizarre conduct leading to diagnoses of "mental disorder," and alcoholism are considerably more in need of study than are belching, facial tics, breaches of etiquette, verbal gaucherie, and the like. We are not interested in preventing others from focusing upon the latter, but we regard some of that endeavor as dangerously close to the study of trivia.

[29] Emile Durkheim, *The Rules of Sociological Method* (New York: Free Press of Glencoe, 1938), p. 68.

[30] Lemert, *Human Deviance, Social Problems, and Social Control;* Lemert, *Social Pathology* (New York: McGraw-Hill Book Co., 1951).

[31] Becker, *Outsiders.*

[32] Kai T. Erikson, "Notes on the Sociology of Deviance," in Howard S. Becker, ed., *The Other Side* (New York: Free Press of Glencoe, 1964), pp. 9–21.

[33] Scheff, *Being Mentally Ill.*

[34] Denzin, "Rules of Conduct and the Study of Deviant Behavior," p. 127.

[35] Clinard, *Sociology of Deviant Behavior.*

[36] Lemert, *Human Deviance, Social Problems, and Social Control.*

[37] Lofland, *Deviance and Identity.*

[38] A detailed review of the data on "hidden delinquency" appears in Gwynn Nettler, *Explaining Crime* (New York: McGraw-Hill Book Co., 1974), pp. 62–97, and in Don C. Gibbons, *Delinquent Behavior* (Englewood Cliffs, N.J.: Prentice-Hall, 1970), pp. 20–46. Much of the research material reviewed appears to indicate that those juveniles who engage in relatively serious violations of the criminal code are most likely to be processed through the juvenile justice system and identified as "juvenile delinquents." Also see Gibbons, *Society, Crime, and Criminal Careers,* 2d ed. (Englewood Cliffs, N.J.: Prentice-Hall, 1973), pp. 59–65

for some data revealing the effects of variations in police practices, social background characteristics of alleged law violators, etc., upon the social responses to these persons. The impact of racial background on police practices toward juveniles is noted in Theodore N. Ferdinand and Elmer G. Luchterhand, "Inner-City Youth, the Police, the Juvenile Court, and Justice," *Social Problems* 17 (Spring 1970): 510–27; Terence P. Thornberry, "Race, Socio-Economic Status and Sentencing in the Juvenile Justice System," *Journal of Criminal Law and Criminology* 64 (March 1973): 90–98.

The issue of whether persons who are publicly identified as "mentally ill" also are involved in marked departures from identifiable behavioral rules is considered in some detail in chapter eight.

[39] Gibbons, *Delinquent Behavior, passim.*

[40] Kingsley Davis, *Human Society* (New York: The Macmillan Co., 1948), pp. 52–82.

[41] Paul E. Mott, *The Organization of Society* (Englewood Cliffs, N.J.: Prentice-Hall, 1965), pp. 24–29.

[42] James B. McKee, *Introduction to Sociology,* 2d ed. (New York: Holt, Rinehart and Winston, 1974), pp. 64–65.

[43] Wheeler, "Deviant Behavior," pp. 604–5.

[44] Jack P. Gibbs, "Norms: The Problem of Definition and Classification," *American Journal of Sociology* 70 (March 1965): 586–94.

[45] Ibid., p. 589.

[46] Ibid., pp. 593–94.

[47] Robin M. Williams, Jr., *American Society,* 3d ed. (New York: Alfred A. Knopf, 1970), pp. 413–37.

[48] Ibid., p. 413.

[49] For another discussion of value and normative pluralism in American society, see Lemert, *Social Pathology.*

[50] Williams, *American Society,* p. 421.

public conceptions
of deviance

W e have observed that there are at present several divergent definitions of deviance forming two main types: "societal" and omnibus definitions. The most frequently employed of these is the "societal" one, which holds that deviance is behavior departing from conduct norms shared by most members of the society. But we argued that norms are societal only insofar as they are binding or enforced upon members of society. The claim that a majority of the population holds some sort of allegiance to norms is often a fiction, for many conduct standards are followed fairly closely because people feel they are compelled to do so, not because they feel the rules are just or honorable. Accordingly, we ought to treat the question of social support for norms and social definitions of deviance empirically by investigating the extent to which different conduct standards are supported within society.

Similarly, we ought to know much more than we do presently about the views in the community regarding those who engage in deviant acts, however these acts are defined; relatively little is known about how the citizenry defines deviance or how it views the deviant actor. The pages to follow present an inventory of studies in these two areas and point to some additional research that needs to be done.

These studies deal with various facets of laymen's perceptions of norms and deviants; that is, relatively few of the research inquiries that have been conducted so far have quizzed people directly about their sentiments regarding a particular legal statute or norm. Many of the studies have produced only tangential observations regarding public views of particular norms,[1] while others have centered not public perceptions of norms, but rather on attitudes toward various deviant actors. In the latter, members of the general public have been asked to indicate their views about homosexuals, alcoholics, or other deviants. Then too, a fair share of the information at hand has to do with public opinions about actions that ought to be taken against deviants rather than about the norms they violate.

PUBLIC VIEWS ON "DEVIANCE"

Most research has dealt with specific forms of deviance rather than with public perceptions of various patterns of nonconformity as a whole. In one exploratory venture, however, J. L. Simmons found that 180 persons listed 1,154 items of behavior as deviant, with an average of 6.4 items per respondent.[2] He concluded that, quite probably, nearly every kind of behavior imaginable is deviant in the eyes of some and normal in the eyes of others.

John I. Kitsuse has also researched public perceptions of various forms of deviance, including homosexuality.[3] He asked college students whether they had ever encountered a homosexual, and about 10 percent answered affirmatively. Those identifying homosexuals frequently employed indirect evidence such as third party claims or social actions which seemed insufficiently "manly," as well as direct evidence including overt sexual propositions. Indeed, one of the most significant findings of this research is that the high frequency with which homosexuality was imputed to individuals on the basis of relatively vague and indirect evidence suggests that these imputations may often be faulty. Further, Kitsuse's subjects showed considerable variability as far as responses to putative (alleged) homosexuals are concerned. Many students said they had not reacted in a hostile fashion to the individual when they discovered evidence that he was a homosexual, and many continued their social affiliations with the alleged homosexual. These findings run counter to the notion that aggression and hostility are always directed at homosexuals by nonhomosexuals.

A third investigation by Elizabeth A. Rooney and Don C. Gibbons dealt with more general attitudes and questioned San Francisco residents regarding abortion, homosexuality, and drug addiction.[4] Some of the findings parallel those of Simmons in that both studies indicated many members of the general public harbor numerous misconceptions about deviance.

Ray C. Rist, Lee J. Haggerty, and Don C. Gibbons conducted another exploratory study in Portland, Oregon, which dealt with citizens' views about what public policies ought to be pursued regarding "adult bookstores" and pornography, homosexuality, prostitution, and other forms of sexual conduct.[5] They also assessed public knowledge about deviance. In general, the researchers found that views of *specific* forms of sexual misconduct tend to cluster but that responses about sexual deviance in general do not; that is, they observed that individuals who agree with one hostile statement toward a specific form of sexual activity such as pornographic theaters tend to respond consistently to other questions on the same subject. However, they found little patterning of responses by individuals toward different forms of sexual conduct. Thus one cannot predict how persons who respond negatively to one form of behavior, such as prostitution, will react to other patterns of conduct, for some who were tolerant toward one kind of activity were tolerant toward other forms, while other respondents were hostile toward some activities and tolerant toward others.

PUBLIC CONCEPTIONS ABOUT "THE CRIME PROBLEM"[6]

During the past decade, many politicians on both the national and local levels have vigorously decried the "breakdown of law and order," "crime in the streets," and similar themes. The mass media have paid much attention to these contentions, and the citizenry has thus been bombarded from all sides with claims that lawlessness has reached epidemic proportions in the United States. It would be little wonder, then, if we were to discover that many members of the general public have come to believe they are surrounded by muggers, rapists, burglars, and other lawbreakers.

A number of studies have dealt with perceptions about the crime problem, and all document the widespread public fears about a breakdown of law and order. Jennie McIntyre has summarized the research undertaken for the President's Commission on Law Enforcement and Administration of Justice which portrayed most people throughout the nation as believing that cime is a worsening problem in their own community.[7] Other inquiries into public conceptions about the crime problem report parallel findings.[8] This research includes a comparative field study by Don C. Gibbons, Joseph F. Jones, and Peter G. Garabedian in Portland and San Francisco, on perceptions about the crime problem in those cities.[9] Other relevant studies are a survey by John E. Conklin in an urban, high crime rate area and a suburban, low crime rate community;[10] a study in Missouri by Sarah L. Boggs;[11] a nationwide random sample survey by Richard A. Block;[12] and a statewide survey in North Carolina.[13] Their evidence points toward widespread apprehensiveness about criminality. Research on this topic has also been conducted in Europe, with similar results.[14]

OPINIONS ABOUT CORRECTIONAL PROCESSES

Although not directly concerned with public views of deviance, there are a number of investigations of opinions about the correctional handling of offenders which ought to be noted. One study by Don C. Gibbons dealt with knowledge possessed by California residents.[15] Few of these persons had any detailed understanding of the workings of the correctional machinery. Similar results were found in a survey commissioned by the California State Legislature Assembly Committee on Criminal Procedure,[16] and in a nationwide study by the Joint Commission on Correctional Manpower and Training.[17] A principle of "out of sight, out of mind" emerges from all of these data, in which we find that public attention soon drifts away from criminal deviants locked up in "people-changing" institutions. Citizens know little about them or their keepers.

Other studies have endeavored to determine what the public sees as appropriate responses to types of criminality. In one investigation, Arnold M. Rose and Arthur E. Prell asked a number of college students to indicate the offenses they regarded as most serious from a list of thirteen minor felonies.[18] Many subjects agreed on those crimes judged to be the most heinous. Examination of the penalties meted out to offenders indicated that many of the crimes viewed as *least* serious by citizens actually received the heaviest penalties in the courts. One parallel investigation to that of Rose and Prell was conducted by Don C. Gibbons in California,[19] while another was carried out in Canada by Craig L. Boydell and Carl F. Grindstaff.[20] Both studies found cases of criminality where public views appear to support penalties that differ from those being handed out by the courts. Donald J. Newman examined food, drug, and cosmetic violations by quizzing a sample of adults about the punishment they regarded as appropriate for such offenses.[21] Most respondents thought these activities should be punished more heavily than they had been in fact.

An indication of historical changes in public attitudes toward drug addiction is found in an investigation by E. M. Pattison, L. A. Bishop, and A. S. Linsky which involves portrayals of drug addiction in popular magazines.[22] The data indicated that in comparison to opinions in 1900, drug addicts are now viewed as less responsible for their behavior, their social milieu is given greater causal emphasis, and rehabilitation, rather than a strictly punitive approach, is now seen as an appropriate response. A second study of public knowledge about drug abuse was conducted by the New York State Narcotic Addiction Control Commission and reported somewhat similar findings.[23]

Reports are also available concerning public perceptions of the juvenile justice system. William P. Lentz surveyed a sample of Wisconsin adults concerning attitudes toward juvenile control.[24] Most favored swift and impartial justice toward juveniles and probation in place of institutional commitment; many asserted that juvenile offenders are "ill" and in need of expert treatment. In another study, Howard Parker examined views of the juvenile court in four Washington state communities.[25] Most of the persons quizzed were ignorant of the workings of the juvenile court and misperceived it as punishing delinquents less severely than they would have preferred. Many asserted that the court was "not tough enough" with juvenile offenders, but when asked to indicate what actions they would have taken against four delinquent cases, most of them opted for penalties that were parallel to, or *less severe,* than those that had actually been meted out by the court.

PUBLIC VIEWS ON ALCOHOL AND ALCOHOLISM

One study of public views of alcohol comes from Harold W. Pfautz's analysis of the image of alcohol in public fiction.[26] Not surprisingly, he reported a trend toward increased social approval of liquor use and a growing tendency to see alcohol as a social instrument rather than a drug. Arnold S. Linsky found that young, relatively well-educated people in a Washington state sample were more favorable to social drinking than were others.[27] They viewed alcoholism as a medical-psychiatric problem and favored medical-psychiatric treatment of it. Somewhat similar observations can be found in an opinion survey in Iowa by Harold A. Mulford and Donald E. Miller.[28] These investigators reported that many of their respondents viewed alcoholics as sick, but they also saw them as weak-willed. Attitudes toward alcoholics varied with age, rural-urban residence, education, and other characteristics of citizens.[29]

PUBLIC PERSPECTIVES ON MENTAL DISORDER

For several decades, vigorous mental health campaigns have made strong efforts to spread the notion that mental illness is like other health problems and should be treated similarly. Lay perspectives on mental health and mental disorders have been examined by Glen V. Ramsey and Melita Seipp,[30] Julian L. Woodward,[31] and Jum C. Nunnally,[32] among others. Gerald Gurin, Joseph Veroff, and Sheila Field have reported a national survey on how people feel about their own mental health.[33]

A collection of studies of public notions about mental disorders has accumulated over the years, which uses a questionnaire with a set of fictitious descriptions of different psychiatric disorders. These descriptions deal with a paranoid individual, a case of simple schizophrenia, a chronic alcoholic, a case of anxiety neurosis, compulsive phobic behavior, and a juvenile delinquency character disorder.[34] The surveys in question included a national study by Shirley A. Star,[35] an inquiry in a small Canadian community by Elaine Cumming and John Cumming,[36] a survey in Baltimore by Paul V. Lemkau and Guido M. Crocetti,[37] an investigation in Easton, Maryland, by John K. Meyer,[38] and two studies in New York City by Bruce P. Dohrenwend and Edwin Chin-Shong.[39]

When taken together several important observations flow out of these surveys. Although psychiatrists apparently tend to agree that all of the described personality-behavior patterns involve relatively severe pathology, the citizens surveyed in these studies did not always see pathology involved. In particular, laymen were most likely to withhold that diagnosis from cases of compulsive phobia, juvenile delinquency, anxiety, and alcoholism. Indeed, only the paranoid case was judged by most respondents as clearly involving pathology. A second conclusion is that there has apparently been a significant shift in public views, and considerably more people are willing to regard these various cases as involving pathology now than in the early 1950s. Third, in several of the investigations, the researchers observed that middle- and upper-status respondents were most likely to see pathology in these cases. Fourth, the laymen tended to judge as most serious those cases of behavior that seemed to involve the greatest physical threat to others. Finally, Dohrenwend and Chin-Shong maintain that, while lower-class individuals regard fewer cases as serious than do middle-class persons, the lower class is not more tolerant of those forms of psychological disorder which it regards as serious than are other classes.

In another recent study using descriptions of mentally ill persons, Derek L. Phillips has noted that citizens stress the degree to which persons are seen to depart from socially approved forms of behavior more than they stress pathology as measured from a mental hygiene point of view.[40] In another investigation, Phillips has also argued that mentally ill persons run the greatest danger of social rejection if they seek help from a mental hospital or psychiatrist and run less risk of rejection by seeking help from a physician or clergyman.[41]

We have seen in this brief review that a number of studies have been conducted on some aspects of public views of deviance. The research by J. L. Simmons and several other investigations have probed the general notions of deviance held by individuals. There have also been many studies of perceptions about crime, surveys of public notions about alcoholism, and investigations of attitudes toward mental illness. Although a fair amount of work has already been accomplished, there are a good many questions that remain to be addressed by research.[42] We now turn to a survey of some of this unfinished business.

WHAT IS "DEVIANCE"?

Spokesmen for the labeling school of deviance analysis have admonished us to note that a social audience is involved in determining that someone is a deviant or that some behavior is deviance. Howard S. Becker's oft-quoted statement asserts that: "... deviance is *not* a quality of the act the person commits, but rather a consequence of the application by others of rules and sanctions to an 'offender.' The deviant is one to whom that label has successfully been applied; deviant behavior is behavior that people so label." (emphasis in the original)[43]

Becker's claim implies that the beholders in whose eyes deviance exists are usually laymen, that it is ordinary citizens who impose social definitions or labels on deviants. In modern societies, of course, the social diagnosis of "hood," "queer," "pimp," or "crazy" is often rendered by a governmental or other public agency such as the police or courts.

We need more research, however, on the question of *public* notions of deviance as contrasted to official definitions. At present, we do not have a very clear understanding of the world view carried about in the heads of citizens. We need more data revealing the range and kinds of behavior they regard as wrong, bad, or in some other way as behavior to be discouraged—in short, deviance as conceptualized by the man on the street. Further, what social labels do people attach to these various lines of conduct, as distinct from official labels such as second degree burglary, statutory rape, or involutional melancholia? Although we know about some labels employed by laymen, we need more inquiry into the vocabularies they use to sort out social conduct and diagnose it.[44] We have some idea of the bases on which legislatures and other governmental structures regard some activities as requiring legislative control, but we still know very little about the lay perspective. Simmons's exploratory studies are a beginning, as are the investigations of public conceptions of mental illness noted previously, in which laymen seem most concerned about behavior seen as dangerous to others; but more work of this nature is in order if we are to achieve anything approaching a comprehensive picture of views of deviance.

ARE VIEWS ON DEVIANCE INTERRELATED?

Investigations of lay views on deviance have nearly all been confined to particular kinds of deviant roles; thus people have been asked to indicate how they react to alcoholics or criminals or mentally disordered persons but have not been asked to differentiate their reactions to assorted kinds of deviants. Commonsense observations suggest that perceptions about deviants are *patterned,* that is, that those who accept the sick view of alcoholics are also more likely to agree that many criminals are characterized by personality pathology, and that drug addicts and homosexuals are psychologically sick. Similarly, these persons perhaps also tend to accept psychiatric notions of mental disorder, while others may be prone to reject the view of deviants as sick persons. Conjecture is, however, different from hard evidence. The question of the extent to which notions about deviance group together in similar attitudes toward different kinds of deviants needs further investigation. The survey data by Rist, Haggerty, and Gibbons alluded to previously represent a beginning in this direction.[45]

IDENTIFYING DEVIANTS AND DEVIANT ACTS

Popular perceptions of deviant conduct seem to be inaccurate on two related counts. First, it is probably the case that laymen frequently attribute a variety of characteristics, usually negatively evaluated, to particular kinds of deviants which these individuals do not, in fact, exhibit. Second, it is also likely that many persons have erroneous understandings of exactly what it is that the deviant does when he is being deviant. The first of these matters is what Edwin M. Lemert designated as putative deviation: "that portion of the societal definition of the deviant which has no foundation in his objective behavior."[46] Thus, criminal lawbreakers are popularly conceived as suffering from personality pathologies and involved in bizarre life styles. Similarly, homosexuality is widely believed to be carried on by persons who are flawed in a variety of other ways as well. The remarks of William L. Shirer, concerning members of the German Nazi party, illustrate some of these putative notions:

> Many of its top leaders, beginning with its chief, Roehm, were notorious homosexual perverts. Lieutenant Edmund Heines, who led the Munich S.A., was not only a homosexual but a convicted murderer. These two and dozens of other quarreled and feuded as only men of unnatural sexual inclinations, with their peculiar jealousies, can.[47]

We have noted several studies of societal conceptions of deviance in which putative elements dominated. Simmons's exploratory work showed that people have many stereotypical and erroneous notions in their heads concerning deviants of one kind or another. Similarly, the Rooney and Gibbons investigation noted that numerous erroneous ideas about abortion and abortionists, homosexuals, and drug addicts have popular support. Much more research could be conducted regarding putative elements and the laymen's notions about the behavior of deviants.

One form of conduct which is probably subject to many mistaken notions is homosexuality. Even the professional literature, particularly the writings of psychiatrists, is permeated with erroneous descriptions of homosexual behavior. For example, Evelyn Hooker has shown that the commonly employed designations of homosexuals as passive and active are not congruent with the sexual behavior of homosexual persons.[48] A thoughtful essay by William Simon and John H. Gagnon. conveys the contrast which probably exists between common notions of homosexuality and the actual social behavior of such persons.[49] These writers remind us that the role of homosexual is often only a relatively minor part of the configuration of social roles occupied by individuals and is frequently not the most salient portion of the person's life style.

Lay notions about sex offenders such as exhibitionists and rapists are also probably equally inaccurate. We probably would find in an inquiry on this matter that many imagine forcible rapists are involved in bizarre, violent assaults on females, quite in contrast to the facts.[50] Along the same line, it seems plausible to expect that notions about other kinds of criminality are also markedly incorrect and filled with putative elements.

THE SOURCES OF NOTIONS ABOUT DEVIANCE

The literature on deviance contains little on the origin of attitudes and beliefs about deviance. Commentary on the social sources of beliefs is found in Howard S. Becker's discussion of *moral entrepreneurs,* that is, those who take a special interest in promulgating a definition of conduct as bad, wicked, or deviant.[51] J. Edgar Hoover's utterances about "mad dogs" and "slimy vermin from the underworld," illustrate moral entrepreneurship, as does the work of the Treasury Department in getting people to identify marijuana smoking as a form of deviance requiring repression. The mass media play a particularly prominent part in creating and diffusing perspectives on deviance.[52]

Relatively little is known about the processes through which persons acquire their views about aberrant conduct. Research should focus attention on young children and examine the process of how attitudes about deviance are learned and the major influences in this process, such as the attitudes of parents, peers, and mass media content.

EMERGING PUBLIC DEFINITIONS OF DEVIANCE

A sexual revolution seems to be underway in the United States, although sociologists have not analyzed these changes extensively. The dramatic success of *Playboy* magazine with its sales of 6,500,000 copies, the proliferation of "skin houses" ("adult" theaters), the spread of adult bookstores, and scholarly and popular press accounts of the development of "swinging" among married persons all seem to indicate changes in sexual activity in contemporary society. Given these shifts in sexual behavior patterns, we might wonder what changes are occurring in public definitions of sexual morality and notions of sexual normality and deviance. For example, how widespread and how accurate is information about activities such as "swinging" among the general public? What view of this behavior do citizens take? How does the public regard adult book stores and sex film theaters? We might examine a recent comment in the *Berkeley Barb* by a reporter who had been studying patrons at a "skin flick" theater. He observed that social definitions of these establishments are ambiguous and said that the audience ". . . responded with applause—a rarity I later learned, since skin flick audiences don't seem to know yet whether society considers them perverts or liberal connoisseurs and thus tend to repress spontaneity."[53] One might add that sociologists don't know how society regards the moviegoers either.

Data are also scarce on such matters as lay opinions of the increased sexual openness among members of the youth culture. We perhaps also ought to be curious about the extent to which such activities as the "Gay Lib" movement have affected the public images of and attitudes toward homosexuality.[54] Finally, although it may be too early to tell, we ought to try to discover the effect on public sentiments of revisions in Connecticut, Colorado, Idaho, Oregon, and Illinois state law, in which private acts of homosexuality among consenting adults are no longer proscribed by the criminal law in those states.

These comments suggest that sociologists might seriously consider monitoring changes in public attitudes toward sexual deviance as laws on obscenity change and magazines portraying various deviant sex acts become more readily available. The rapid diffusion of marijuana smoking throughout the general population has probably attenuated traditional hostile attitudes toward marijuana use; study of this area of social change might also provide valuable information on how lay opinions of deviance are modified.

WORDS AND DEEDS[55]

The studies summarized and the research problems examined to this point have all involved survey research techniques which focus on attitudes and beliefs about deviance. Fear of crime, perspectives on mental disorder, and putative beliefs about deviants are all personal, individual thought patterns. But what conclusions can be drawn from the responses of people to questionnaires about crime, alcoholism, mental disorder, and other forms of deviance? What do these responses tell us about social behavior? What relationship, if any, exists between words and deeds?

Little is known, however, about how people's behavior relates to their perceptions about deviance. Are those individuals who verbalize the greatest apprehensiveness about crime in the streets more likely than others to buy guns or large dogs, increase their insurance, or engage in other protective actions? Do individuals who express hostile attitudes toward homosexuals convert their negative views into behavioral responses different from the responses of those who express more tolerant opinions? Do the people who openly fear the mentally disordered or who express hostile sentiments about "hippies" have certain parallel behavioral responses? No answers to these questions are now available.

Nor is the relationship of social policy to public opinions about deviance understood. Whose perspectives influence most strongly the enforcement policies of police or the actions of city officials? The usual answer is the kind offered by Michael Banton who claims that city police agencies are attuned to popular morality and try to enforce the laws most congruent with the sentiments of most citizens.[56] Similarly, sociologists generally believe that policemen and city officials are often most responsive to the standards and attitudes of the middle- and upper-classes. Although there is little doubt that these broad arguments hint at the truth, these contentions are little more than unsubstantiated hypotheses at present. We know very little about how the police or other officials are informed about popular morality, or how pressure groups representing a selected view of popular morality function.

SUMMARY

This chapter has examined a variety of research investigations into social definitions of deviance. We have also commented on issues that need to be covered in future research. Our attention will turn in the next chapter to theories that have been offered regarding the social structural forces impelling persons into norm violating acts.

NOTES

¹ For example, see Joseph R. Gusfield, *Symbolic Crusade* (Urbana, Ill.: University of Illinois Press, 1963). This research indicated that the Volstead Act designed to enforce prohibition of alcohol consumption was not supported by the general public in the United States. However, the research did not deal directly or in detail with the views of individual citizens. For a discussion of public views of other criminal laws, see Don C. Gibbons, *Society, Crime, and Criminal Careers,* 2d ed. (Englewood Cliffs, N.J.: Prentice-Hall, 1973), pp. 35–39.

² J. L. Simmons, "Public Stereotypes of Deviants," *Social Problems* 13 (Fall 1965): 223–32.

³ John I. Kitsuse, "Societal Reaction to Deviant Behavior: Problems of Theory and Method," *Social Problems* 9 (Winter 1962): 247–57.

⁴ Elizabeth A. Rooney and Don C. Gibbons, "Social Reactions to 'Crimes Without Victims,' " *Social Problems* 13 (Spring 1966): 400–10.

⁵ Ray C. Rist, Lee J. Haggerty, and Don C. Gibbons, "Public Perceptions of Sexual 'Deviance': A Study of the Interrelations of Knowledge and Values," mimeographed (Center for Sociological Research, Portland State University, 1973). See also C. Ronald Huff and Joseph E. Scott, "Public Attitudes on Deviance: The Case for Patterned Perspectives," paper presented at Pacific Sociological Association meetings, March 1974.

⁶ For a detailed bibliography of studies of public views on the crime problem, see Albert D. Biderman, Susan S. Oldham, Sally K. Ward, and Maureen A. Eby, *An Inventory of Surveys of the Public on Crime, Justice, and Related Topics* (Washington, D.C.: National Institute of Law Enforcement and Criminal Justice, Law Enforcement Assistance Administration, 1972).

⁷ Jennie McIntyre, "Public Attitudes Toward Crime and Law Enforcement," *Annals of the American Academy of Political and Social Science* 374 (November 1967): 34–46.

⁸ However, somewhat different observations were obtained in a survey of the readers of *Psychology Today.* These relatively young and well-educated citizens were of the opinion that current crime rates are higher than in the past. Most of them held that some kind of treatment rather than punishment should

be given to drug addicts, alcoholics, prostitutes, and homosexuals. Many of them asserted that white-collar criminals are dealt with too leniently, most of them opposed the death penalty, and most felt that juveniles should receive different and less severe penalties than adult offenders. Liberal respondents voiced approval of Supreme Court decisions in the area of due process, while conservatives opposed these rulings. Most of the respondents held that responsibility for crime rests on the individual, not upon adverse societal conditions. See "Your Thoughts on Crime and Punishment," *Psychology Today* (May 1969): 53–58.

[9] Don C. Gibbons, Joseph F. Jones, and Peter G. Garabedian, "Gauging Public Opinion About the Crime Problem," *Crime and Delinquency* 18 (April 1972): 134–46.

[10] John E. Conklin, "Dimensions of Community Responses to the Crime Problem," *Social Problems* 18 (Winter 1971): 373–85.

[11] Sarah L. Boggs, "Formal and Informal Crime Control: An Exploratory Study of Urban, Suburban, and Rural Orientations," *Sociological Quarterly* 12 (Summer 1971): 319–27.

[12] Richard A. Block, "Fear of Crime and Fear of the Police," *Social Problems* 19 (Summer 1971): 91–101.

[13] Richard J. Richardson, Oliver Williams, Thomas Denyer, Skip McGaughey, and Darlene Walker, *Perspectives on the Legal Justice System: Public Attitudes and Criminal Victimization* (Chapel Hill, N.C.: Institute for Research in Social Science, University of North Carolina, 1972).

[14] Wolfgang Kaupen, Holger Volks, and Raymund Werle, *Compendium of Results of a Representative Survey Among the German Population on Knowledge and Opinion of Law and Legal Institutions* (Cologne, Germany: Working Group on Sociology of Law, 1970).

[15] Don C. Gibbons, "Who Knows What About Correction?" *Crime and Delinquency* 9 (April 1963): 137–44.

[16] Assembly Committee on Criminal Procedure, *Deterrent Effects of Criminal Sanctions* (Sacramento: California State Legislature, 1968).

[17] Joint Commission on Correctional Manpower and Training, *The Public Looks at Crime and Corrections* (Washington, D.C.: Joint Commission on Correctional Manpower and Training, 1968).

[18] Arnold M. Rose and Arthur E. Prell, "Does the Punishment Fit the Crime? A Study in Social Valuation," *American Journal of Sociology* 61 (November 1955): 247–59.

[19] Don C. Gibbons, "Crime and Punishment: A Study in Social Attitudes," *Social Forces* 47 (June 1969): 391–97.

[20] Craig L. Boydell and Carl F. Grindstaff, "Public Opinion and the Criminal Law: An Empirical Test of Public Opinions Toward Legal Sanctions," in Boydell, Grindstaff, and P. C. Whitehead, eds., *Deviant Behavior and Societal Reaction* (Toronto: Holt, Rinehart and Winston, 1972).

[21] Donald J. Newman, "Public Attitudes Toward a Form of White-Collar Crime," *Social Problems* 4 (January 1957): 228–32.

[22] E. M. Pattison, L. A. Bishop, and A. S. Linsky, "Changes in Public Attitudes on Narcotic Addiction," *American Journal of Psychiatry* 125 (August 1968): 160–67.

[23] Daniel Glaser and Mary Snow, *Public Knowledge and Attitudes on Drug Abuse in New York State* (New York: New York State Narcotic Addiction Control Commission, 1969).

[24] William P. Lentz, "Social Status and Attitudes Toward Delinquency Control," *Journal of Research in Crime and Delinquency* 3 (July 1966): 147–54.

[25] Howard Parker, "Juvenile Court Actions and Public Response," in Peter G. Garabedian and Don C. Gibbons, eds., *Becoming Delinquent* (Chicago: Aldine Publishing Co., 1970), pp. 252–65.

[26] Harold W. Pfautz, "The Image of Alcohol in Public Fiction: 1900–1904 and 1946–1950," *Quarterly Journal of Studies on Alcohol* 23 (March 1962): 131–46.

[27] Arnold S. Linsky, "The Changing Public Views of Alcoholism," *Quarterly Journal of Studies on Alcohol* 32 (September 1970): 692–704; see also Linsky, "Religious Differences in Lay Attitudes and Knowledge on Alcoholism and Its Treatment," *Journal for the Scientific Study of Religion* 5 (1965): 41–50.

[28] Harold A. Mulford and Donald E. Miller, "Measuring Public Acceptance of the Alcoholic as a Sick Person," *Quarterly Journal of Studies on Alcohol* 25 (June 1964): 314–23; see also Mulford and Miller, "Public Definitions of the Alcoholic," *Quarterly Journal of Studies on Alcohol* 12 (June 1961): 312–20.

[29] Studies of attitudes toward Skid Road alcoholics are summarized in Howard M. Bahr, *Skid Row* (New York: Oxford University Press, 1973), pp. 39–86.

[30] Glen V. Ramsey and Melita Scipp, "Public Opinions and Information Concerning Mental Health," *Journal of Clinical Psychology* 4 (October 1948): 397–406.

[31] Julian L. Woodward, "Changing Ideas on Mental Illness and Its Treatment," *American Sociological Review* 16 (August 1951): 443–54.

[32] Jum C. Nunnally, Jr., *Popular Conceptions of Mental Health* (New York: Holt, Rinehart and Winston, 1961).

[33] Gerald Gurin, Joseph Veroff, and Sheila Field, *Americans View Their Mental Health* (New York: Basic Books, 1960); see also Leo Srole, Thomas S. Langner, Stanley T. Michael, Marvin K. Opler, and Thomas A. C. Rennie, *Mental Health in the Metropolis: The Midtown Manhattan Study* (New York: McGraw-Hill Book Co., 1962).

[34] Shirley A. Star, *The Public's Ideas About Mental Illness* (Chicago: National Opinion Research Center, 1955).

[35] Ibid.

[36] Elaine Cumming and John Cumming, *Closed Ranks* (Cambridge, Mass.: Harvard University Press, 1957).

[37] Paul V. Lemkau and Guido M. Crocetti, "An Urban Population's Opinion and Knowledge About Mental Illness," *American Journal of Psychiatry* 117 (February 1962): 692–700.

[38] John K. Meyer, "Attitudes Toward Mental Illness in a Maryland Community," *Public Health Reports* 79 (September 1964): 769–72.

[39] Bruce P. Dohrenwend and Edwin Chin-Shong, "Social Status and Attitudes Toward Psychological Disorder: The Problem of Tolerance of Deviance," *American Sociological Review* 32 (June 1967): 417–33.

[40] Derek L. Phillips, "Rejection of the Mentally Ill: The Influence of Behavior and Sex," *American Sociological Review* 29 (October 1964): 679–87.

[41] Derek L. Phillips, "Rejection: A Possible Consequence of Seeking Help for Mental Disorders," *American Sociological Review* 28 (December 1963): 963–72.

[42] A pioneering inquiry into another area of behavior is Julian B. Roebuck and Bruce Hunter, "The Awareness of Health-Care Quackery as Deviant Behavior," *Journal of Health and Social Behavior* 13 (June 1972): 162–66.

[43] Howard S. Becker, *Outsiders* (New York: Free Press of Glencoe, 1963), p. 9.

[44] Several illustrations of the matters which need to be studied can be offered. For one, Polsky has noted that American slang contains a term for mother-son incest but none for sibling or father-daughter forms of incest. But, mother-son incest is extremely rare, so that in this case, the public use (or non-use) of a term for deviant behavior is not an accurate indicator of prevalence of deviance. See Ned Polsky, *Hustlers, Beats, and Others* (Garden City, New York: Doubleday and Co., 1969), p. 123. A second illustration is statutory rape. Laymen often refer to the female participants in statutory rape as "jail bait" or "San Quentin quail," suggesting that the girls are guilty of bringing rape upon themselves and that statutory rape is inconsequential. However, the criminal law and the criminal courts do not take this view. Persons who get into court on charges of statutory rape often receive quite severe sentences.

[45] Rist, Haggerty, and Gibbons, "Public Perceptions of Sexual 'Deviance.'"

[46] Edwin M. Lemert, *Social Pathology* (New York: McGraw-Hill Book Co., 1951), p. 56. A closely related matter has to do with imputations of deviance based on indirect evidence. Many of these surmises that someone is a deviant because of other activities in which he is involved are probably incorrect and constitute wrongful accusations. For example, incumbents of certain occupational roles such as hairdresser or professional dancer-chorus member in stage musicals are frequently believed to be homosexuals. Similarly, it is apparently the case that many citizens believe that movie actors and actresses lead bizarre, sexually uninhibited lives. These imputations of deviance are probably incorrect in many instances.

[47] William L. Shirer, *The Rise and Fall of the Third Reich* (New York: Simon and Schuster, 1960), p. 120.

[48] Evelyn Hooker, "An Empirical Study of Some Relations Between Sexual Patterns and Gender Identity in Male Homosexuals," in John Money, ed., *Sex*

Research: New Developments (New York: Holt, Rinehart and Winston, 1965), pp. 20–52.

[49] William Simon and John H. Gagnon, "Homosexuality: The Formulation of a Sociological Perspective," *Journal of Health and Social Behavior* 8 (September 1967): 177–85.

[50] Empirical evidence on rape is discussed in Gibbons, *Society, Crime, and Criminal Careers*, pp. 390–94.

[51] Becker, *Outsiders*, pp. 147–63.

[52] See Gusfield, *Symbolic Crusade*, for a discussion of the efforts of moral entrepreneurs that led to the Volstead Act.

[53] *Berkeley Barb*, January 22–28, 1971.

[54] See for example Laud Humphreys, *Out of the Closets* (Englewood Cliffs, N.J.: Prentice-Hall, 1972); Joseph A. McCaffrey, ed., *The Homosexual Dialectic* (Englewood Cliffs, N.J.: Prentice-Hall, 1972).

[55] Irwin Deutscher, "Words and Deeds: Social Science and Social Policy," *Social Problems* 13 (Winter 1966): 235–54; see also Deutscher, *What We Say/ What We Do* (Glenview, Ill.: Scott, Foresman and Co., 1973).

[56] Michael Banton, *The Policeman in the Community* (New York: Basic Books, 1964), pp. 127–55.

social structure
and
deviant behavior

Suppose we observe that crime rates, suicide statistics, or other indicators of forms of deviance vary greatly among social classes or between metropolitan and rural areas. How are these differences explained? Although sociologists offer many arguments about the social sources of deviant behavior, the most important theoretical perspective attempting to account for differences in *rates* of deviance within society has been the anomie tradition which can be traced back to Emile Durkheim. In this chapter we note Durkheim's conceptualization of anomie, along with some critical comments that have been advanced regarding that formulation. Additionally, we shall identify the major outlines of anomie theory as it is represented in work of the contemporary sociologist, Robert K. Merton,[1] together with some critical observations of that argument. Finally, this discussion will touch on some alternative formulations regarding social structure and deviance which have been offered in recent writings on deviant behavior.

DURKHEIM'S WORK

Durkheim's views on anomie initially grew out of his effort to explain "pathological" forms of the division of labor, particularly the frequent tendency of an expanding division of labor and social complexity to result in imperfect coodination of the parts of social organization, a decline in bonds of solidarity, and conflicts among social classes.[2] According to Durkheim, these conditions arise when those who perform specialized tasks in the division of labor lack intimate and continuous interaction with each other, such that common rules and understandings to guide social relationships fail to develop. The resulting condition, which he labeled *anomie,* is a state of deregulation or normlessness.

Durkeim's most well known version of anomie was advanced as an explanation of certain forms of suicide.[3] According to Durkheim, the social needs or desires of humans are potentially insatiable; thus the collective order of norms and values is necessary as an external regulating force to define and limit goal seeking. The collective order defines the goals to which men are encouraged to aspire, thus it regulates and disciplines their aspirations; if the collective order is disrupted, men's aspirations may increase until they outdistance all possibilities of fulfillment. Traditional rules then lose their authority over behavior, and a state of deregulation, normlessness, or anomie is said to exist. Durkheim argued that the regulatory functions of the collective order most commonly break down following sudden depression, sudden prosperity, or rapid technological change, when people are misled into aspirations that are almost impossible to achieve. When a sudden depression occurs, individuals are unable to adapt readily to a diminished state of existence; sudden prosperity, on the other hand, seduces people into believing that they are capable of attaining unlimited wealth and achievement. A similar effect stems from rapid technological change, which leads some to imagine that they have boundless possibilities of achievement.[4] These conditions, according to Durkheim, engender pressures toward suicide, particularly in Western, industrialized societies. Individuals commit suicide because the stability and meaning in their lives provided by the social order has disappeared or been greatly weakened.

SOME CRITICAL VOICES

Although Durkheim's explication of anomie and its effects on suicide has been generously applauded, it has also been the target of much critical commentary. For example, Marvin E. Olsen has observed that the version of anomie presented in Durkheim's discussion of the division of labor differs somewhat from the one put forth in the analysis of suicide.[5] Olsen points out that: "Anomie, as Durkheim first conceived of it in *The Division of Labor in Society,* might be defined as a condition of *inadequate procedural rules to regulate complementary relationships among the specialized and interdependent parts of a complex social system.*" (emphasis in the original)[6] On the other hand, anomie, as it was used in Durkheim's inquiry into suicide, described a situation of inadequate moral norms to guide and control the actions of individuals and groups in the interests of the total social system. In short, one meaning of anomie centered on inadequate *procedural* rules governing the behavioral actions of persons, while a second and more well known notion of anomie stressed deficiencies in the system of *moral* norms defining the goals that men should pursue. Because the concept has usually been restricted to the area of inadequate moral norms by most social analysts,

Olsen suggests a new term, *discordance,* to refer to situations of inadequate procedural rules.

In his discussion, Olsen elaborates on Durkheim's argument and indicates the varieties of social malintegration or disorganization which can be observed in societies. He concludes that:

> We are at last in a position to link together the concepts of integration and anomie. Anomie, in its new limited meaning, is obviously *one source of normative malintegration* within social systems, since all social organizations are constructed around bodies of moral norms. Other common sources of normative malintegration might include (a) inconsistency between the values and norms of a society, (b) failure of the social structure to reflect the underlying values and norms of the society, and (c) conflict among groups and organizations in the society with differing goals. Discordance (as defined above) is meanwhile *one source of functional malintegration* within social systems, since symbiotic relationships are always dependent on an established body of procedural rules. Other common sources of functional malintegration might include (a) a low degree of task specialization, or division of labor, in the system, (b) lack or weakness of a centralized coordinating structure to control interdependent relationships, and (c) failure of groups or organizations in the society to adequately fulfill necessary operating requirements of the total social system. (emphasis in the original)[7]

A different commentary is offered by A. R. Mawson, who points out that there are a number of ambiguities in Durkheim's assertions.[8] He also notes that contemporary versions of anomie often depart rather markedly from the meanings given this term by Durkheim. Anomie is sometimes used to refer to normlessness, but the concept of norm remains undefined. Still others confuse anomie with Karl Marx's term, alienation. The thrust of Mawson's critique is to identify the conceptual or logical shortcomings of the anomie perspective.

John Horton has noted a number of differences between Durkheim's notion of anomie and contemporary uses of the concept.[9] He observes that contemporary versions of both Durkheim's anomie and Marx's alienation have altered the classical or original meanings of the terms. Both Durkheim and Marx were involved in radical attacks on the status quo, but from vastly different perspectives. Horton claims that contemporary users of anomie and alienation assert that they are involved in value-free sociology but are in fact expounding a defense of the status quo in the way they use these concepts.

According to Horton, when Durkheim used the term anomie he referred to a state of normlessness or anarchy in which social controls to harness the strivings of men were inadequate. For Marx, alienation was seen as a condition in which men are caught up in economic values and activities that prevent them from actualizing their human potentialities. Workers are alienated because they are captives of productive activities which value the products of labor more highly than the values and interests of the laborers. Workers are unable to derive a sense of personal worth, competence, and accomplishment from the industrial activities which they perform.

Marx and Durkheim criticized the economic individualism of their day, both felt that economic interests and values had become separated from and commanded all other spheres of collective life, and both were angry about this condition. In Horton's words:

> Thus, Durkheim believed that the reification of self-interest was a contradiction of man's social nature, which required restraint through social control. Marx, on the other hand, contended that any reification of man's activity and products contradicted human nature, which developed fully only in the absence of reification and constraint. Far from being the natural disposition of man, whose dispositions are historically relative, the doctrine of the pursuit of self-interest was the propaganda of the capitalistic ruling class, the ideological expression of class society and the alienating division of labor.[10]

In short, Durkheim complained that those values stressing economic self-interest are destructive of an older and preferable moral order, while Marx regarded the pursuit of economic self-interest as impeding the realization of a higher order of humanistic values.

In Horton's view, modern sociologists have usually avoided taking explicit judgmental positions on the desirability of current social arrangements. Instead, they have adopted several evasive stratagems in analyzing anomie and alienation. They have shifted their attention to the study of *persons,* so that investigators go about measuring whether particular individuals feel alienated, powerless, or adrift; this method avoids passing judgment on the adequacy of existing *societal* arrangements. According to Horton, such a tactic involves an implicit assumption in favor of the status quo, that is, contemporary social structure.

Another approach found in contemporary applications of anomie notions such as those of Merton formulates theories in terms of dominant social values. As we shall see, Merton asserts that a state of anomie occurs when barriers exist to the achievement of dominant American success goals. But he does not raise the question of whether those values are the morally proper ones to be pursued; instead, they are accepted as given. In contrast, Durkheim was involved in the condemnation of moral values which stress self-interested striving for material ends. In his view, even if the barriers to achievement of success goals were removed, the pursuit of these ends would continue as a matter to be attacked.

Contemporary sociologists have thus assumed a posture of dispassionate objectivity that masks a basic conservatism and refrains from questioning the prevailing social order. Instead of serving as vigorous social critics, sociologists have become exponents of the status quo in their guise as social scientists. These conservative sociologists see social ills as temporary irregularities within a system which they regard as inherently proper and valuable. That brand of sociology does not object to exploitive capitalism, for the only viable societal structure it considers is one modeled after the contemporary situation.[11]

χ MERTON AND ANOMIE THEORY[12]

The contemporary American sociologist, Robert K. Merton, has elaborated greatly on the earlier notions of Durkheim concerning the breakdown of regulatory norms and deviant behavior. Others in turn have added to his theorizing, Richard A. Cloward's work is particularly important. The resulting set of ideas has served as probably the single most influential argument in the sociology of deviance during the past several decades, as attested by the copious citations in sociological treatises.[13] Merton has consistently emphasized the sociologist's operating premise that "some unknown but substantial proportion of deviant behavior does not represent impulses of individuals breaking through social control, but, on the contrary, represents socially induced deviations—deviations which the culture and the social organization conjoin to produce."[14] The major thrust of his work has been to sketch the details of the processes by which societally produced deviance allegedly occurs.

Merton distinguishes two major elements of social and cultural structures, the culturally defined goals that men are encouraged to pursue, and the social structure which regulates and controls the acceptable modes or means for the pursuit of goals and interests. He observes that goals and institutionalized norms governing the means of goal striving may vary independently of each other, sometimes leading to malintegrated states, one extreme case being the instance of inordinate stress on goals with little concern for prescribed means of obtaining them. In this instance, a situation of "anything goes" prevails, and goal striving is governed only by considerations of technical expediency. Merton discusses the example of unethical activities in athletics, particularly college football, as a situation in which institutionalized norms have become attenuated in favor of excessive concern with certain goals. The great stress placed on winning often leads to various violations of recruiting regulations, eligibility requirements, and other kinds of rule breaking. The other extreme of goals-means malintegration involves undue stress on ritualistic conformity to norms. Between these two extremes are systems that maintain a rough balance between accent on goals and emphasis on norms, and it is these systems that consitute relatively stable societies.[15]

Merton argues that contemporary American society is anomic, for it represents a polar type in which success goals are emphasized without equivalent emphasis on institutionalized conduct norms:

> The emphasis upon this set of culture goals is imperfectly integrated with the organization of our society, which, as a matter of objective and generally recognizable fact, does not provide equal access to those goals for all members of the society. On the contrary, there are heavily graded degrees of access to this, in terms not only of class and ethnic origins, but also in terms of less immediately visible differentials.
>
> Given the composite emphasis of this uniform cultural value of success being enjoined upon all irrespective of origins, and given the fact of a social organization which entails differentials in the availability of this goal, pressure is exerted upon certain classes of individuals to engage in deviant behavior, particularly those classes or strata or groups which have the least direct access to the goal.[16]

Merton's central proposition is that the cultural system of American society commands all men to strive for success goals by means of certain normatively regulated or approved forms of activity. At the same time, opportunities to reach these goals through socially approved means are differentially distributed. According to Merton: "It is only when a system of cultural values extols, virtually above all else, certain *common* success-goals *for the population at large* while the social structure rigorously restricts or completely closes access to approved modes of reaching these goals *for a considerable part of the same population,* that deviant behavior ensues on a large scale." (emphasis in the original)[17] He presents a typology of five modes of adaptation to this situation of disjunction, *conformity, innovation, ritualism, retreatism* and *rebellion* (see table 3).

Innovation refers to those cases in which persons continue to pursue approved goals but whose means are deviant or illegitimate. The armed robber is an illustration of innovation involving the use of illegal means to pursue conventional goals such as monetary success. *Ritualism* involves persistence in conformist behavior, but without any hope of realizing one's aspirations. The ritualist adaptation frequently includes

table 3 A Typology of Modes of Individual Adaptation[18]

MODES OF ADAPTATION	CULTURAL GOALS	INSTITUTIONALIZED MEANS
I Conformity	+	+
II Innovation	+	−
III Ritualism	−	+
IV Retreatism	−	−
V Rebellion	±	±

+ = Acceptance; − = Rejection; ± = Rejection of prevailing values and substitution of new values.

blaming scapegoats for personal failure. *Retreatism* involves withdrawal from the competitive struggle and rejection of both the approved goals and the socially approved paths to achieve them. The retreatist adaptation leads to involvement in passive deviance such as alcoholism, through which the person demonstrates that he has ceased to hold allegiance to the conventional values of hard work and respectability presumably held by others. Finally, *rebellion* is that adaptation in which disgruntled individuals actively reject goals which they view as unattainable and means which they hold to be unworkable and substitute new, socially unapproved goals toward which they strive by nonnormative means. In his commentary on these adaptations, Merton made no systematic attempt to identify the various real life deviants who fall within these categories. Instead, he merely offered one or two examples of deviant responses which may fit within each category.

Richard A. Cloward has further developed anomie theory. First, he directed attention to the differentials which exist in *illegitimate* opportunities, as well as in legitimate opportunity structures, and he noted that the forms taken by deviant behavior depend *both* on the situation of disjunction *and* the opportunities to engage in deviant conduct.[19] Just as the prospects for achieving cultural goals through institutionalized means are differentially distributed, so are the opportunities for various careers in deviant conduct. For example, the use of illegal drugs depends in part on contacts with illicit suppliers. Similarly, development of a professional criminal career is partially contingent on contact with individuals who will induct the actor into this deviant pattern.

Cloward has also been involved in two major applications of anomie theory to specific cases of social deviation. In one, he studied a military prison in which prisoners were encouraged to aspire to goals which were not, in fact, often available to them.[20] As a result, deviant behavior became widespread among the offenders. This prison investigation by Cloward stands as a microcosmic illustration of the societal pattern described by Merton. In their explanation of gang or subcultural delinquency,[21] Cloward and Lloyd E. Ohlin claim that working-class boys are drawn into delinquent conduct as a response to the disjunction which they perceive between their aspirations and their prospects for attaining them.[22]

CRITICISMS OF MERTONIAN ARGUMENTS

The Mertonian schema represents an elegant, plausible, and appealing formulation, but it needs much further expansion and revision. Albert K. Cohen has noted several points where the perspective needs to be elaborated.[23] His essay on "The Sociology of the Deviant Act" represents a major effort to effect a theoretical marriage between the structural argument of Merton and some of the social-interactional and deviant career perspectives considered in chapters seven and eight.

A principal inadequacy of anomie theory, according to Cohen, is that it puts too much emphasis on individual adaptations to disjunction. He observes that:

> As far as the formal and explicit structure of Merton's first formulation is concerned, it is, in certain respects, atomistic and individualistic. Within the framework of goals, norms, and oppoortunities, the process of deviance was conceptualized as though each individual—or better, role incumbent—were in a box by himself. He has internalized goals and normative, regulatory rules; he assesses the opportunity structure; he experiences strain; and he selects one or another mode of adaptation. The bearing of others' experience—their strains, their conformity and deviance, their success and failure—on ego's strains and consequent adaptation are comparatively neglected.[24]

In endeavoring to build on Merton's anomie theory, Cohen indicates that the sense of strain or disjunction perceived by an individual is not determined by the objective returns on his efforts alone, for the person is likely to measure himself and his situation against others in his reference groups. The unsuccessful individual who is surrounded by associates who have been successful in pursuing conventional goals by legitimate means may well react to his own situation differently from the person who is in contact with others who have gotten ahead by cutting corners or by using illegitimate means. Accordingly, in order to explain deviance, we must examine interaction patterns and reference group ties of individuals, as well as their general placement within the American social structure.

Cohen's discussion of needed revisions and additions in anomie theory also notes that discontinuity is implied in the anomie argument, in that "it treats the deviant act as though it were an abrupt change of state, a leap from a state of strain or anomie to a state of deviance."[25] By contrast, Cohen argues that deviant acts usually unfold in a tentative, groping fashion, with some persons retreating from further involvement in norm violation and others drifting into greater entanglement in it. Then too, he argues that anomie theory would be improved if more attention were given to the ways in which the responses of others affect the deviant career patterns developed by different actors.

The unfinished nature of the anomie argument, despite its popularity, is also revealed by the remarkably few applications that have been made of it to specific patterns of deviance. Instead, the anomie propositions have been employed most commonly as a high-level explanatory metaphor, with no real attempt to assess their theoretical utility by formulating specific hypotheses about forms of deviant conduct. Aside from the two cases of Cloward's work criminological explanations have been little influenced by the theory.

The exact scope of the anomie theory and its relation to deviance are still in question. Is anomie an explanation of all forms of deviance, or is it relevant only to some kinds of nonconformist action? Merton speaks rather vaguely about deviance, without indicating whether he intends his argument to apply to all or only to some forms of deviant conduct. We hold that some kinds of deviance are not explained by this argument, but the nature of that which is included or excluded from the explanation remains to be specifed. Commonsense observations suggest that the perspective has little applicability to homosexuality, forcible rape, or other forms of sexual deviance, or to much other deviant conduct. For example, the activities of "hippies" do not arise out of situations in which these persons lack access to opportunities for achievement of success goals. Conventional success goals appear to have been rejected by many hippies, but not because legitimate means were unavailable. Instead, hippies have often "dropped out" of middle-class families.

More work is also in order on the *translation* of the view to coordinate its terms for the modes of adaptation (innovation, rebellion, retreatism, ritualism, conformity) with the social labels for deviance familiar in everyday life. In other words, the empirical indicators of adaptations must be made evident if we are to use Merton's argument to explore the real world. The theorist who advocates the use of anomie theory is obliged to tell us how to know when we are looking at instances of innovation, rebellion, etc.

Marvin B. Scott and Roy Turner have discussed some of the problems of Mertonian theory.[26] They point out that anomie is not explicitly defined, and that Merton makes no attempt to ascertain the range and variety of real-life forms of deviation or to fit his theory to these patterns. Instead, he selectively discusses a few kinds of behavior which intuitively appear to illustrate the means-ends disjunction situation. Scott and Turner also contend that Merton's conception of anomie is actually closer to the ideas of Max Weber than it is to Durkheim's theories. For Durkheim, anomie was the product of periods of rapid social change and dislocation; in Merton's theory, anomie tends to center about a relatively permanent state of affairs involving disjunction. Merton's deviants resemble Weber's Western men pursuing unlimited goals, while Merton's modes of adaption parallel Weber's four types of social action.

Edwin M. Lemert and Jack D. Douglas, among others, have offered some even harsher views of Merton's formulation, suggesting that some full-scale alternative theories regarding the social sources of deviance are needed. We turn to their contentions in the discussion below.[27]

VALUE-PLURALISM AND DEVIANCE

The writings of Edwin M. Lemert contain a major alternative to Merton's anomie argument.[28] Lemert attacks Merton's portrayal of cultural structure as a set of hierarchical values which defines, regulates, and controls behavior. He contends this concept views culture as a reified entity which operates independently of the specific persons who comprise the societal members. He insists that "only individuals have hierarchies of values, which by minimal agreement specify affective as well as cognitive responses."[29]

Lemert acknowledges that in addition to values exhibited by individuals, it is possible to speak of values which group members as a whole come to stress through social interaction and control. Hence one can speak of group values in a meaningful fashion, but the step beyond to cultural values is a giant one. In Lemert's view, those who speak of cultural values as an entity are involved in projecting a sociological fiction. These observations undermine the notion of universal cultural goals and values that are shared by most members of a society. Particularly in a large, complex society with many associational networks, the identifiable values are likely to be multiple in number and shared only by segments of the population. *Value pluralism* is more descriptive of the cultural structure of American society than is Merton's picture.

A closely related objection by Lemert to anomie notions is that the distinction between values (ends) and means is difficult, if not impossible, to apply to actual human behavior. Instead, the same acts can be identified as end-oriented from one perspective and as means-oriented from another. It could be argued, for example, that individuals who are involved in college attendance are pursuing educational ends or a culturally valued occupational career. But, it could also be said that these goals are the means by which those persons hope to achieve some higher set of ends.

In expanding the idea of value pluralism, Lemert points to a number of cases, such as violation of fish and game laws by Indians, in which deviance arises out of the pursuit of traditional values by some group which has had alien standards imposed upon it. The lack of socially structured means to broad cultural ends of which Merton speaks is absent in these cases. Lemert also observes that deviance and conformity are not always closely in tune with the value commitments of persons. He suggests that instances of conforming or deviant behavior on the part of particular actors may not be an accurate index of internalized support or hostility toward norms. Deviant conduct often flows out of considerations of cost to the individual, rather than out of antagonism toward some specific norm. For example, white-collar criminals sometimes engage in violations of statutes regulating the conduct of business such as price fixing because they feel driven to these acts by harsh competition. At the same time, many of them acknowledge the moral superiority of honest business conduct and agree that price fixing is undesirable behavior. Lemert admonishes us to make the question of relationships between individual and group values, individual choice, and conformity and deviance a matter for empirical inquiry, rather than to establish some presumed relationships by fiat, as in the manner of Merton.

Lemert's critique also draws attention to Merton's lack of concern for empirical facts, some of which appear to show that deviance is not socially distributed in the manner hypothesized by him. Then too, Merton has little to say about group dynamics and group processes in the genesis of deviance or conformity, nor does he acknowledge the possibility that some deviance arises out of technological pressures rather than from lack of legitimate opportunities for the achievement of success goals.

In general, Lemert despairs of identifying some single source of initial acts of deviant conduct, or in his terms, of *primary deviance*.[30] The forms of deviant conduct and the factors that give rise to them are so numerous and varied that no theoretical formulation will adequately account for primary deviance. Furthermore, according to Lemert, the more important task centers about the study of *secondary deviation,* which refers to repeated involvement in deviance, accompanied by a role-conception of oneself as a nonconformist.[31]

The importance of studying secondary deviation is captured in the following passage from Lemert:

> Primary deviation is assumed to arise in a wide variety of social, cultural, and psychological contexts, and at best has only marginal implications for the psychic structure of the individual; it does not lead to symbolic reorganization at the level of self-regarding attitudes and social roles. Secondary deviation is deviant behavior, or social roles based upon it, which becomes means of defense, attack, or adaptation to the overt and covert problems created by the societal reaction to primary deviation. In effect, the original "causes" of the deviation recede and give way to the central importance of the disapproving, degradational, and isolating reactions of society. The distinction between primary and secondary deviation is deemed indispensable to a complete understanding of deviation in modern, pluralistic society. Furthermore, it is held that the second research problem is pragmatically more pertinent for sociology than the first.[32]

As we shall see in more detail in the chapter on the labeling approach to the study of deviance to which Lemert has made major contributions, social control is identified as a causal force in deviant behavior rather than simply a reaction to deviance as in the work of Merton; that is, social control efforts are seen as often unintentionally driving individuals into deviant careers.

The major outlines of a pluralistic society-multiple values argument are discernible in the writings of Lemert, as is a fairly complex articulation of the major forces behind primary deviance and secondary deviation. Thus we find ourselves with two major theoretical positions concerning social structure and deviance: the anomie argument of Merton and a value-pluralism position represented by Lemert.

Some closely parallel views on deviance and the etiological backgrounds from which it develops have been offered by Jack D. Douglas.[33] He begins by outlining the nature of the structural-functional position to which he takes exception. His somewhat overdrawn portrait includes the claim that sociologists of a traditional, structural persuasion believe norms and moral values are self-evident. Because traditional sociologists think they know which values characterize American society, they don't need to investigate the viewpoints and moral perspectives of common citizens. Further, according to Douglas, traditional viewpoints favor the use of statistical methods of analysis involving examination of relationships between social variables and official rates of deviance. Traditionalists thus regard official statistics on crime and deviance as relatively adequate and valid. Then too, the older views give short shrift to the workings of official agencies of social control. The causes of deviance are thought to occur before the onset of norm-violating acts, so that social control agencies operate only after deviance has broken out.

According to Douglas, the older perspective holds that American core values are few in number, stable over time, and congruent with each other. Deviance is defined as behavioral violations of these core values. Regarding the individual deviant, he says:

> To the extent that individual decisions and actions are relevant to explaining deviance, the individual can be assumed to know non problematically . . . that these actions are deviant and that they are associated with certain negative sanctions. In choosing or deciding to commit a deviant act he is, therefore, choosing to commit it as (or *qua*) a deviant act and is, thereby, choosing to be a deviant. In simplest terms, deviant acts are committed by deviant persons. Moreover, these deviant choices are normally believed to represent the "real selves"—the *substantial selves* of deviants. Consequently, deviants are believed to be very different types of persons from nondeviants. (emphasis in the original).[34]

Douglas claims that the deviance-defining process in society is much more complex and ambiguous than suggested by the older views. He also argues against the use of official data, holding these to be unreliable and defective indicators of the true extent and character of deviance. He takes exception to the picture of the deviant as a motivated actor who consciously opts for behavior which violates clear-cut values. In his view, a more accurate characterization would stress moral ambivalence and risk taking. Finally, he maintains that American society is changing rapidly, and that numerous moral or value conflicts exist as a result of the value-pluralism of modern societies.

Both the value-pluralism notions of Lemert and the related ones of Douglas are, at present, general orientations toward deviance, not fully developed theories. In our view, these arguments contain considerable plausibility and explanatory power when contrasted to formulations such as the anomie argument of Merton. But, the social terrain of value conflict and normative variation is still relatively unmarked. Accordingly we are not yet in a position to explain in precise detail how these social patterns are implicated in particular forms of deviant conduct.

EMERGING CONFLICT PERSPECTIVES ON DEVIANCE

In our opening chapter, we noted some recent conflict and radical arguments about deviance. In one of these, Alexander Liazos has charged that sociologists have been too preoccupied with the study of "nuts, sluts, and preverts" and have paid too little attention to what he terms "covert institutional violence."[35] Covert institutional violence represents repressive actions by the power structure, exploitation of the powerless by the powerful, and other forms of oppression that are held to be central to the economic, political, and social order of American society. In Liazos's view, the United States is a tortured, mortally ill nation suffering from the ravages of a capitalistic system which inevitably produces immoral exploitation of the masses of citizens, both in this country and elsewhere in the world. Liazos would have us discontinue inquiry into those mundane forms of deviance that have captured our interest in the past, such as crime, drug addiction, and prostitution in favor of the study of racism, inequality, powerlessness, and institutionalized violence that grow out of exploitive capitalism.

Alex Thio leveled similar charges against the version of deviance analysis that has dominated in sociology. He holds that investigators have centered their efforts on powerless underdogs, such as unskilled criminals and prostitutes, and he contends that sociological curiousity ought to turn toward the deviant activities of the overdogs, that is, members of the political-economic power structure who control American society.[36] This study would scrutinize the deviant endeavors of overdogs and how their actions create deviance on the part of the underdogs. According to Thio, this work would indicate that prostitution and conventional crime on the part of underdogs are the rational and almost inevitable consequences of the exploitation of the powerless by the overdogs in capitalistic societies.

Two related propositions are involved in the calls for new directions; one insists that traditional interests in mundane forms of deviance be abandoned entirely in favor of the study of racism, sexism, exploitation, and repression, and the other asserts that we should investigate the ways in which the latter phenomena and the activities of the power elite are involved in garden-variety forms of deviant conduct. In either case detailed theoretical expositions dealing with these matters have not yet been produced.[37]

CONFLICT THEORY AND CRIME

The most detailed theorizing that has been produced regarding social conflict and deviance has appeared in the criminological literature. Twentieth-century criminological analysis has changed over the decades from a conservative to a dominant liberal-cynical posture, and now is leaning in the direction of radical criminological thought.[38]

In liberal-cynical criminological thought, the social order or societal structure is seen as relatively viable and stable. Liberal-cynical criminology acknowledges, however, that the criminogenic influences which produce criminality are exceedingly pervasive and intimately bound up with the core institutions of modern society. Thus, uncovering the etiological forces of lawbreaking requires a penetrating examination of many central features of American society.[39] Even so, this brand of criminological thought has tended to emphasize normative consensus and to de-emphasize the role of social conflict among competing interest groups in the creation of criminal laws. Similarly, conventional criminology has avoided arguments that widespread criminality is an inevitable by-product of capitalistic societies. Liberal criminologists have argued for repair work on the social and economic structure of society to reduce crime, but they have not advocated wholesale revolutions of any kind. On the other hand, these themes, on which liberal criminology has been relatively silent, form some of the core propositions of emerging radical criminological thought.

The earlier generation of criminologists, however, has not been entirely mute regarding the role of social power and conflicts among interest groups in the origin of laws and criminality. For example, Edwin H. Sutherland sketched the beginnings of a social conflict perspective on the law about forty years ago when he observed that:

> [Crime] is a part of a process of conflict of which law and punishment are other parts. This process begins in the community before the law is enacted, and continues in the community and in the behavior of particular offenders after punishment is inflicted. This process seems to go somewhat as follows: A certain group of people feel that one of their values —life, property, beauty of landscape, theological doctrine—is endangered by the behavior of others. If the group is politically influential, the value important, and the danger serious, the members of the group secure the

enactment of a law and thus win the co-operation of the State in the effort to protect their value. The law is a device of one party in conflict with another party, at least in modern times. Those in the other group do not appreciate so highly this value which the law was designed to protect and do the thing which before was not a crime, but which has been made a crime by the co-operation of the State. This is a continuation of the conflict which the law was designed to eliminate, but the conflict has become larger in one respect, in that the State is now involved. Punishment is another step in the same conflict. This, also, is a device used by the first group through the agency of the State in the conflict with the second group. This conflict has been described in terms of groups for the reason that almost all crimes do involve either the active participation of more than one person or the passive or active support, so that the particular individual who is before the court may be regarded as merely a representative of the group.[40]

Another relatively early statement of parallel views regarding the criminal law and its implementation can be found in the writings of George B. Vold,[41] while more recent, detailed explications of conflict theory appear in the work of Austin Turk,[42] Richard Quinney,[43] Stuart Hills,[44] and Ian Taylor, Paul Walton, and Jock Young.[45]

William J. Chambliss and Robert B. Seidman have produced one of the most complete sociological statements to date on power conflicts, criminality, laws, and the legal machinery.[46] They view law making and the implementation of criminal laws by the criminal justice system as reflecting power struggles in modern society. Hence, they assert:

It is our contention that, far from being primarily a value-neutral framework within which conflict can be peacefully resolved, the power of the state is itself the principal prize in the perpetual conflict that is society. The legal order—the rules which the various law-making institutions in the bureaucracy that is the State lay down for the governance of officials and citizens, the tribunals, official and unofficial, and the bureaucratic agencies which enforce the law—is in fact a self-serving system to maintain power and privilege. In a society sharply divided into haves and have nots, poor and rich, blacks and whites, powerful and weak, shot with a myriad of special interest groups, not only is the myth false because of imperfections in the normative system: It is *inevitable* that it be so. (emphasis in the original)[47]

The Chambliss and Seidman volume is a beginning venture in the direction of a propositional inventory about power relations and their impact on law making and law implementation in complex societies.[48]

Another recent commentary on crime from a radical perspective is that of economist David M. Gordon who contrasts liberal and conservative views of the crime problem against the radical position.[49] He notes five major hypotheses in the radical view of crime in the United States, including the following proposition:

Capitalist societies depend . . . on basically competitive forms of social and economic interaction. Individuals cannot depend on society for economic security; they must fend for themselves, finding the best opportunities for providing for themselves and family. At any point in time, many of the best opportunities for economic survival open to different citizens will violate a historically determined set of statutes and laws. Although these activities are therefore technically illegal, they nonetheless constitute functionally similar responses to the organization of institutions in capitalistic societies; they represent a means of survival in a society which does not guarantee survival to its citizens. Three kinds of crime in the United States provide the most important examples of this functional similarity: ghetto crime, organized crime, and corporate crime.[50]

Gordon's exposition then discusses the extent to which crime in the ghetto is a rational response of young black males to the uncertainties of the economic world and the pains of unemployment they experience. He indicates how organized crime and business violations occur as almost inevitable products of capitalistic, exploitive social organization.[51] Organized crime provides illicit services to large numbers of customers who clamor for them. The secrecy, relative efficiency, and occasional violence of organized crime result because the services in demand are illegal. Turning to business violations (white-collar crime), Gordon argues that these offenses grow up as corporate responses to the uncertainties of the marketplace.

Other propositions within the radical view as enunciated by Gordon include the observation that differential enforcement of the law is practiced against those with low social power, hence the ghetto strong armed robber goes to prison while the corporation executive who has been convicted of antitrust violations receives probation (if he appears in court at all, which is unlikely). Then too, the radical position is that current patterns of law enforcement and "corrections" play a crucial part in legitimizing and perpetuating existing class distinctions and victimizing the powerless. In summary, Gordon avers that:

In short, radicals argue that the problem of urban crime as we know and fear it should be regarded as a specific and inevitable feature of the

American class and institutional structure. Like many of our crimes, it flows from a rational response to the competitiveness of our institutions. Unlike most other crimes, it is prosecuted heavily. The continued effect of this institutional pattern of prosecution and punishment exacts a heavy and deadening price from its victims; in that sense it plays a functional role in the context of larger social institutions by removing many from the labor force and by obviating the need to find decent work for those criminals. To eradicate urban crime, one would need both fundamentally to change the institutions which produce it and somehow to replace the functions it serves within these institutions. Since one of its principal functions is to help perpetuate the lower-class status of blacks without recourse to overt racism, eliminating the prevalence of crime among blacks would probably require more overt racism in order to preserve necessary class divisions. More overt racism would necessarily accentuate the kinds of social forces which currently produce urban crime. If we eliminated urban crime, our institutions would tend to reproduce it. And it is in that sense that we must change the entire set of institutions in order to solve the problem.[52]

CONFLICT THEORY: AN ASSESSMENT

The suspicion that struggles between interest groups, differentials in social power, and related factors are implicated in deviance is not entirely a new one. Indeed, many of those currently involved in the development of radical-conflict perspectives contend that their efforts are Marxist in nature and linked to the writings of Karl Marx (1818–1883).[53] Thus, the basic claims being advanced are probably not new; the interest in conflict theories has simply been renewed.

A closely related observation is that many of the recent radical or conflict statements represent departures only in degree from other formulations that have been advanced regarding the social-structural sources of deviance. These newer views are not totally divergent from the anomie or value-pluralism arguments examined earlier. For example, Gordon's assertions about the economic pressures that operate to produce ghetto crime are not wholly unlike many of the analyses of ghetto lawbreaking that have appeared in standard (liberal-cynical) criminology textbooks.[54]

Conflict theorists are correct in asserting that criminal laws are often the outgrowth of power struggles between interest groups in society.[55] The major argument between conflict theorists and other criminologists regarding the processes that produce criminal laws is that conflict theorists would contend that nearly all criminal laws arise out of interest group struggles, while other criminologists believe a significant portion of criminal statutes reflects relatively widespread value consensus in American society. Thus in the latter view, a fair share of the criminal laws develop in response to broader, more widely shared concerns than implied in conflict perspectives. The gaps in the available data regarding law-making processes are so large that it is not yet possible to decide this debate unequivocally.

Conflict theorists also accurately identify widespread discriminatory and differential enforcement of laws and direct attention to examples of unskilled offenders involved in garden-variety crimes such as burglary, robbery, and assault who are the criminals most likely to be incarcerated in prison or to receive some other harsh penalty. At the same time, most antitrust violators and other high-status lawbreakers avoid entanglement in criminal court processing entirely, or if they do end up in a criminal court, they receive exceedingly lenient penalties. Then too, there is abundant evidence indicating that black citizens frequently are the targets of differentially harsh responses at nearly every stage of the legal-correctional process.[56] Discriminatory processing of lawbreakers, based largely on social status and social power differentials among these individuals, has been pointed out both by conventional liberal theorists and by radical criminologists. The controversy between these two groups again centers mainly on the specific nature and precise degree of discriminatory processing of offenders, rather than on the proposition that differential reactions do occur.

In our estimation, the principal inadequacy of conflict theories on deviance and criminality lies in the area of causal or etiological hypotheses. Conflict or radical arguments have said much about social power struggles in the enactment of laws and creation of other rules and in differential enforcement of these standards; but these formulations have sketched the workings of these phenomena as causes of deviance and lawbreaking only in very broad strokes. In short, complete, detailed conflict theories regarding the social origins of deviant conduct have not yet been developed.

Existing social conflict theories are also unclear regarding those forms of deviance that they are intended to explain.[57] Although arguments such as those of Gordon regarding the origins of ghetto crime and business offenses are plausible, it is much less clear that homicides, various sexual crimes, and a number of noncriminal forms of deviance can be accounted for within conflict formulations. Then too, existing radical-conflict theorizing has not yet indicated, in precise detail, the causal connections between such matters as economic exploitation within the capitalistic system and forms of deviance.

THE SOCIAL FUNCTIONS OF DEVIANCE

It must be acknowledged that some sociological arguments identify *positive* social functions made by deviance to the social order. Such contentions can be traced to Durkheim who argued that criminality is often functional, since it identifies the limits of permissible behavior in a society.[58] If it were possible to repress these major violations of normative sentiments, men would become sensitive to the less marked deviations which they now overlook, and these acts would be regarded as crimes. At some point, intolerable demands for conformity would be imposed on individuals. These demands for conformity would be inimical to social progress, for according to Durkheim: "to make progress, individual originality must be able to express itself. In order that the originality of the idealist whose dreams transcend his century may find expression, it is necessary that the originality of the criminal, who is below the level of his time, shall also be possible. One does not occur without the other."[59]

Somewhat later, George Herbert Mead advanced the argument that punishment of the crimes of identified miscreants is functional for the affirmation of social solidarity.[60] Recent writers who have noted some positive contributions that deviance may make to social stability include Lewis A. Coser,[61] Albert K. Cohen,[62] Ned Polsky,[63] and Kai T. Erikson.[64] Erikson has also conducted a fascinating historical inquiry into these matters, researching the accounts of the witchcraft trials and other events involving deviants among the Puritans of the Massachussetts Bay Colony.[65] He indicates that these episodes, involving public clamor over misbehaving persons, greatly affected the crystallizing of social boundaries within the fledgling colony.

SUMMARY

We have now concluded a brief summary of the principal theories of social structure and deviance. The major point that emerges from our commentary is the existence of large gaps and holes in the fabric of these sociological explanations. It thus seems clear enough that anomie arguments are both somewhat defective and also inapplicable to many forms of deviance. At the same time, the value-pluralism theories and conflict perspectives under development are still quite unfinished. The next several generations of sociologists have much work ahead in constructing valid theories of social structure and deviance.

In addition, when sociologists turn attention from deviance in the abstract and general explanatory theories to analysis of various forms of concrete deviant conduct such as crime, mental disorder, alcoholism, and sexual deviation, the theoretical picture becomes somewhat more blurred than implied in this chapter. Many who have written about the causes of various specific kinds of deviance show much eclecticism in the explanatory theories they use. Patterns of deviance are explained by a blend of causal propositions which includes anomie notions, value-conflict hypotheses, urbanism and its correlates, and other factors as well.[66] Thus many sociological theorists cannot be classified as strict advocates of either anomie or value-conflict theories.

Let us now turn attention from the broad formulations discussed in this chapter to a closer look at those hypotheses advanced about the socialization processes leading to deviant acts and careers.

NOTES

[1] A brief useful outline of Durkheim's views and those of Merton concerning anomie can be found in Albert K. Cohen, *Deviance and Control* (Englewood Cliffs, N.J.: Prentice-Hall, 1966), pp. 74–83; Harry M. Johnson, *Sociology* (New York: Harcourt Brace Jovanovich, 1960), pp. 552–86.

[2] Emile Durkheim, *The Division of Labor in Society* (New York: Free Press of Glencoe, 1964), Book 3, Chapter 1, pp. 353–73.

[3] Emile Durkheim, *Suicide,* trans. by J. A. Spaulding and George Simpson (New York: Free Press of Glencoe, 1951).

[4] A modern exposition of the negative aspects of rapid social change can be found in Alvin Toffler, *Future Shock* (New York: Random House, 1970). Toffler claims that we are overwhelmed by social change in modern society, and we are ill-equipped to deal with it.

[5] Marvin E. Olsen, "Durkheim's Two Concepts of Anomie," *Sociological Quarterly* 6 (Winter 1965): 37–44.

[6] Ibid., p. 40.

[7] Ibid., p. 43.

[8] A. R. Mawson, "Durkheim and Contemporary Social Pathology," *British Journal of Sociology* 21 (September 1970): 298–311.

[9] John Horton, "The Dehumanization of Anomie and Alienation: A Problem in the Ideology of Sociology," *British Journal of Sociology* 15 (December 1964): 283–300.

[10] Ibid., p. 288.

[11] A full scale attack on "scientism" and a brand of sociology which disguises its conservative bias under a camouflage of scientific rhetoric is found in Alvin

W. Gouldner, *The Coming Crisis of Western Sociology* (New York: Basic Books, 1970). See also Don C. Gibbons and Peter G. Garabedian, "Conservative, Liberal, and Radical Criminology: Some Trends and Observations," in Charles E. Reasons, ed. *The Criminologist: Crime and the Criminal* (Pacific Palisades, Calif.: Goodyear Publishing Co., 1974), pp. 51–65; see also Alex Thio, "Class Bias in the Sociology of Deviance," *The American Sociologist* 8 (February 1973): 1–12.

[12] This section on Merton's ideas closely parallels the material originally appearing in Don C. Gibbons, *Society, Crime, and Criminal Careers*, 2d ed. (Englewood Cliffs, N.J.: Prentice-Hall, 1973), pp. 184–88.

[13] Some important cases of anomie analysis by Merton and other contributors include: Robert K. Merton, *Social Theory and Social Structure* rev. and enl. ed. (New York: Free Press of Glencoe, 1957), pp. 131–94; Merton, "Social Conformity, Deviation, and Opportunity Structures: A Comment on the Contributions of Dubin and Cloward," *American Sociological Review* 24 (April 1959): 177–89; Merton, "The Social-Cultural Environment and Anomie," in Helen L. Witmer and Ruth Kotinsky, eds., *New Perspectives for Research on Juvenile Delinquency* (Washington, D.C.: U.S. Department of Health, Education, and Welfare, 1955), pp. 24–50; Merton, "Anomie, Anomia, and Social Interaction: Contexts of Deviant Behavior," in Marshall B. Clinard, ed., *Anomie and Deviant Behavior* (New York: Free Press of Glencoe, 1964), pp. 213–42; Richard A. Cloward, "Illegitimate Means, Anomie, and Deviant Behavior," *American Sociological Review* 24 (April 1959): 164–76; Robert Dubin, "Deviant Behavior and Social Structure: Continuities in Social Theory," *American Sociological Review* 24 (April 1959): 147–64; Albert K. Cohen, "The Study of Social Disorganization and Deviant Behavior," in Robert K. Merton, Leonard Broom, and Leonard S. Cottrell, Jr., eds., *Sociology Today* (New York: Basic Books, 1959), pp. 461–66; Cohen, "The Sociology of the Deviant Act: Anomie Theory and Beyond," *American Sociological Review* 30 (February 1965): 5–14; Marshall B. Clinard, "Theoretical Implications of Anomie and Deviant Behavior," *Anomie and Deviant Behavior,* pp. 10–23; An inventory of empirical and theoretical studies of anomie can be found in Stephen Cole and Harriet Zuckerman, "Appendix: Inventory of Empirical and Theoretical Studies of Anomie," in Clinard, *Anomie and Deviant Behavior.,* pp. 243–313. Many of the cited works are only tangentially linked to Merton's formulation.

[14] Merton, in Witmer and Kotinsky, *New Perspectives for Research,* p. 29.

[15] Merton, *Social Theory and Social Structure,* pp. 131–36.

[16] Merton, in Witmer and Kotinsky, *New Perspectives for Research,* p. 30.

[17] Merton, *Social Theory and Social Structure,* p. 146.

[18] Ibid., p. 140.

[19] Cloward, "Illegitimate Means, Anomie, and Deviant Behavior."

[20] Witmer and Kotinsky, *New Perspectives for Research,* pp. 80–92.

[21] Richard A. Cloward and Lloyd E. Ohlin, *Delinquency and Opportunity* (New York: Free Press of Glencoe, 1960).

[22] This theory is discussed in detail in Don C. Gibbons, *Delinquent Behavior* (Englewood Cliffs, N.J.: Prentice-Hall, 1970), pp. 119–39. A good deal of the research evidence relating to that theory is also discussed in these pages. On the whole, that evidence indicates that most of the Cloward and Ohlin formulation is incorrect.

[23] Cohen, "The Sociology of the Deviant Act."

[24] Ibid., p. 6.

[25] Ibid., p. 8.

[26] Marvin B. Scott and Roy Turner, "Weber and the Anomic Theory of Deviance," *Sociological Quarterly* 6 (Summer 1965): 233–40.

[27] Talcott Parsons has developed a number of ideas concerning deviance which parallel those of Merton. See Talcott Parsons, *The Social System* (New York: Free Press of Glencoe, 1951), pp. 249–325; see also Johnson, *Sociology.*, pp. 652–66. Parson's work focuses most heavily on the *forms* of deviance, rather than on the *sources* of deviant behavior as in the anomie argument. Parsons argues that some degree of ambivalence toward norms is extremely common, and that many individuals uphold the moral validity of norms at the same time that they exhibit attenuated allegiance to them for one reason or another. In other words, many persons agree in principle with a particular norm but are nonetheless motivated to violate it. Those actors who are ambivalent toward a rule are likely to engage in deviant conduct relative to that norm. In some cases, the individual may deal with his norm ambivalence by *stressing* the alienative side, thus tending toward *under*conformity. Or, he may handle ambivalence by *repressing* the alienative component, thereby engaging in *over*conformity.

But, there is more to the directions taken by deviance. Parsons also notes that alienation from norms can be of either an avoidance or active form. Some actors engage in active violation of norms, while others exhibit relatively passive deviations. Finally, deviant acts are sometimes directed at persons, as in assault, while other deviations such as property crimes, are directed more at general norms from which the actor feels alienated.

We are not inclined to devote much discussion to Parson's analysis, for his taxonomy is closely related to that of Merton. Most importantly, the Parsons argument has been almost totally ignored in the actual study of deviant conduct, so that it cannot be regarded as a major perspective.

The anthropologist, S. F. Nadel, attempted to deal with the issues involved in defining deviance in a pluralistic society from the standpoint of structural-functional theory. Nadel's work relied heavily on the formulation of Parsons, but has had even less impact on the study of deviance. See S. F. Nadel, *The Theory of Social Structure* (New York: Free Press of Glencoe, 1957). See especially chapter three, "Conformity and Deviance," pp. 45–62.

[28] Edwin M. Lemert, *Human Deviance, Social Problems, and Social Control,* 2d ed. (Englewood Cliffs, N.J.: Prentice-Hall, 1972), pp. 26–61.

[29] Ibid. p. 29.

[30] Ibid. p. 40.

[31] Ibid. pp. 47–48.

[32] Ibid. p. 48.

[33] Jack D. Douglas, "Deviance and Order in a Pluralistic Society," in John C. McKinney and Edward A. Tiryakian, eds., *Theoretical Sociology* (New York: Appleton-Century Crofts, 1970), pp. 367–401.

[34] Ibid. p. 370.

[35] Alexander Liazos, "The Poverty of the Sociology of Deviance: Nuts, Sluts, and Preverts," *Social Problems* 20 (Summer 1970): 103–20.

[36] Thio, "Class Bias in the Sociology of Deviance."

[37] One effort to spell out some of the ways in which racism is linked to American crime can be found in Gibbons, *Society, Crime, and Criminal Careers*, pp. 195–98.

[38] These trends in criminological thought are discussed in detail in Gibbons and Garabedian, "Conservative, Liberal, and Radical Criminology." Conservative criminology refers to the kind of endeavor represented in the writings of scholars in the period up to the 1950s, characterized, first by a relatively *low level of conceptualization*. A "good guy" and "bad guy" image of criminality was often advocated, in which it was asserted that criminality was the result of some stew or admixture of negative social factors.

[39] It should not be supposed that liberal-cynical criminological thought is monolithic or focused on a single theme. For a discussion of the variants of liberal-cynical arguments, see ibid. Also see Gresham M. Sykes, "The Future of Criminality," *American Behavioral Scientist* 15 (February 1972): 409–19.

A word or two also is in order regarding our use of the label "cynical" to characterize modern criminological thought. Perhaps "pessimistic" would be a more appropriate adjective for theories of causation, since the growing awareness that crime causation is an exceedingly complex phenomenon tends to make the criminologist chary about his ability to completely account for it. Then too, contemporary criminologists who are armed with an appreciation of the complex interweaving of factors in lawbreaking are not likely to be very sanguine about the prospects for its amelioration.

The cynical posture of the modern criminologist emerges more strikingly in observations about the criminal justice and correctional systems. The sociologist is an "inside dopester" who is aware that correctional organizations often operate in ways quite different from those sketched out in organizational charts or manuals of procedure. This growing sophistication of criminological analysis has been paralleled by a marked decline in the criminologist's faith in the perfectability of the legal-correctional machinery.

[40] Reprinted by permission of Indiana University Press from the *Sutherland Papers*, edited by Albert Cohen, Alfred Lindesmith, and Karl Schuessler, © 1956 by Indiana University Press, Bloomington. Now available from the University of Chicago Press in a revised edition as *Edwin H. Sutherland: On Analyzing*

Crime, © 1973. An earlier and briefer version of social conflict notions and the criminal law can be found in the first American criminology text. See Maurice F. Parmelee, *Criminology* (New York: The Macmillan Company, 1918), p. 34.

[41] George B. Vold, *Theoretical Criminology* (New York: Oxford University Press, 1958), pp. 203–19.

[42] Austin T. Turk, *Criminality and Legal Order* (Chicago: Rand McNally and Co., 1969).

[43] Richard Quinney, *The Social Reality of Crime* (Boston: Little, Brown and Co., 1970). A more polemical version of radical criminology has been offered in another essay by Quinney in which he rails against the criminal law in contemporary society, claiming that it is the instrument through which the dominant class maintains its power over the weak. See Quinney, "The Ideology of Law: Notes for a Radical Alternative to Legal Repression," *Issues in Criminology* 7 (Winter 1972): 1–35; see also Quinney, *Critique of Legal Order* (Boston: Little Brown, and Co., 1974) for an extended version of this argument.

Quinney would do away with monolithic criminal law as we presently know it and replace it with decentralized law. This law would be consistent with "natural law" which endeavors to maximize the individual's efforts to develop his own human potentialities. In the kind of society envisioned by Quinney, "Communities would then be free to develop their own systems of regulation, if such systems are at all necessary." (p. 26)

The kind of analysis found in Quinney's essay is not adequate. Although his commentary is liberally sprinkled with quotes and comments from such authorities as Fuller, Pound, and Hart, his essay is bombastic and polemical. We do not agree that modern law in its entirety is a tool by which a handful of powerful persons manage to oppress the rest. Then too, we find unconvincing Quinney's contention that bodies of general law are not really required in complex societies in order to maintain a degree of social order which at the same time promotes individual freedom. Finally, it is by no means clear that Quinney's alternative of decentralized law is a viable alternative to the existing system of laws and legal machinery. Assuming that his proposal is practical and realisitic, who is to say that there would be any less tyranny under a decentralized system of laws determined by "the people"?

[44] Stuart L. Hills, *Crime, Power, and Morality* (Scranton, Pa.: Chandler Publishing Co., 1971).

[45] Ian Taylor, Paul Walton, and Jock Young, *The New Criminology* (London: Routledge and Kegan Paul, 1973). Although this book presents an incisive critique of many lines of contemporary theorizing about deviance and criminality, it does not spell out in much detail the nature of "the new criminology" promised in its title. Very few specific propositions about criminality that flow out of radical or Marxist thought are found in the volume. The Taylor, Walton, and Young book reflects the newness and relative immaturity of this brand of theorizing.

[46] William J. Chambliss and Robert B. Seidman, *Law, Order, and Power* (Reading, Mass.: Addison-Wesley Publishing Co., 1971).

[47] Ibid. p. 4.

[48] Chambliss and Seidman have considerably less to say about how differences in social power, interest group conflicts, and the like are implicated in the genesis of acts of criminal behavior.

[49] David M. Gordon, "Crime: Editor's Introduction," in Gordon, ed., *Problems in Political Economy: An Urban Perspective* (Lexington, Mass.: D. C. Heath Co., 1971), pp. 273–314; see also Gordon, "Class and the Economics of Crime," in James Weaver, ed., *Political Economy: Radical and Orthodox Approaches* (Rockleigh, N.J.: Allyn and Bacon, 1972).

[50] Gordon, "Crime: Editor's Introduction," p. 276; for a recent evaluation of the general radical attack on big business, see Charles Perrow, *The Radical Attack on Business* (New York: Harcourt Brace Jovanovich, 1972).

[51] An important, revealing ethnography of unemployment, social disorder, and crime in the ghetto is Elliot Liebow, *Tally's Corner* (Boston: Little, Brown and Co., 1967).

[52] Gordon, "Crime: Editor's Introduction," p. 279.

[53] However, Taylor, Walton, and Young have pointed out that this link is a tenuous one, in that Marx had little to say about criminality and deviance *per se*. See Taylor, Walton, and Young, *The New Criminology*, p. 209–21.

[54] However, Gordon and other radical theorists also offer claims that the correctional system serves the social function of locking up potential black leaders who might otherwise provide opposition to the current system of economic oppression and exploitation. These theorists also argue that the correctional system functions to keep large numbers of blacks out of the labor market. Arguments such as these are less frequently encountered in standard textbooks and kindred sources.

[55] Studies of the social origins of criminal laws are reviewed in Gibbons, *Society, Crime, and Criminal Careers,* pp. 29–35.

[56] A sizeable share of the evidence on discriminatory and differential reactions to lawbreakers is examined in ibid.

[57] For a brief critique of conflict theory, see Ronald L. Akers, *Deviant Behavior* (Belmont, Calif.: Wadsworth Publishing Co., 1973), pp. 19–21. Akers argues that there are at least some important values, commonly shared across different groups in society, that provide some of the glue that binds the social structure together. Stated differently, he contends that there is more to society than a congeries of competing and conflicting groups. Then too Akers questions the arguments of conflict theories that would attribute all forms of deviance to group conflict. He maintains that such activities as murder, rape, and arson derive out of other sources. In general, he conjectures that conflict approaches do a better job of explaining deviant behavior arising out of ideological and political confrontations than they do of accounting for a number of other forms

of deviance, particularly those centering around personal "vices." Finally, Akers offers a judgment close to ours when he asserts (p. 20): "the conflict approach is *potent as an explanation of the formation and enforcement of the norms themselves; it is less powerful as an explanation of deviant behavior.*" (emphasis in the original)

[58] Lewis A. Coser and Bernard Rosenberg, eds., *Sociological Theory: A Book of Readings* (New York: The Macmillan Co., 1964), pp. 584–91.

[59] Ibid. p. 588.

[60] George Herbert Mead, "The Psychology of Punitive Justice," *American Journal of Sociology* 23 (March 1918): 585–92.

[61] Lewis A. Coser, "Some Functions of Deviant Behavior and Normative Flexibility," *American Journal of Sociology* 68 (September 1962): 172–81. For some devastatingly critical observations on the claims advanced by Coser and others relative to the alleged social functions of deviance, see Travis Hirschi, "Procedural Rules and the Study of Deviance," *Social Problems* 21 (Fall 1973): 161–63.

[62] Cohen, *Deviance and Control,* pp. 6–11.

[63] For a discussion of the social functions of pornography, see Ned Polsky, *Hustlers, Beats, and Others* (Garden City, N.Y.: Doubleday and Co., 1969), pp. 183–200.

[64] Kai T. Erikson, "Notes on the Sociology of Deviance," *Social Problems* 9 (Spring 1962): 307–14.

[65] Kai T. Erikson, *Wayward Puritans* (New York: John Wiley and Sons, 1966).

[66] For example, see Marshall B. Clinard, *The Sociology of Deviant Behavior,* 4th ed. (New York: Holt, Rinehart and Winston, 1974); Gibbons, *Society, Crime, and Criminal Careers.*

SELECTED READINGS

CLINARD, MARSHALL B., ed. *Anomie and Deviant Behavior.* New York: Free Press of Glencoe, 1964. A high-level compendium of essays on anomie arguments, including reports of research investigations and a detailed bibliography of published statements on anomie.

COHEN, ALBERT K. *Deviance and Control.* Englewood Cliffs, N.J.: Prentice-Hall, 1966. A brief exposition on theories of deviance which outlines many of the main features of sociological arguments on social structure and deviance.

DOUGLAS, JACK D. "Deviance and Order in a Pluralistic Society." In *Theoretical Sociology,* John C. McKinney and Edward A. Tiryakian, eds., pp. 367–401. New York: Appleton-Century-Crofts, 1970. Presents a value-pluralism argument regarding deviance in modern societies.

DURKHEIM, EMILE. *Suicide.* Trans. by J. A. Spaulding and George Simpson. New York: Free Press of Glencoe, 1951. A sociological classic, dealing with suicide rates and social-structure factors thought to produce them.

LEMERT, EDWIN M. *Human Deviance, Social Problems, and Social Control* (2d ed.). Englewood Cliffs, N.J.: Prentice-Hall, 1972. Presents a value-pluralism argument about the causes of deviance. A major alternative to anomie formulation.

MERTON, ROBERT K. *Social Theory and Social Structure* (rev. and enl. ed.). New York: Free Press of Glencoe, 1957. Contains several seminal essays on social structure and deviance centered about the concept of anomie.

deviant acts
and
deviant careers

W e have now examined theories about the discovery of those elements in the social structure that produce the rates and patterns of deviance in a particular society. But most of us are at least as curious about how specific individuals become enmeshed in deviant acts. How do actual persons get involved in norm violations and thereby become units in crime rates or some other statistics on deviance?

Ideally, theoretical formulations regarding "the sociology of deviance" (social-structural theories) ought to have analogs dealing with what we identified in chapter three as "the social-psychology of deviant acts and deviant careers." A complete theory of deviance emphasizing notions such as anomie thus ought to contain propositions which spell out the ways in which anomic conditions get "inside the heads" of specific persons, so to speak, and impel them into deviant acts. But as we have noted earlier, theory building has generally been bifurcated, with one group paying most attention to social-structural arguments and another concentrating on explaining the involvement of individuals in deviance.[1]

This chapter centers about a relatively brief examination of some varied answers to the question of how persons become engaged in deviance. Since large numbers of very simple and very complex formulations have been offered to explain the causes of deviance, we cannot deal in detail with even a generous sample of them. In addition, no effort is made here to articulate a theoretical synthesis that would combine different etiological arguments into a new explanatory statement. Such an endeavor would be a truly heroic task far surpassing the aims of this text.

TYPES OF THEORY

If we were to ask laymen about the causes of crime, homosexuality, delinquency, prostitution, or other forms of deviance, we would probably receive a bewildering assortment of answers. Some would invoke faulty biology as an answer, some would stress defective family experiences, while others would point to situational pressures, and still others would claim that deviants are psychologically disordered individuals. The writings of behavioral and social scientists contain similar notions about the causation of deviance. Accordingly, some kind of classification scheme must be employed if we are to make sense of the myriad forms the explanation takes.

Albert K. Cohen has provided a useful categorization in which he indicates that some explanatory theories stress most strongly the *characteristics of persons* thought to propel some into deviance and others into conformity.[2] "Kinds of people" hypotheses contend that such elements as biological characteristics or psychological variables lead persons into different lines of conduct. For example, this argument would hold that homosexuals differ in biological or psychological makeup from non-homosexuals. According to Cohen, the theoretical and research task for persons of this persuasion is twofold. First, there is a search for "a classification or typology of personalities, of which each type has a propensity to certain kinds of behavior."[3] The second, related chore pertains to discovering the different backgrounds or developmental processes that produced the different types of individuals. Tables 4 and 5 illustrate these research strategies.[4]

table 4 Kinds of People and Frequencies of Deviant Behavior

	BEHAVIOR	
KINDS OF PEOPLE	*Deviant*	*Nondeviant*
P (people)$_1$	High percent	Low percent
P (people)$_2$	Low percent	High percent

Table 4 shows the investigative strategy that has often been followed in delinquency research where, for example, the researcher has selected a sample of delinquents and another of nondelinquents and then has sought to find personal characteristics that differentiate them. Quite commonly the search has focused on personality problems and the hypothesis that delinquents are "psychologically disturbed" while the nonoffenders are "normal." Table 5 sketches the succeeding step of the research in which attempts are made to uncover developmental background differences (such as family interaction patterns) linked to the personality types, which in turn are related to delinquent or nondelinquent involvement.

table 5   Developmental Background and Kinds of People

	KINDS OF PEOPLE	
DEVELOPMENTAL BACKGROUND	P (people)$_1$	P (people)$_2$
B (background)$_1$	High percent	Low percent
B (background)$_2$	Low percent	High percent

A second kind of explanation identified by Cohen emphasizes mainly different *situations* or the circumstances that push one person toward deviant behavior and another toward conformity. These situational variations are thought to produce either particular pressures toward deviance or patterns of deviant motivation that result in individuals being implicated in norm violation. Laymen frequently verbalize this kind of argument about delinquency, for example, when they explain a youth's misbehavior in terms of "bad companions" or "bad apples" who led him astray. Table 6 sketches this form of argument.[5]

table 6   Kinds of Situations and Frequencies of Deviant Behavior

	BEHAVIOR	
KINDS OF SITUATIONS	*Deviant*	*Nondeviant*
S (situation)$_1$	High percent	Low percent
S (situation)$_2$	Low percent	High percent

Conjunctive theories are formulations that emphasize the joint involvement of both actor and situation variables in the production of the deviant act. These contend that deviance is most likely when certain personality types become involved in particular situations conducive to

table 7   Conjunction of Persons, Situations, and Frequencies of Deviant Behavior

	KINDS OF SITUATIONS	
KINDS OF PEOPLE	S (situation)$_1$	S (situation)$_2$
P (people)$_1$	Highest percent deviant	Intermediate percent deviant
P (people)$_2$	Intermediate percent deviant	Lowest percent deviant

deviance. Thus embezzlement would be most likely to occur when individuals with certain personality weaknesses become entangled in situations of financial stress. Table 7 shows the nature of this viewpoint.[6]

Conjunctive theories argue that deviance results from interaction between actor and situation. These theories treat the interaction as a single episode, that is, the explanation is considered complete when the particular combination of personality characteristics and situational forces that is involved in some initial act of deviance has been identified. A fourth form of theory, however, emphasizes *interaction* processes; that is, deviant patterns are viewed as developing over time through a series of stages. The nature of this image of the developmental process in deviance is indicated by Cohen:

> Some individual, in the pursuit of some interest or goal, and taking account of the situation, makes a move, possibly in a deviant direction, possibly with no thought of deviance in mind. However, his next move —the continuation of his course of action—is not fully determined by the state of affairs at the beginning. He may, at this juncture, choose among two or more possible directions. Which it will be will depend on the state of the actor and situation at *this* point in time, and either or both may, in the meantime, have undergone change. . . . In short, what these theories add is a conception of the act itself as a tentative, groping, feeling-out process, never fully determined by the past alone but always capable of changing its course in response to changes in the current scene. (emphasis in the original)[7]

Figure 1 illustrates the general form of interaction process views of deviance.[8]

In figure 1, some initial act A on the part of an individual leads either to another act, AA or AB, depending on circumstances following the beginning action. In turn, different pathways of behavior stem from these experiences, again contingent upon the varied situations and differential experiences encountered by specific persons. Initial acts of flirtation or experimentation along potentially deviant lines are seen as leading to several possible outcomes rather than to a single fate for the actor. The sense of this model can be illustrated by an example of juveniles who become involved in vandalism, petty thievery, and other casual flirtations with delinquency. Some of them ultimately become enmeshed in criminal careers, in part because they are arrested, incarcerated, and acquire various social liabilities that "lock them in" to lawbreaking careers. Others drift out of misconduct because they manage to avoid some of these experiences.

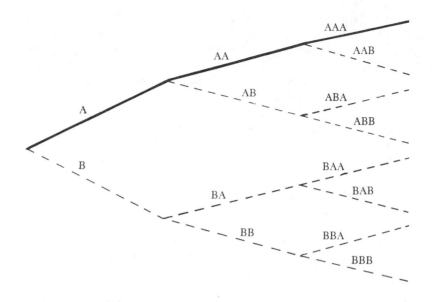

figure 1 Interaction Process and Deviant Outcomes. (Reprinted with permission from *Deviance and Control* by Albert K. Cohen. © 1966 by Prentice-Hall, Inc.)

Cohen's characterization of explanatory theories emphasizes the *form* taken by different perspectives rather than the *content* of these arguments. If we look at different "kinds of people" propositions, for example, we see that some assert that deviants are biologically flawed, others contend that norm violators are psychologically aberrant types, while still others maintain that deviants are normal persons who have become entangled in peculiar social situations that impel them into nonconformity. Similarly, conjunctive theories vary in terms of the weight they give to biological, psychological, or sociological variables.

In examining the content of explanatory theories about deviant acts and careers, the classification into categories of *biogenic, psychogenic,* and *sociogenic* is often used.[9] These three rubrics are very broad, and each contains a wide variety of specific claims. Briefly, biogenic hypotheses locate the genesis or origins of deviant acts in biological factors, psychogenic claims center on psychological imperfections of deviants, and sociogenic arguments stress the workings of social structure and differential learning opportunities in deviance.

Laymen have always favored biological hypotheses about deviance, and researchers have also paid much attention to them.[10] Lay versions of these notions include the belief that homosexuality is a biological quirk and that criminals are the products of hereditary transmission of faulty traits. Behavioral science hypotheses include the early work of criminologists who endeavored to uncover evidence of hereditary transmission of criminality, physical inferiority which predestined persons to deviance, or biological links between body type, temperament patterns, and propensities toward lawbreaking.

Critics have not been kind to biological theories. Concerning earlier attempts to uncover physical types predisposing persons to criminality, George B. Vold has observed: "Physical type theories turn out to be a more-or-less sophisticated form of shadow boxing with a much more subtle and difficult to get at problem, namely, that of the constitutional factor in human behavior."[11] Similarly, Richard R. Korn and Lloyd W. McCorkle have indicted the exponents of genetic theories of criminality for failure to develop arguments consistent with modern knowledge of genetics.[12] Critics have also voiced extreme skepticism about such modern biogenic arguments as those of William H. Sheldon, who has attempted to show that particular body types result in related temperament patterns, some of which predispose persons to delinquency and criminality.[13]

It is still too early to reject totally the possibility of biological correlates of deviant behavior. There is a good deal of current interest on this point in the XYY chromosomal abnormality found among some males.[14] Current evidence indicates that somewhat larger numbers of incarcerated persons than normal members of the population have the XYY pattern, although some XYY males are not abnormal or criminal. On the other hand, contrary to widely publicized claims in the mass media, XYY males apparently are not markedly aggressive, nor do the data indicate that they are characterized by physical, neurological, or physiological abnormalities. Ernest B. Hook has amalgamated much evidence on the XYY genotype and contends that: "There is a definite association between the XYY genotype and presence in mental-penal settings, but both the nature and extent of this association are yet to be determined."[15] In summary, although much work remains to be accomplished before the relationship between this chromosomal pattern and deviant behavior becomes entirely clear, the data that have been accumulated make it impossible for us to declare unequivocally that there are no biological correlates of deviance.[16]

PSYCHOGENIC THEORIES OF DEVIANCE

Psychogenic formulations include a wide range of different, specific arguments about deviance, all of which contend that psychological aberrations, usually thought to be the product of unusual or distorted socialization experiences, lead individuals to engage in deviance. Thus homosexuality is held to be the result of psychological maladjustment in which homosexuals exhibit atypical motivation and perceptions concerning masculinity and heterosexuality, while crime is alleged to be the work of persons with defective superegos or some other psychological impairment. In criminology, these views take three general forms: psychoanalytic claims, arguments about psychopathy and its relationships to criminality, and general emotional disturbance views that are eclectic and do not stem directly from psychoanalytic thought.[17]

Don C. Gibbons has reviewed a sizeable body of empirical evidence regarding the relationship of psychological problems and emotional disturbance to criminality.[18] The survey concludes that those claims characterizing criminal offenders as suffering from gross psychological pathology, such as psychoses, are demonstrably false; the extent of psychotic disorders among offenders is no greater than among noncriminals. Second, the survey found that conventional psychoanalytic theories about criminality must be rejected because they are hopelessly ambiguous, and rigorous scientific tests of them are not possible. Third, the survey evaluated the argument that criminals are often psychopaths or sociopaths as worthless. Used in analyses of criminality, both the psychopathy and the sociopathy arguments represent nothing more than a deceptive form of name calling. In nearly every case, the principal evidence used to establish either the psychopathy or sociopathy of an offender is the same behavior that one is endeavoring to explain, namely, persistent involvement in lawbreaking. We hold that the conclusions of this survey apply equally well to psychogenic arguments claiming that other deviants are psychologically abnormal persons. Much evidence to the contrary is available, indicating that many individuals caught up in deviant lines of conduct are no more psychologically impaired than are nondeviants.[19]

At the same time, we believe that the full story has yet to be told regarding psychological factors.[20] Our views on personality are similar to those of Alex Inkeles, who argues:

> Sociologists have traditionally explained the fact that most people fulfill their major social obligations by referring to the system of sanctions

imposed on those who fail to meet, and the rewards granted to those who do meet, the expectations of society. Performance is thus seen as largely dependent on factors "outside" the person. The only thing that need be posited as "inside," in this view, is the general desire to avoid punishment and to gain rewards. Important as such "drives" may be, they do not seem sufficient to explain the differences in the way people perform their assigned social roles. While accepting the crucial importance of the objective factors which determine social behavior, we must recognize that recruitment into occupational and other status-positions, and the quality of performance in the roles people are assigned, may, to an important degree, be influenced by personal qualities in individuals. It may be assumed, further, that this happens on a sufficiently large scale to be a crucial factor in determining the functioning of any social system. To the degree that this is true, to predict the functioning of a particular institution, of a small- or large-scale system, we need to know not only the system of status-positions but also the distribution of personality characteristics in the population at large and among those playing important roles in the system.[21]

The form of explanation that is probably required to account for particular lines of conduct by specific individuals is one in which personality elements are joined with social-structural ones. Our judgment is that there probably are many deviants who are psychologically well adjusted and who exhibit quite conventional personality configurations. There are other norm-violators, including some "mentally disordered," who have fairly disordered thought processes.[22] In addition, the behavior of some deviants is partially accounted for by specific personality factors that differentiate them from other individuals but that are not indicators of personality abnormality. For example, it may be that "dependency" is a personality attribute that is relatively frequent on the part of naive check forgers, middle-class alcoholics, and certain other deviants, although dependency would not usually be regarded as sufficiently debilitating to be thought of as an indicator of abnormality. In the same way, other deviants may exhibit personality patterns centering around "masculinity concerns" or similar dimensions. But individuals showing conventional personality structures, patterns of abnormality, or characteristics such as "dependency" are all found also among those persons *not* identified as deviants.

Assume for a moment that this line of argument is correct and that persons showing "dependency" are to be found occupying a variety of social roles. How are we to account for these varied lines of activity? These different outcomes probably result from variations in "career contingencies" or life events encountered by specific individuals. Thus some dependent persons become involved in check forgery, others in alcoholism, and still others in nondeviant conduct, depending on the various contingent social experiences that vary from one actor to another. The behavioral model articulated here is similar to the interaction process identified by Albert K. Cohen discussed earlier.

Sufficient data already exist concerning psychological correlates of deviance patterns to indicate that this question is worthy of further exploration and study.[23] Some of the relevant research includes Edwin M. Lemert's study of dependency on the part of alcoholics,[24] John W. Kinch's evidence regarding self-concept variations among juvenile delinquents,[25] and some tentative findings pointing to dependency on the part of check forgers.[26]

The question of the psychological elements of deviance will again be raised when we deal with the labeling perspective on deviance. When we turn to that version of theorizing, we shall see that a frequent complaint is that it seems to posit an empty organism to which things happen, but which has no control over life events that are visited upon it. The human is thus a kind of billiard ball, buffeted about by experiences which he can neither determine nor control; that is, labeling exponents sometimes seem to imply that individuals are singled out capriciously by social control agencies or other social audiences which tag them as a "nut," "pervert," or "second-degree burglar." In turn, the stigmatizing conquences of such experiences are viewed as inexorably driving those persons into further involvement in norm violation. In all of this, the image of the individual as a thinking, reacting, motivated actor who possesses some degree of autonomy and freedom to determine the course of his behavior receives little emphasis. In the opinion of some critics, labeling arguments will remain incomplete until they are expanded in the direction of a fuller treatment of the deviant as an active agent in his own fate.

SOCIOGENIC PERSPECTIVES ON DEVIANCE

Although sociologists disagree regarding the nature of the social processes thought to be the major forces in the genesis of deviance, their theoretical positions can be sorted into a relatively small set of general categories. Representative classifications of theoretical viewpoints have been offered by Gresham M. Sykes (criminological arguments,)[27] Ronald L. Akers,[28] and Travis Hirschi.[29]

Sykes, Akers, and Hirschi note *social learning* theories that have enjoyed considerable popularity among sociologists which assert that deviance comes about through experiences in which persons acquire deviant attitudes and motivation by means of the same general learning processes that are involved in nondeviant behavior. The learning experience thus differs from that involved in nondeviant behavior only in the *content* of what is learned and not in the *form* of the learning.

These three sociologists identify *social control* viewpoints as a second perspective. These theories maintain that conformity is usually produced through the ties of the person to the conventional moral order which bind him to other persons and exert pressure on him to refrain from deviance.[30] Crudely put, the individual behaves himself only to the extent that he values the good opinion others have of him. If these ties become weakened for some reason, social control breaks down, and the individual is then free to engage in norm-violating acts. This perspective does not posit any special motivation toward deviance; rather, it argues that most of us would violate norms if we were not discouraged from doing so by a concern for the responses of others to our conduct. In Hirschi's explication of social control theory applied to juvenile delinquency, he identifies several dimensions along which social control varies, including attachment, commitment, involvement, and belief.[31] Attachment refers to the strength of links to others such as parents or peers, while commitment relates to the devotion of the person to conformist lines of conduct. Individuals also vary in the degree to which they are involved in activities that restrict the time they have available for deviant acts, and they differ in the strength of their attitudes toward conformity. In general, the weaker these ties are, the more likely it is that the person will engage in deviance.

A third etiological perspective identified by all three sociologists is the *anomie-social disorganization* view, which is an elaboration on social-structural formulations considered earlier in this book. These theorists contend that during periods of anomie or social disorganization, large numbers of quite normal persons will be bombarded by strains, pressures, and deleterious life circumstances that will push them into deviance.[32]

A related scheme is offered by David Matza, who has sorted theories into those that stress *affinity, affiliation,* or *signification.*[33] Affinity refers to arguments that persons "catch a deviance" through proximity to various adverse social situations or conditions of social disorganization, and affiliational contentions posit the social learning of deviance through a process akin to what Edwin H. Sutherland termed "differential association."[34] These two orientations sketched by Matza are basically very similar to the cultural learning and anomie views identified in the classifications above. Signification is Matza's term for labeling claims, the subject of the latter part of this chapter.

A final observation on perspectives on deviance is that our comments are misleading if they imply the existence of clear-cut schools of thought in which the advocates of one orientation adhere to it religiously, giving no credence to other points of view. In fact, sociological theorists show much eclectic appreciation of differing hypotheses about norm violation.[35] Additionally, other explanatory variants not mentioned here are also entertained by many, including contentions about "risk-taking" processes in which some deviants are pictured as drifting into norm violation or being drawn into it from the force of situational pressures.[36]

INTERACTIONAL AND LABELING THEORIES OF DEVIANCE

In examining several theories regarding social-structural forces thought to produce deviance, we observed that most of these theories regard deviance as behavior which violates a common cultural value system or norms shared by most citizens and which disrupts social equilibrium. Also, in these perspectives, central cultural values are seen as relatively few in number and generally shared by citizens throughout the society. Little attention is paid in these arguments to reactions to deviance or social control processes; the implicit assumption is that societal responses play only a minor role. These structural-functional formulations have sometimes been identified as an Eastern school of thought, in that they have been most in vogue in Eastern universities of the United States.[37]

By contrast, a different set of orientations, which is sometimes identified as the Western or Pacific Coast school,[38] has sprung up in recent years and is currently receiving the heaviest attention in theoretical and research literature. This very lively perspective is most commonly designated as the *social-interactional* or *labeling* view. Although it would be misleading to imply that there is a single theoretical position which can be identified as labeling theory,[39] a collection of themes or viewpoints is shared by a sizeable and growing body of sociologists,[40] and a generous supply of critical commentary exists regarding this perspective.[41]

What are the central arguments of the labeling view?[42] First, it stresses that deviance is problematic and a matter of social definition, because the standards or norms which are violated are not universal or unchanging in character. Then too, deviance is the result of social judgments imposed on persons by a social audience. Howard S. Becker reminds us that:

Social groups create deviance by making the rules whose infraction constitute deviance, and by applying those rules to particular people and labeling them as outsiders. From this point of view, deviance is *not* a quality of the act the person commits, but rather a consequence of the application by others of rules and sanctions to an "offender." The deviant is one to whom that label has been applied; deviant behavior is behavior that people so label. (emphasis in the original)[43]

Such statements are sometimes taken to mean that only those persons who have been involved in nonconformity *and* who have been subjected to specific labeling or defining experiences are deviants. But labeling theorists usually equivocate on this point, often speaking of secret deviants who have not been publicly identified, or of primary deviance which has not received a societal reaction.[44] Either way, nearly all agree that those nonconformists who are singled out by the police, mental health personnel, or other social audiences face adjustment problems concerning spoiled identity that hidden deviants do not encounter. This proposition is at the center of the labeling orientation.

Another theme is that *deviance arises out of diverse sources* or circumstances. Labelers do not believe that some small core of cultural values and differentially available opportunity structures accounts for the varied forms of deviance in complex societies. Instead, they stress value pluralism and underscore the significance of subcultural normative patterns in nonconformity.[45] Acts of deviance often occur when individuals find themselves pulled and tugged by competing interests and values. Whatever the circumstances producing norm violation, they cannot be subsumed under some all-embracing theory such as anomie.

Views differ somewhat among labeling theorists on the importance of studying the etiology of initial acts of norm violation and on whether such causes can be identified at all. Some have given minimal attention to the question of initial causation, seemingly because they assume that it is not possible to specify the myriad circumstances out of which these events flow. Others have offered value-pluralism and risk-taking notions designed to suggest the range of circumstances producing nonconformity and have discussed the origins of deviant acts in much detail. In either case, labeling arguments have paid relatively little attention to rates of deviance and structural factors accounting for them and we can see that the labeling tradition and the social-structural or anomie perspectives have developed as divergent alternatives. Few attempts have been made by sociologists to develop detailed formulations that deal both with causal concerns of deviance rates and with processes operating in individual deviant careers. Nanette J. Davis has commented that the labeling theory, "as practiced, has been largely astructural, ahistorical, and noncomparative, and tends to promote a sociology of the segmental, the exotic, and the bizarre."[46]

Labelers agree that deviant behavior ought to be examined as a *social process* involving *both* the acts of nonconforming individuals and the responses of others to these deviations. They draw attention to careers in which persons who become caught up in nonconformity exhibit changes in behavior and self-concept patterns over time. In turn, careers change in response to social reactions directed toward the deviant person.

In many of the examples offered by labelers, initial acts of deviance are denied or disavowed by the actors, so that their acts are "normalized." Thus at first, the person or his social audience, or both, are able to define the misbehavior as unimportant or peripheral to his real self. But if social reactions that are directed at the individual ultimately undermine his claim to normality, he is driven toward an altered social identity as a deviant, or less frequently, propelled away from norm violation.

Labeling theorists have examined organizations and agencies which function ostensibly to rehabilitate the violator or in other ways to draw him back into conformity. They contend that various people-changing organizations frequently produce results quite different from those intended, often operating to seal off opportunities for the individual to withdraw from deviance, as they stigmatize him and create other social impediments to his rehabilitation. Labeling theorists are generally pessimistic about training schools, prisons, mental hospitals, and other similar institutions, for they suspect that these places often exacerbate the adjustment problems of their inmates.

To date, labeling views have contained much speculation and little empirical evidence. The labeling perspective on mental disorder, for example, does not seem to correspond with the empirical facts currently at hand.[47] Similarly, the evidence regarding alleged deleterious effects of correctional organizations is less clear than implied in labeling arguments. We shall say more about these matters in chapter eight.

EDWIN M. LEMERT

Edwin M. Lemert has written one of the earliest and most sophisticated versions of labeling theory in which he analyzes extensively the nature of the processes by which persons are singled out as nonconformists and the life-careers of some become organized around deviant statuses.[48] He emphasizes deviant individuals and their immediate social interactions with others rather than rates of deviance and the larger social structures producing these rates. He assumes that "behavioral deviations are a function of culture conflict which is expressed through social organization."[49] As we noted in chapter six, he rejects structural-functional arguments such as the anomie view in favor of value pluralism which emphasizes subcultural values and value conflicts as the sources of deviance.[50]

Lemert's writings identify several origins of deviant conduct, and he employs the rubrics of *individual, situational,* and *systematic* deviation for these different sources.[51] Individual deviation refers to acts which emanate from internal psychic pressures, while situational deviation develops as a function of situational stresses or pressures. Acts of situational deviation are relatively independent of psychic pressures among actors, thus different individuals placed in the same stressful setting would be expected to respond in similar ways.

It is possible to observe behavioral instances which approximate the limiting cases identified by Lemert. For example, some kinds of sexual misconduct can be explained only as the consequence of the idiosyncratic motives of the offender. Nearly pure illustrations of situational deviation also exist, such as the individual implicated in cumulative, catastrophic financial strain to whom theft appears the only problem-solving pattern of activity open. As Lemert would acknowledge, however, these examples are polar extremes on a causal continuum. In real life, deviant conduct often arises as the joint product of pressures of social situations and factors from one's inner life. In many actual cases, the etiological task requires evaluating the relative contribution of each motivational source to the behavioral product under examination. This job is often at the heart of satisfactory explanation; a critical need in many areas of deviant behavior is for theoretical models which clarify and weight these two factors.

By *systematic* deviation, Lemert refers to patterns of deviant behavior which take on the coloring of subcultures or behavior systems. He says: "When such communication [between deviants] carries specific content, when rapport develops between deviants and common rationalizations make their appearance, the unique and situational forms of deviation are converted to organized or systematic deviation."[52] Systematic or organized forms of deviance arise from cases of conduct which were individual or situational in genesis. Lemert indicates that systematic deviation is most likely to occur when society makes survival of the deviant individual problematic unless he can become absorbed into some kind of protective social system. Accordingly, the existence of homosexual subcultures in American society is explained, at least in part, as a consequence of the harrassment and hostility which the identified homosexual encounters in society.[53] One point Lemert makes regarding systematic forms of deviant conduct is particularly worth emphasizing, namely, that most deviant subcultures follow a limited or circumscribed set of deviant mores, for most of the members' values are those of the dominant culture.[54] Drug addicts, homosexuals, or other social pariahs hold allegiance to most conventional values of society, and their deviant beliefs and conduct are specific and few in number.

Much of the emphasis in Lemert's presentation is on *processual* aspects of nonconforming behavior, in which he shows that deviant careers often undergo marked changes over time. In the past, the more common model of explanation has been of a simple stimulus-response or cause-effect kind, endeavoring to discover some set of influences which antedated the deviant behavior under study, often with a considerable time span separating the causal factors and present behavior. Furthermore, older causal formulations have tended to assume that once the causes of initial deviance have occurred, little remains to be explained. Longitudinal models of analysis were rarely employed; thus little attention was paid to changes in careers flowing out of differential experiences the deviant undergoes in his life history.

By contrast, Lemert argues that initial acts of nonconformity are frequently instances of risk taking, representing tentative flirtations with proscribed behavior patterns.[55] Whatever the reasons for these actions, many of them are subjected to societal reactions when they are observed by someone else and made the focus of concern. The subsequent career experiences of the deviant may thus be more heavily influenced by these societal reactions than by anything else that has occurred to him before his involvement in disapproved conduct. Lemert notes that societal definitions and reactions in complex societies are often markedly *putative,* so that beliefs having no foundation in actual behavior become attached to deviant persons. The "drug fiend" mythology which holds that addicts are generally depraved and immoral illustrates this point clearly.[56]

One major distinction introduced by Lemert is between *primary deviance* and *secondary deviation.*[57] These concepts reflect his concern with deviance as a social process and with the impact of societal reactions on persons. He claims that primary deviation is polygenetic, arising from a variety of social, psychological, cultural, and physiological sources; it represents that state of affairs in which an individual engages in norm-violating conduct which he regards as alien to his true self. Secondary deviation, on the other hand, develops when the actor reorganizes his social-psychological characteristics around the deviant role. Lemert declares that: "The deviant individuals must react symbolically to their own behavior aberrations and fix them in their sociopsychological patterns. The deviations remain primary deviations or symptomatic and situational as long as they are rationalized or otherwise dealt with as functions of a socially acceptable role."[58]

Primary deviance sometimes escalates to secondary deviation, but in other cases it remains primary. Secondary deviation most often arises out of (a) repeated acts of norm violation, and (b) the experience of societal reactions. A feedback process often occurs in which repeated misconduct or deviation triggers societal reactions to the behavior, which then stimulate further deviant acts. According to Lemert, "The sequence of interaction leading to secondary deviation is roughly as follows: (1) primary deviation; (2) societal penalties; (3) further primary deviation; (4) stronger penalties and rejections; (5) further deviation, perhaps with hostilities and resentments beginning to focus upon those doing the penalizing; (6) crisis reached in the tolerance quotient, expressed in formal action by the community stigmatizing of the deviant; (7) strengthening of the deviant conduct as a reaction to the stigmatizing and penalties; (8) ultimate acceptance of deviant social status and efforts at adjustment on the basis of the associated role."[59]

In his analysis of forms of deviant behavior, Lemert goes on to show how these theoretical notions can be applied to varied forms of misconduct and pathological behavior. He has also noted how development of a deviant status can result in a variety of limitations being imposed upon the social participation of the deviant actor, so that his economic activities, mobility experiences, and so on, become markedly circumscribed as he progresses in deviant conduct. Lemert has also applied these insights on deviant behavior to research studies on alcoholic persons,[60] the development of paranoid social patterns,[61] and the genesis of certain forms of criminality.[62]

HOWARD S. BECKER

Howard S. Becker has also made early and important contributions to labeling views, particularly in his book, *Outsiders.* His arguments are very similar to those of Lemert. Becker points out that there is no automatic, fixed and invariant relationship between behavioral acts and societal reactions to the conduct as deviant. Instead, the likelihood that behavioral occurrences will be identified publicly as deviant varies in accordance with the time at which they occur, the place where they transpire, and the individuals who observe the conduct.[63] Becker notes that some individuals are falsely accused as deviants, for although they have been labeled as outsiders, their behavior has actually been conforming in character. Other persons are secret deviants; although they misbehave, their misconduct does not come to the attention of any significant public. Still other individuals who acquire a public identity as "queer," "crazy," or some other deviant tag behave in ways which warrant this social judgment.

One of Becker's major contributions is his stress on the temporal patterning of deviant behavior, arguing that sociologists need to pay attention to *sequential models of deviance,* that is, to orderly changes in the actions of the person over time. He offers the concepts of *deviant careers* and *career contingencies* as useful explanations of career development. A career contingency is a factor or set of influences which results in the movement of a career incumbent from one position to another in a career pattern.[64] Becker suggests that interest in deviant careers ought to concentrate on the processes and variables which sustain a pattern of deviance over a lengthy period of time, rather than on isolated and fugitive deviant escapades. He argues that: "One of the most crucial steps in the process of building a stable pattern of deviant behavior is likely to be the experience of being caught and publicly labeled as a deviant. . . . The most important consequence is a drastic change in the individual's public identity."[65]

Other major insights in Becker's work center on his distinction between *master* and *subordinate* statuses, in which he argues that a particular deviant status, such as that of "hood," "fairy," "speed freak," or "hustler" may become superordinate over the other statuses occupied by the individual, with the result that most of the social relationships of the person become heavily colored by his public identity as a deviant or discredited individual.[66] Finally, Becker, like Lemert, regards the development of deviant groups (subcultures or systematic deviation) as a profoundly important determinant of the course of a deviant career.[67]

CRITICAL ASSESSMENTS OF LABELING ARGUMENTS

Although labeling formulations have enjoyed great popularity, a considerable quantity of critical comment about them has also been produced. Jack P. Gibbs correctly contends that the labeling argument is a relatively vague perspective rather than a full-blown theory;[68] that is, the labeling view is a general orientation to deviance which still needs conceptual clarification as well as research testing. Gibbs contrasts various "old" conceptions of deviance with the "new" one revolving around labeling arguments. His own preference is for that version of older thoughtways which identifies deviance as behavior violating a conduct norm and criminality as activity running counter to a legal prohibition. By contrast, a literal reading of some labeling arguments seems to suggest that only that behavior which has been subjected to a societal reaction constitutes deviance. Gibbs maintains that this version of labeling theory cannot provide adequate answers to three major questions: "(1) Why does the incidence of a particular act vary from one population to the next? (2) Why do some persons commit the act while others do not? (3) Why is the act in question considered deviant and/or criminal in some societies but not in others?"[69]

It is true that labeling theorists do sometimes sound as though they are arguing that deviants are not behaviorally different from nondeviants and that the only thing that differentiates them is societal reaction. One could almost read that interpretation into the work of Thomas J. Scheff, who argues that mental illness is a label attached to some persons who engage in residual rule breaking, but that almost all persons are involved in residual rule breaking.[70] Scheff uses the term residual rule breaking to refer to diverse kinds of violations for which the culture provides no explicit label, in contrast to those deviant acts that are publicly identified by terms such as "crime," "perversion," and so forth. The sense of residual rule breaking conveyed by Scheff is of widespread petty, innocuous acts characteristic of most of us at one time or another.

It is this version of labeling theory that Ronald L. Akers has in mind when he asserts: "One sometimes gets the impression from reading this literature that people go about minding their own business, and then— 'wham'—bad society comes along and slaps them with a stigmatized label."[71] Or, in another place, Akers offers this critical judgment about labeling theory and its inattention to primary deviation: "When carried too far, however, this insight serves as a blinder. The labelling creates the deviance, yes, and often operates to increase the probability that certain stigmatized persons will commit further deviance, and to promote deviant behavior that might not have occurred otherwise. But the label does not create the behavior in the *first place*." (emphasis in the original)[72]

Similar sentiments have been expressed by David J. Bordua, who asserts that labeling theory: " . . . assumes an essentially empty organism, or at least one with little or no autonomous capacity to determine conduct. The process of developing deviance seems all societal response and no deviant stimulus."[73] Bordua argues that such a view of the deviant actor hardly squares with the facts of human behavior. More specifically, he asks how the successes of the social control machinery are to be explained within labeling theory. Some persons do opt out of deviance even after being processed through some kind of people-changing machinery, contrary to what would be expected from labeling theory. Bordua contends that labeling theory will have to take more account of the prereaction social history characteristics of individual deviants if it is to attain maximum utility as an explanation.[74]

If one were to stick to a strict interpretation of the assertions that social groups create deviance through their reactions and that deviance is a consequence of applications by others of rules and sanctions, then the questions of Gibbs above are indeed unanswerable. However, not all labeling writers make such claims. Indeed, Lemert, who might be regarded as the intellectual father of these views, defines deviance in terms of rule violation rather than social reactions. Hence he regards the societal reaction as a variable to be studied, rather than a defining characteristic of deviance. Actually, as we have already noted, most labeling theorists hold less than complete allegiance to the view that societal reaction defines deviance. For example, Becker speaks of secret deviants, which contradicts the notion that deviance is a consequence of a societal reaction directed at a person.

Nanette J. Davis has found other flaws in labeling arguments, and she maintains that: "Labeling theory, characteristically oriented within a symbolic interaction framework, has suffered from a 'methodological inhibition' often associated with this social psychological approach. Conceptual impoverishment is facilitated by an absorption with general imagery, with unsystematic, elusive, and suggestive empirical presentations, rather than definitive tests of interaction framework."[75] She contends that the interactional stance of labelers beclouds the phenomena of deviance in romanticism, as when it offers up a picture of "Hell's Angels" members as noble ruffians or prostitutes as "happy hookers," rather than describing these individuals more accurately. It also encourages the sociologist to project a "hip" posture of one who is privy to the bizarre scenes wherein deviant acts are played out.[76] Then too, it emphasizes tactics for penetrating the social worlds of nonconformists, often by means of unobtrusive or disguised research procedures. "Soft" methodology is stressed, and the sociologist is encouraged to engage in relatively unsystematic observations.

Another serious criticism offered by Davis is that labeling views tend toward an actor-dominated form of analysis, rather than one that is organization-centered; labeling hypotheses emphasize the effects of labeling on the actor while ignoring the organizational side of social control.[77] She remarks: "The core propositions of Lemert's social control model included the structural emphasis on social differentiation, power exchanges, and conflict as a basis for the sociologist's coming to terms with social control and social change. Lemert's lineal descendents, however, in taking the *reaction* of the labeled person as the starting point for research, rather than the policies and decisions of the *reactors,* have bypassed the rich field of social control." (emphasis in the original)[78] Quite obviously, Davis would have us devote considerably more attention to social conflict, the workings of social control bureaucracies, and similar subjects.

Our own position on labeling theory is similar to that of Edwin M. Schur[79] and Ronald L. Akers.[80] First, they express a sense of appreciation for labeling views, holding that these perspectives have highlighted certain aspects of deviance which have gone unnoticed in other orientations. It is doubtless this aspect of labeling arguments which is most responsible for their great current popularity. These notions have provided us with a theoretical breakthrough, and we are now in a position to make explanatory advances that would not have occurred with older theories. Then too, we agree with Schur in his opinion that the general outlines of labeling arguments have been drawn from the mainstream of sociology and do not constitute an entirely novel orientation.[81] Schur has pointed out, for example, that there is a close affinity between a number of the main tenets of labeling theory and those of symbolic interactionism.

We hasten to add, however, that we also agree with Schur, Akers, and others in their judgment that labeling viewpoints represent embryonic theory at best. Extant labeling views operate mainly as sensitizing claims. For example, they advise us to pay attention to social definitions of deviance and social reactions to deviant persons; although that is good advice, we have already seen in chapter five that not much empirical investigation of these matters has yet occurred. Consequently, we are not yet in a position to articulate a series of empirical generalizations about societal definitions or their relationship to other social factors.

Much the same commentary applies to another core contention of labelers, namely, that societal reactions directed at deviants, such as penal incarceration or commitment to a mental hospital are negative career contingencies. What little evidence we have at hand indicates that reality is a good deal more complex than implied in such views. For example, we can find data suggesting that training schools or other custodial institutions sometimes have benign or positive effects on some who are placed in them, as well as other pieces of evidence indicating that claims about the deleterious effects of labeling experiences are sometimes not warranted. We will return to this question in detail in chapter eight where we shall attempt to spell out some of the relationships which probably exist between kinds of deviants and various societal reactions.

SUMMARY

This chapter has glanced at the many answers that have been offered to the question: "Why do they do it?" Various biogenic, psychogenic, and sociogenic formulations have been advanced as explanations of deviance, but most of our attention has centered on labeling views because these are the most commonly encountered arguments in the contemporary sociological literature on deviance.[82] Even so, there is much more work to be done on these perspectives before they can be described as full-blown theories and before they approach empirical adequacy as accounts of how individuals become involved in primary deviance or in careers in nonconformity.

NOTES

[1] Some exceptions would be Albert K. Cohen, "The Sociology of the Deviant Act: Anomie Theory and Beyond," *American Sociological Review* 30 (February 1965): 5–14; Edwin H. Sutherland and Donald R. Cressey, *Principles of Criminology,* 8th ed. (Philadelphia: J. B. Lippincott, 1970). Cohen has suggested some revisions and extensions of Merton's anomie theory that would direct attention to social-psychological hypotheses. Sutherland and Cressey offer paired arguments regarding differential social organization and differential association as answers to the two causal questions relating to criminal deviants.

[2] Albert K. Cohen, *Deviance and Control* (Englewood Cliffs, N.J.: Prentice-Hall, 1966), pp. 42–45.

[3] Ibid., pp. 42–43.

[4] Adapted from ibid., p. 42.

[5] Adapted from ibid.

[6] Adapted from ibid.

[7] Ibid., pp. 44–45.

[8] Ibid., p. 43.

[9] These categories are employed in Don C. Gibbons, *Society, Crime, and Criminal Careers,* 2d ed. (Englewood Cliffs, N.J.: Prentice-Hall, 1973), pp. 125–149. A fairly detailed review both of historical and contemporary theories in criminology can be found in ibid., pp. 125–251.

[10] A large sampling of biogenic theories regarding criminality is presented in ibid., pp. 136–49; one example of biogenic notions is reported in Jonathan O. Cole, "The Drug Approach to Mental Illness," in Samuel Prager, ed., *The Medicated Society* (New York: The Macmillan Co., 1968), p. 106. Cole reports that " . . . one famous Nobel laureate, Dr. Linus Pauling coined a wonderful phrase, 'For every twisted mind, a twisted molecule.' Though he may ultimately turn out to be correct, to date the twisted-molecule cause has not been found for

most conditions. In fact, even if this rather optimistic concept were found to be true, there is certainly no assurance that one could immediately find a drug that would untwist the molecule."

[11] George B. Vold, *Theoretical Criminology* (New York: Oxford University Press, 1958), p. 74.

[12] For an incisive critique of theories seeking to find the causes of deviance in genetically inherited traits, see Richard R. Korn and Lloyd W. McCorkle, *Criminology and Penology* (New York: Holt, Rinehart and Winston, 1959), pp. 199–204.

[13] William H. Sheldon, Emil M. Hartl, and Eugene McDermott, *Varieties of Delinquent Youth* (New York: Harper and Row, Publishers, 1949). The criticisms of this work are reviewed in Gibbons, *Society, Crime, and Criminal Careers,* pp. 142–44.

[14] The XYY chromosome hypothesis and the relevant evidence are discussed in Gibbons, *Society, Crime, and Criminal Careers,* pp. 146–49; Stephen Schafer, *Theories in Criminology* (New York: Random House, 1969), pp. 190–94; and Ernest B. Hook, "Behavioral Implications of the Human XYY Genotype," *Science* 179 (January 1973): 139–79.

[15] Hook, "Behavioral Implications of the Human XYY Genotype," p. 147.

[16] Also, it is not the case that all advocates of biogenic hypotheses have advanced unsophisticated or unidimensional arguments. For example, see Juan B. Cortés with Florence M. Gatti, *Delinquency and Crime: A Biopsychosocial Approach* (New York: Seminar Press, 1972). These investigators carried on a detailed, careful, sophisticated investigation of the linkages between biological, psychological, and social factors and delinquency. They report that mesomorphic bodily structure, temperament patterns, and delinquency are related. They also present a complex biopsychosocial theory of delinquency. Although we think this theory is not entirely adequate in terms of the logical requirements of formal theory, it certainly cannot be faulted as unsophisticated. Parenthetically, these authors take Gibbons to task for his evaluation of the research of the Gluecks concerning bodily structure and delinquency [Sheldon and Eleanor Glueck, *Physique and Delinquency* (New York: Harper and Row, Publishers, 1956)]. Gibbons, commenting on the Gluecks' findings, noted: "However, a sociologist would be quick to point out that a process of *social selection,* rather than biological determinism, probably explains the results." [Don C. Gibbons, *Delinquent Behavior* (Englewood Cliffs, N.J.: Prentice-Hall, 1970), pp. 75–76, emphasis in the original.] Regarding this statement, Cortés and Gatti point out: "For one thing, nobody nowadays speaks of biological *determinism;* but second, the fact that there may be a process of social selection, does not detract in the least from the relevance of many other variables." (emphasis in the original), Cortés and Gatti, *Delinquency and Crime,* p. 40. Although Gibbons's comment has been cited favorably by several others in the sociological literature as a seemingly devastating blow to the Gluecks' thesis, we acknowledge the Cortés and Gatti rejoinder contains much merit.

[17] Gibbons, *Society, Crime, and Criminal Careers,* pp. 151–79.

[18] Ibid.

[19] For example, with regard to psychological patterns among homosexuals, see Evelyn Hooker, "The Adjustment of the Male Overt Homosexual," *Journal of Projective Techniques* 21 (March 1957): 18–31; William Simon and John H. Gagnon, "Homosexuality: The Formulation of a Sociological Perspective," *Journal of Health and Social Behavior* 8 (September 1967): 177–85.

[20] See the discussion of this argument in Gibbons, *Society, Crime, and Criminal Careers,* pp. 175–79.

[21] Alex Inkeles, *What is Sociology? An Introduction to the Discipline and Profession* (Englewood Cliffs, N.J.: Prentice-Hall, 1964), p. 57.

[22] There is considerable controversy over the question of the degree to which the "mentally ill" are truly ill or disordered, as opposed to being simply social nuisances or burdensome to someone. We shall examine this matter later in this chapter and in chapter eight.

[23] For reviews of that data concerning criminals and delinquents, see Gibbons, *Society, Crime, and Criminal Careers,* pp. 151–78; Gibbons, *Delinquent Behavior,* pp. 76–89.

[24] Edwin M. Lemert, "Dependency in Married Alcoholics," *Quarterly Journal of Studies on Alcohol* 23 (December 1962): 590–609.

[25] John W. Kinch, "Self Conceptions of Types of Delinquents," *Sociological Inquiry* 32 (Spring 1962): 228–34.

[26] Gibbons, *Society, Crime, and Criminal Careers,* p. 311.

[27] Gresham M. Sykes, "The Future of Criminality," *American Behavioral Scientist* 15 (February 1972): 409–19.

[28] Ronald L. Akers, *Deviant Behavior* (Belmont, Calif.: Wadsworth Publishing Co., 1973), pp. 9–31.

[29] Travis Hirschi, *Causes of Delinquency* (Berkeley, Calif.: University of California Press, 1969), pp. 3–15.

[30] See ibid. for a version of social control theory applied to delinquency. See also Akers, *Deviant Behavior,* pp. 26–29.

[31] Hirschi, *Causes of Delinquency.*

[32] Akers also identifies social conflict views as another argument on the sources of deviance. Akers, *Deviant Behavior.* As we indicated in chapter six, social conflict arguments about deviance speak most strongly to the matter of value pluralism and normative conflict in American society. They have drawn our attention to the fact that many rules, criminal laws, in particular, represent the special interests of some particular powerful group that has managed to get its preferences incorporated into law. However, to date, this approach has been more promissory than productive, particularly with regard to hypotheses about the development of deviance on the part of particular individuals. As Akers has observed (p. 20): "the conflict approach *is potent as an explanation of the formation and enforcement of norms themselves; it is less powerful as an explanation of deviant behavior.*" (emphasis in the original)

[33] David Matza, *Becoming Deviant* (Englewood Cliffs, N.J.: Prentice-Hall, 1969), chapters 5 and 7.

[34] Sutherland and Cressey, *Principles of Criminology*, pp. 71–93.

[35] For example, see Gibbons, *Society, Crime, and Criminal Careers*, where a variety of hypotheses is advanced to account for different types or "role-careers" in criminality. In that work, a number of psychogenic contentions about particular offender types are also explored.

[36] Cf. Don C. Gibbons, "Observations on the Study of Crime Causation," *American Journal of Sociology* 77 (September 1971): 262–78; Edwin M. Lemert, *Human Deviance, Social Problems, and Social Control*, 2d ed. (Englewood Cliffs, N.J.: Prentice-Hall, 1972), pp. 38–40; David Matza, *Delinquency and Drift* (New York: John Wiley and Sons, 1964).

[37] The central propositions of structural-functional theories on deviance are summarized in Jack D. Douglas, "Deviance and Order in a Pluralistic Society," in John C. McKinney and Edward T. Tiryakian, eds., *Theoretical Sociology* (New York: Appleton-Century-Crofts, 1970), pp. 367–401.

[38] These distinctions appear in David J. Bordua, "Recent Trends: Deviant Behavior and Social Control," *Annals of the American Academy of Political and Social Science* 369 (January 1969): 149–63; Lemert, *Human Deviance, Social Problems, and Social Control*, pp. 14–15.

[39] On this point, Edwin M. Lemert is frequently identified as the main architect of the labeling school of thought. It is surely proper to accord major importance to his work, for his writings have had a seminal influence on theorizing in this area during the past several decades. But, although Lemert is often described as a central figure in a "labeling school," he has voiced a good deal of criticism regarding the theoretical excesses he perceives in the work of others who claim to be elaborating on his ideas. See Lemert, *Human Deviance, Social Problems, and Social Control*, pp. 16–25.

[40] Some of the major works which have advanced this perspective are Lemert, *Human Deviance, Social Problems, and Social Control;* Lemert, *Social Pathology* (New York: McGraw-Hill Book Co., 1951); Howard S. Becker, *Outsiders* (New York: Free Press of Glencoe, 1963); Douglas, "Deviance and Order in a Pluralistic Society," pp. 367–401; Douglas, *American Social Order* (New York: Free Press of Glencoe, 1971); Douglas, ed., *Deviance and Respectability* (New York: Basic Books, 1970); Kai T. Erikson, "Notes on the Sociology of Deviance," *Social Problems* 9 (Spring 1962): 307–14; John I. Kitsuse, "Societal Reaction to Deviant Behavior: Problems of Theory and Method," in Howard S. Becker, ed., *The Other Side* (New York: Free Press of Glencoe, 1964), pp. 87–102; John Lofland, *Deviance and Identity* (Englewood Cliffs, N.J.: Prentice-Hall, 1969); David Matza, *Becoming Deviant* (Englewood Cliffs, N.J.: Prentice-Hall, 1969); Thomas J. Scheff, *Being Mentally Ill* (Chicago: Aldine Publishing Co., 1966); Edwin M. Schur, *Labeling Deviant Behavior* (New York: Harper and Row, Publishers, 1971); John DeLamater, "On the Nature of Deviance," *Social Forces* 46 (June 1968): 445–55; Eliot Freidson, "Disability as Social Deviance," in Marvin B. Sussman,

ed., *Sociology and Rehabilitation* (Washington, D.C.: American Sociological Association, 1965), pp. 71–99; Robert A. Scott and Jack D. Douglas, eds., *Theoretical Perspectives on Deviance* (New York: Basic Books, 1972); Earl Rubington and Martin S. Weinberg, *Deviance: The Interactionist Perspective,* 2d ed. (New York: The Macmillan Co., 1973).

[41] These include David J. Bordua, "Recent Trends: Deviant Behavior and Social Control," *Annals of the American Academy of Political and Social Science* 369 (January 1969): 149–63; Ronald L. Akers, "Problems in the Sociology of Deviance: Social Definitions and Behavior," *Social Forces* 46 (June 1968): 455–65; Jack P. Gibbs, "Conceptions of Deviant Behavior: The Old and the New," *Pacific Sociological Review* 9 (Spring 1966): 9–14; Gibbs, "Issues in Defining Deviant Behavior," in Scott and Douglas, *Theoretical Perspectives on Deviance,* pp. 39–68; Edwin M. Schur, "Reactions to Deviance: A Critical Assessment," *American Journal of Sociology* 65 (November 1969): 309–22; Nanette J. Davis, "Labeling Theory in Deviance Research: A Critique and Reconsideration," *Sociological Quarterly* 13 (Autumn 1972): 447–74; Peter K. Manning, "Survey Essay: On Deviance," *Contemporary Sociology* 2 (March 1973): 123–28; Milton Mankoff, "Societal Reaction and Career Deviance: A Critical Analysis," *Sociological Quarterly* 12 (Spring 1971): 204–18; Ian Taylor, Paul Walton, and Jock Young, *The New Criminology* (London: Routledge and Kegan Paul, 1973), pp. 139–71; Paul G. Schervish, "The Labeling Perspective: Its Bias and Potential in the Study of Political Deviance," *The American Sociologist* 8 (May 1973): 47–57; John I. Kitsuse, "Deviance, Deviant Behavior, and Deviants: Some Conceptual Problems," in William J. Filstead, ed., *An Introduction to Deviance* (Chicago: Markham Publishing Co., 1972), pp. 233–43.

[42] Good summaries of the main elements of labeling theory can be found in Schur, "Reactions to Deviance": 7–13; Schur, *Labeling Deviant Behavior,* pp. 7–36; Lemert, *Human Deviance, Social Problems, and Social Control,* pp. 16–25; Douglas, "Deviance and Order in Pluralistic Society," pp. 372–401.

[43] Becker, *Outsiders,* p. 9.

[44] This point has been noted by Akers, "Problems in the Sociology of Deviance"; Gibbs, "Conceptions of Deviant Behavior"; Bordua, "Recent Trends," among others.

[45] For example, value pluralism can be seen at work in cases of incest in rural areas. See Christopher Bagley, "Incest Behavior and Incest Taboo," *Social Problems* 16 (Spring 1969): 505–19; for some parallel views regarding working class delinquents, see Walter B. Miller, "Lower Class Culture as a Generating Milieu of Gang Delinquency," *Journal of Social Issues* 14 (1958): 5–19.

[46] Davis, "Labeling Theory in Deviance Research," p. 453.

[47] The labeling view of mental illness is most explicit in Scheff, *Being Mentally Ill*; an evaluation of the empirical adequacy of this argument can be found in Walter R. Gove, "Societal Reaction as an Explanation of Mental Illness: An Evaluation," *American Sociological Review* 35 (October 1970): 873–84.

⁴⁸ Lemert, *Social Pathology*; Lemert, *Human Deviance, Social Problems, and Social Control*. It ought to be noted that Lemert's writings on deviance date back to 1951, long before most other labeling theorists were active. One forerunner of modern labeling views is Frank Tannenbaum, *Crime and the Community* (New York: Ginn and Co., 1938), pp. 19–21. In that work, Tannenbaum drew attention to "dramatization of evil," which was his term for the societal reaction experiences which drive the deviant further into misconduct.

⁴⁹ Lemert, *Social Pathology*, p. 23.

⁵⁰ Lemert, *Human Deviance, Social Problems, and Social Control*, pp. 26–61.

⁵¹ Lemert, *Social Pathology*, p. 23; for a detailed discussion of situational factors in criminal behavior, see Gibbons, "Observations on the Study of Crime Causation."

⁵² Ibid., p. 44; compare this argument with Nadel's commentary, in which he tells us: "But if deviance is widespread and frequent, we should expect the nonconformists to defend their conduct. They could do so only by insisting that their reading of the situation . . . is the correct one, even though opposed to that of their critics, which means that their assertions would break the common consensus as their actions break the presumed norm." S. F. Nadel, *The Theory of Social Structure* (New York: Free Press of Glencoe, 1957), p. 48.

⁵³ Maurice Leznoff and William A. Westley, "The Homosexual Community," *Social Problems* 3 (April 1956): 257–63.

⁵⁴ Lemert, *Social Pathology*, pp. 48–50.

⁵⁵ Lemert, *Human Deviance, Social Problems, and Social Control*, pp. 38–40.

⁵⁶ Lemert, *Social Pathology*, pp. 55–57; see our discussion in chapter five.

⁵⁷ Lemert, *Human Deviance, Social Problems, and Social Control*, pp. 62–92.

⁵⁸ Lemert, *Social Pathology*, p. 75.

⁵⁹ Ibid., p. 77.

⁶⁰ Lemert, "Dependency in Married Alcoholics."

⁶¹ Lemert, "Paranoia and the Dynamics of Exclusion," *Sociometry* 25 (March 1962): 2–20.

⁶² Lemert, "The Behavior of the Systematic Check Forger," *Social Problems* 6 (Fall 1958): 141–49; Lemert, "An Isolation and Closure Theory of Naive Check Forgery," *Journal of Criminal Law, Criminology, and Police Science* 44 (September-October 1953): 296–307.

⁶³ Becker, *Outsiders*, pp. 3–22.

⁶⁴ Ibid., pp. 22–39. Some of the difficulties in the utilization of career notions in the study of criminality are noted in Don C. Gibbons, "Offender Typologies —Two Decades Later," *British Journal of Criminology*, forthcoming.

⁶⁵ Becker, *Outsiders*, p. 30.

⁶⁶ Ibid., p. 31–34.

[67] Ibid., p. 36–39.

[68] Gibbs, "Issues in Defining Deviant Behavior." See also Paul Rock, "Phenomenalism and Essentialism in the Sociology of Deviance," *Sociology* 7 (January 1973): 17–29.

[69] Ibid., p. 37.

[70] Scheff, *Being Mentally Ill,* pp. 31–40.

[71] Akers, "Problems in the Sociology of Deviance," p. 463.

[72] Akers, *Deviant Behavior,* pp. 141–42.

[73] Bordua, "Recent Trends," p. 53.

[74] Taylor, Walton, and Young also charge that labeling arguments are weak because they fail to specify the varied sources of primary deviation and they assume an essentially mindless organism, thereby failing to provide a sociology of deviant motivation. See Taylor, Walton, and Young, *The New Criminology,* pp. 139–71. They aver (p. 171): "What is required is a sociology that combines structure, process and culture in a continuous dialectic." Davis is also critical of the labeling argument holding that deviant careers develop from labeling to isolation from conventional persons to an acquired sense of a common fate and commitment to deviant norms, that is, secondary deviation. She observes: "The socialization and career analysis approach posits that movement into deviance creates a deviant way of life. Yet this ignores the fact that much of what is considered deviant in our society is highly situational, or behavior that constitutes only a small part of the person's life." Davis, "Labeling Theory in Deviance Research," p. 457. On this point, also see Gibbons, "Observations on the Study of Crime Causation"; Gibbons, "Crime in the Hinterland," *Criminology* 10 (August 1972): 177–91; Gibbons, "Offender Typologies—Two Decades Later."

[75] Davis, "Labeling Theory in Deviance Research," pp. 457–60.

[76] Recent deviance texts which have a fairly pronounced "hip" tone to them are H. Taylor Buckner, *Deviance, Reality, and Change* (New York: Random House, 1971); Lewis Yablonsky, *The Hippie Trip* (New York: Pegasus, 1968); J. L. Simmons and Barry Winograd, *It's Happening* (Santa Barbara: Marc-Laird Publications, 1966); Simmons, *Deviants* (Santa Barbara: The Glendessary Press, 1969); Jerry Jacobs, *Deviance: Field Studies and Self-Disclosures* (Palo Alto: National Press Books, 1974).

[77] Davis, "Labeling Theory in Deviance Research," pp. 448–56.

[78] Ibid., p. 452. For a recent statement on social control, see Jack P. Gibbs, *Social Control* (Andover, Mass.: Warner Modular Publications, 1972).

[79] Schur, *Labeling Deviant Behavior.*

[80] Akers, "Problems in the Sociology of Deviance."

[81] Schur, *Labeling Deviant Behavior.*

[82] Not all recent texts on deviance qualify as labeling treatises. For example, Aker's *Deviant Behavior* utilizes operant conditioning and differential associa-

tion-reinforcement as central organizing principles. Bell has put together an eclectic treatment of various "problems," including premarital sexual behavior, extramarital sexual activity, birth control, alcoholism, homosexuality, prostitution, etc. See Robert R. Bell, *Social Deviance* (Homewood, Ill.: The Dorsey Press, 1971). H. Taylor Buckner has produced an odd text employing an individual experience-social reality orientation. Buckner maintains that deviance centers about conflicts between individual perspectives on the social world and prevailing cultural views of "normal" behavior. See Buckner, *Deviance, Reality, and Change.* Buckner's book strikes us as a curious hodgepodge. For example, he presents an expanded version of Merton's typology of modes of adaptation (pp. 68–71) in which one type is illustrated by "a socialist revolutionary who believes in free enterprise." We think it would take a diligent search indeed to turn up that kind of deviant!

Finally, Winslow and Winslow have recently produced a deviance text that is rich with details on how certain deviants "do" deviance but which is somewhat impoverished in terms of conceptual sophistication. See Robert W. Winslow and Virginia Winslow, *Deviant Reality: Alternative World Views* (Boston: Allyn and Bacon, 1974).

SELECTED READINGS

BECKER, HOWARD S. *Outsiders.* New York: Free Press of Glencoe, 1963. An early and influential statement of arguments on labeling processes and deviance.

LEMERT, EDWIN M. *Human Deviance, Social Problems, and Social Control* (2d ed.). Englewood Cliffs, N.J.: Prentice-Hall, 1972. A collection of essays which amplify many themes first presented in *Social Pathology.*

_____. *Social Pathology.* New York: McGraw-Hill Book Co., 1951. A sociological classic, outlining many basic arguments and propositions that are incorporated into modern labeling views on deviance.

LOFLAND, JOHN. *Deviance and Identity.* Englewood Cliffs, N.J.: Prentice-Hall, 1969. A detailed and thoughtful discussion of deviance and social processes in deviant behavior from a symbolic interactionist perspective.

MATZA, DAVID. *Becoming Deviant.* Englewood Cliffs, N.J.: Prentice-Hall, 1969. A detailed exposition of the processes of career development of deviants.

SCHEFF, THOMAS J. *Being Mentally Ill.* Chicago: Aldine Publishing Co., 1966. An application of a labeling perspective to explanation of mental illness and to the career of mental patients.

effects of
labeling experiences

The preceding chapter introduced the labeling or societal reaction perspective on deviance. We noted that this theoretical orientation has produced significant new insights, but much unfinished business remains to be addressed. Many presentations of labeling notions in the sociological literature grossly oversimplify and distort the real world by advancing arguments and propositions which fail to reflect the richness and diversity of actual social life. In particular, the aspect of labeling arguments that deals with the career effects of labeling experiences upon deviant actors needs more conceptual and theoretical precision and more testing through research studies.

Relatively little research has been produced regarding the effects of societal reactions. Most essays in sociological publications on the impact of labeling experiences have been highly speculative, and their generalizations are not based on empirical research. Although their claims often seem plausible, most are of indeterminate factual accuracy. Thus, the claim that mental hospitals, juvenile training schools, prisons, treatment facilities for alcoholics, and kindred "people-changing" organizations have deleterious effects on those processed through them seems credible, but there is little firm evidence to support this contention. In spite of the paucity of hard evidence, a number of sociologists have put forth unqualified claims that training schools are "crime schools," that mental hospitals create mental illness, and other similar assertions.[1]

Some of the unequivocal versions of these claims about labeling effects stand as instances of the sociological imagination gone beserk. We do have some data concerning the impact of social control and societal reaction experiences on deviants, and much of it hints that these phenomena often have effects other than those alleged by some labeling theorists. A judicious sociologist aware of the fragmentary nature of the evidence would refrain from making bold assertions about social reaction effects on nonconformists.

The theorist striving for a factually adequate analysis of the effects of labeling experiences needs to explore a number of possible consequences which these events have on nonconformists. These consequences probably range along a continuum from one extreme involving complete castigation and ostracism of the misbehaver to experiences at the other end of the scale in which the social reaction events successfully deter any recurrence of that deviant activity by the person.[2] In short, some social reactions may drive some persons into careers in deviance, while other experiences propel other individuals out of further nonconformity.[3] Then too, there are many instances in which labeling events have only a benign effect on the labeled targets, so that they are relatively untouched by these experiences; these instances stand as examples of unsuccessful degradation ceremonies.[4]

These varied outcomes probably are to be explained by such things as variations among deviants which render some more susceptible than others to the influence of these events. We also need to note the great diversity of activities and structures which are bunched together under the conceptual umbrella of societal reaction. Who would be so bold as to argue that a traffic fine, for example, has the same psychological impact as being hauled off to a prison or mental hospital? Clearly, we need to examine closely the forms of societal reaction as they combine with various patterns of deviant conduct if we are to make sense of this complex bundle of phenomena.

We shall now examine some of the commentary which has appeared in the sociological literature regarding the alleged effects of labeling and the relationships of these experiences to deviant careers. We then discuss several specific forms of deviance, such as delinquency, criminality, mental illness, and homosexuality, and we will marshal the available empirical evidence concerning the ways in which labeling experiences facilitate or deter further deviance. Our discussion will not produce a full-blown theory, but our commentary should reveal the richness and diversity of the phenomena with which theorists must contend.[5]

SOME VIEWS ON THE CAREER
EFFECTS OF LABELING PROCESSES

One of the most well known works dealing with the responses of social audiences to persons seen as deviants is Erving Goffman's *Stigma*.[6] Goffman offers the concept of spoiled identity and applies it across a broad range of socially disvalued categories: the blind, prostitutes, the ugly, the mentally ill, and so forth. Although Goffman's discussion surely is insightful and suggestive of a great many ideas that merit further exploration, it does not contain a tight logical structure.

Many of his concepts are introduced in an *ad hoc* fashion, leaving the formalization and integration of them to others.

By contrast to Goffman's work, Shlomo Shoham has recently attempted a logically rigorous analysis of social responses to social stigmas or discrediting characteristics, including both physical and social attributes of persons.[7] He examines the social control functions served by social processes in which certain behavior patterns or physical characteristics of individuals are singled out by social audiences as discrediting stains on the identities of those persons. Although Shoham does acknowledge that labeling experiences may sometimes have deterrent effects on the deviant, he concentrates on the processes whereby negative responses and social rejection push an actor toward continued involvement in deviant careers; Shoham pays little attention to how some persons may overcome their stigmas and move toward conformity. In short, his exposition is an instance of lopsided labeling theory which concentrates too much on the negative impact of these events.

Bernard A. Thorsell and Lloyd W. Klemke offer another explication of the effects of labeling experiences in an essay which resulted from their survey of deviance literature.[8] They note six general observations on labeling that are frequently encountered, including the propositions that labeling has different effects at separate stages of a deviant career, some labeling occurs in more private settings and circumstances than does other labeling, with differential effects on the deviants, and so on. Further, these writers derive from this material six hypotheses dealing with the conditions under which the labeling process is more likely to terminate existing deviant behavior and to deter future misbehavior. According to them, labeling is most likely to lead to disengagement of the actor from deviance: "(1) if the labeled person is a primary rather than a secondary deviant, (2) if the labeling is carried out in a confidential setting with the understanding that future deviance will result in public exposure, (3) if the labeling has been carried out by an in-group member or significant other, (4) the more easily the label is removable when the deviant behavior has ceased, (5) the more the labeling results in efforts to reintegrate the deviant into the community, and (6) if the label is favorable rather than derogatory."[9] These·authors conclude their discussion with the usual call for more research on these matters.

A more exhaustive examination of the relationship between the concepts of deviance and identity is presented by John Lofland.[10] He relies heavily on authors closely identified with the labeling perspective for supportive material in his analysis of the ways the process he terms "escalation" operates to transform one's identity from a normal to a deviant person or from a deviant to a normal individual.[11] Throughout his discussion, the effects on the person of the attitudes of others and the labels they employ are given heavy emphasis as features of the process whereby an actor comes to construct and reconstruct his ongoing identity.

A major defect in Lofland's work is that his discussion is structured around deviance in the abstract, with little concern for particular patterns of behavior. As a result, he outlines a range of social mechanisms that allegedly apply to norm violation generally, but he fails to identify those specific labeling processes that operate to produce any given type of deviant or any specific type of deviant identity. Further, in his effort to develop a theoretical statement which can embrace norm violation in its manifold forms, he apparently found it necessary to introduce a host of concepts such as "strangership"[12] and "facilitating actor"[13] which require the reader to assimilate an esoteric vocabulary in order to grasp his arguments. While the introduction of a new vocabulary is not in itself undesirable, in this instance it seems to have obfuscated the study of deviance as much as it has facilitated understanding.

Edwin M. Schur's *Labeling Deviant Behavior*[14] attempts to codify writings on labeling deviant behavior and investigate the implications of labeling in such matters as collective rule making, morals, and public policy. In discussing the adequacy of the hypothesis that societal reactions lead to continued involvement in deviant behavior, Schur concludes that: "an absolutely central consideration for the labeling orientation is that the generalizations presented here cannot adequately account for the diverse processing contingencies arising at the different levels and operating at least somewhat independently of the predictor variables in question."[15] The thrust of Schur's commentary is to point out that labeling experiences have varied effects, depending on a host of other factors which interact with these contingencies to produce behavioral outcomes. He would eschew simple and unequivocal claims about societal reactions and deviant careers, so that his conclusion is similar to ours.

Another general review of the relationship between labeling and deviant careers is provided by Daniel Glaser.[16] His point that some kinds of deviance are more psychologically and financially rewarding than other kinds is worth emphasizing. Individuals may be recruited into these attractive career lines by the implicit rewards in those roles, rather than being nudged into them by adverse societal responses. It may be, for example, that many women find the occupation of prostitute exciting and appealing so that neither the workings of "White

Slavers" nor societal condemnation explains their involvement in this activity. Similarly, criminological observers have noted that some criminal roles are avidly pursued by persons who find these endeavors exciting and see them as preferred alternatives to the straight life.[17]

One of the earliest and best formulations of the process linking labeling with increasing social involvement in deviant behavior is Edwin M. Lemert's *Social Pathology*.[18] Lemert indicated that the societal reaction to an initial act of deviation may pressure the individual from primary deviance toward total reorganization of his social roles, social obligations, and social opportunities.[19] He had relatively little to say, however, about those factors, including societal reactions, which sometimes lead to secondary deviation but sometimes result in the termination of nonconformity at the primary stage.[20]

An inventory of essays on labeling and its effects on deviants could continue indefinitely. For example, Milton Mankoff's essay claims that one of the labeling perspective's most profound derivative theories is: *"rule-breakers become entrenched in deviant roles because they are labeled 'deviant' by others and are consequently excluded from resuming normal social roles in the community"* (emphasis in the original).[21] This analysis, however, contains a number of flaws.[22]

Jack D. Douglas also credits the official people-processing organizations with primary responsibility for the creation of career deviance.[23] In his words, "official stigmatization does more than anything else to change an individual's (substantial) social self and his own self-image, thereby leading to commitments to deviant patterns of action."[24] But Douglas's analysis remains abstract, for he does not demonstrate that a career in deviance is most frequently engendered by official stigmatization nor that it is an invariable outcome. Along the same line, David Matza discusses labeling effects, but his work deals primarily with only one substantive area of deviance, marijuana smoking, which is not likely to lead to a deviant career.[25] Then too, his concepts and claims are so abstract that it is difficult to determine what empirical facts the argument might explain.

The various attempts to explicate the relationship between the norm-violating act, the societal reaction to that act, and a career in deviance are thus far from clear. Still, they all imply that the societal response of hanging a negative tag on an individual is an important first step on the path of his continued involvement in deviant activity and the acquisition of a nonconformist identity. A closer look at some of the evidence on this matter is now in order. Let us begin with criminals and delinquents, to whom this argument has most frequently been applied.[26]

THE IMPACT OF SOCIETAL REACTIONS
ON DELINQUENT AND CRIMINAL CAREERS

The claim that the stigma of the criminal label drives persons further into deviance is frequently found in the labeling literature, as is the companion hypothesis that "people-changing" institutions such as prisons and training schools actually push persons further into criminality, foreclosing their chances of withdrawing from lawbreaking.

How are these negative consequences produced? One answer is that correctional organizations are defective in providing the therapy and assistance to help the offender escape from his lawbreaking ways. There is little doubt that correctional agencies and institutions in American society are woefully lacking in resources for therapeutic intervention in lawbreaking careers.[27] These organizations contain few vocational instructors, psychiatrists, social workers, or other treatment agents. The few available treatment workers are deluged with huge caseloads, making it almost impossible for them to engage in positive intervention. Finally, the most crucial defect of correctional organizations is that we almost completely lack any kind of social engineering skills which can be directed at offenders. Correctional treatment is not an application of scientific skills or high-powered professional social work. Instead, it is intuitive, trial-and-error fiddling with persons and one of the "tinkering trades" identified by Erving Goffman.[28] No wonder, then, that informed observers are not very sanguine about the rehabilitative potential of correctional agencies.[29]

Additionally, many would argue that even if correctional organizations were upgraded, large numbers of psychiatrists added to their staffs, and improvements made in their training and therapy programs, they might continue to operate as negative career contingencies. Briefly stated, the argument runs: Criminal status is negatively evaluated by significant others even when the offender has been publicly identified only as a petty misdemeanant. Persons involved in felonies or who have been incarcerated in penal institutions are even more severely stigmatized by others. The criminal tag which the identified lawbreaker acquires serves as a "master status," coloring all reactions of others to him; he is seen by others as a thoroughly disreputable and discredited character. Other facts about him which are discordant with his "bad guy" public identity recede into the background and are given little attention by the social audiences who view his behavior. Finally, once the individual's public identity has been spoiled by the criminal-identification process, nothing that he does subsequently is likely to change that situation. In the eyes of others, "once a crook, always a crook."

These claims have been made frequently in recent years, both in the mass media discussions of prison reform and allied issues and in the deviance literature—no wonder, for the deficiencies of correctional organizations have been well documented. The labeling contentions about the stigmatizing effects of criminal sanctions have always had a plausible sound, starting with Frank Tannenbaum's early observations regarding "dramatization of evil."[30] Further layers of credible conjecture have been added in recent years by Edwin M. Lemert, Howard S. Becker, John I. Kitsuse, and other contemporary students of deviance.

But plausibility is no guarantee of validity; we have already examined some credible but probably incorrect claims about deviance. Labeling notions concerning the alleged harmful effects of correctional experiences are at present quite inchoate and, most likely, they are defective. Stated another way, whatever the relationships between correctional intervention activities and deviant careers, they are complex and multifaceted. We now have many extremely simple and gross claims rather than a well-developed formulation which directs attention to the whole complex of factors, events, and experiences which make up labeling effects on lawbreaking deviants. At the very least, when we ultimately devise this kind of theory and engage in research to test it, we are likely to find that current formulations are sometimes polemical and exaggerated in general statement as well as erroneous in their particulars.

There have recently been murmurings in the direction of explicit theorizing about effects of societal reactions on offenders (and potential deviants), along with the accumulation of some empirical evidence bearing upon these questions. Examination of a sample of that material should reveal something of the complexity of the real world with which theories will ultimately have to contend.

deterrence[31]

To deter someone from crime means to stop him from lawbreaking by threats of one kind or another. The subject of deterrent effects of penal sanctions (punishments) is one on which visceral feelings tend to be more frequently expressed than cerebral responses. Discussions of deterrence have been permeated with half-truths, nonsequiturs, shibboleths, and often, utter nonsense.

To begin with, many persons fail to distinguish between *specific* and *general* deterrence.[32] Specific deterrence refers to punishment which curtails further lawbreaking on the part of an already identified offender, as when we imprison a person in hopes that he will thereby be intimidated or resocialized and will sin no more when released from custody. A general deterrent is expected to forewarn, frighten, and impress a *potential* deviant sufficiently that he will refrain from the lawbreaking he may have been contemplating. For example, Alcatraz Prison in San Francisco Bay may have discouraged many potential lawbreakers who gazed upon it from putting their deviant impulses into operation. The empirical possibilities are four in number: some particular penal sanction may be effective as a specific deterrent but be ineffective as a general one; it might work as a general deterrent but not as a specific one; or it may either succeed or fail in both capacities.

The simple-mindedness of many current discussions of deterrence can be seen in commentaries on capital punishment. First, it is not entirely clear that capital punishment completely fails as a specific or general deterrent of homicides, kidnapping, and other capital offenses. Second, the giant leap in logic from the contention that capital punishment is ineffective to the conclusion that no form of punishment works as a deterrent is surely unwarranted.

Another markedly deficient argument points to the Prohibition experience as proof that people cannot be deterred from activities in which they are motivated to engage. In truth, all that the Prohibition episode proves is that a highly unpopular law, lacking normative support even from many of those persons who sponsored and enacted it, and enforced by only a handful of policemen, was consequently disobeyed by large numbers of persons. Similarly, one oft-repeated allegation that prisons are abject failures since three-fourths or more of the persons who go through them are subsequently reincarcerated is undocumented. Daniel Glaser has presented a body of factual data which shows quite convincingly that this claim is simply untrue, and markedly fewer individuals are actually being returned to prison.[33]

The outline of a theory of deterrence has been offered by Franklin E. Zimring,[34] who introduces a number of important distinctions, including that between partial and marginal deterrence. The former relates to threats or punishment that reduce the magnitude of the threatened or punished behavior but do not curb it entirely. Marginal deterrence refers to the degree to which a specific punishment reduces the rate of illegal behavior below that produced by a lesser penalty. For example, marginal deterrence would be seen in the instance of prison sentences that reduce the rate of reinvolvement in criminality below that brought about by placing offenders on probation.

Research studies of deterrence include the work of William J. Chambliss dealing with parking violations on a midwestern university campus.[35] He reports that these acts decreased following an increase in the severity and certainty of punishments. Jack P. Gibbs has calculated indexes of certainty and severity of punishment for homicide in the United States and reports that homicide rates appear to be lower in states where the risks of apprehension were most certain and where prison sentences were relatively severe.[36] Other studies parallel to Gibb's have been conducted by Charles R. Tittle,[37] and by Theodore G. Chiricos and Gordon P. Waldo,[38] with results generally similar to those by Gibbs. Finally, an inquiry by Donald T. Campbell and H. Laurence Ross dealt with a "crackdown" on speeding motorists in Connecticut in 1955.[39] In response to a much-publicized rash of traffic fatalities, the governor ordered that persons convicted of speeding be deprived of their licenses for thirty days on a first speeding charge, with more serious penalties for repeaters. Researchers found that traffic fatalities decreased after these changes in enforcement policies. However, the period of high fatalities preceding the crackdown was atypical of longer-term trends in that state; thus, the reduction in accidents may have been the consequence of factors other than the changes in punitive policies.

stigma

We have already noted that the claim that various labels which become attached to deviants and blot their public identity has been explored in great detail by Erving Goffman.[40] This general argument has become a familiar refrain concerning publicly identified lawbreakers. Even so, relatively little evidence exists dealing in a direct way with the stigmatizing effects of criminal status.

The most well known report on stigma and criminal labels is that of Richard D. Schwartz and Jerome H. Skolnick, who conducted a field study in which they endeavored to assess the degree to which a criminal record for a relatively petty offense operates as a liability in the case of an unskilled job seeker.[41] They found that a fictitious job applicant with a minor criminal record received fewer job offers than did an unblemished applicant. Even more striking, an applicant whose dossier showed that he had been acquitted of an offense fared no better than the convicted individual. In this example, the criminal tag did appear to operate as a stigmatizing influence. On the other hand, in a second study, Schwartz and Skolnick report that doctors who had been charged with malpractice suffered no apparent negative consequences from having been so identified.

Mary Owen Cameron's observations regarding amateur shoplifters ("snitches") also bear upon the question of stigmatizing effects.[42] She reports that most of the nonprofessional shoplifters she studied who had been apprehended in larcenies by department stores in Chicago refrained from further misbehavior after having been compelled by store personnel to admit that they were "thieves" and "criminals." Apparently that admission was so discordant with their self-images as housewives and law-abiding citizens that the painful encounters with the store employees (definers of deviance) operated to drive them out of deviant conduct.

"people-changing" processes

The topics of deterrence and stigma are closely related, and a discussion of specific deterrence is also linked to the effects of "people-changing" organizations and institutions. Most of the commentary on deterrence has paid relatively slight attention to the details and nuances of correctional operations and their effects; instead, it has been content with broad analyses of recidivism rates and has not examined in detail the organizational processes and their impact. Focusing our attention on the influence of correctional structures on lawbreakers should point out the complex interrelationships of deterrence, stigma, and "people-changing" institutions.

Correctional experiences are extremely varied in modern societies, ranging from warnings and small fines to incarceration in prisons or, in a few instances, execution. These operations may produce any of three general effects. Criminals or delinquents may be impelled further into misconduct by the negative force of correctional handling; on the other extreme, these events may have positive consequences, pushing the deviant out of further illegality. Third, it is possible that these experiences may have neutral effects, such that the offender is neither harmed nor helped by them. The best guess is that some correctional actions do produce positive results, others operate negatively and still others have neutral consequences.

A complete theoretical exposition on correctional effects would at least have to recognize differences among types of offenders. Quite probably, the impact on a working-class, "crime-wise" delinquent of being incarcerated in a penal institution would differ from that on a rural, unsophisticated first-time offender in the same setting. Similarly, correctional experiences probably do not mean the same thing to amateur "snitches," gang delinquents, embezzlers, white-collar criminals, members of the Mafia, pimps, "psychopathic killers," or other deviants.

A complete theory of correctional impact would also have to observe the marked differences between various kinds of intervention procedures. Placement on probation is probably less stigmatizing and traumatic than being put in prison, fines may well have different effects than jail sentences, and so on. Additionally, there are important variations among specific correctional structures such as penitentiaries or probation agencies. Some prisons are maximum security bastilles with a harsh and austere custodial regimen while others place heavy emphasis on programs of resocialization. Several investigations point to differential effects of these varied organizational climates of correctional structures. These studies include Bernard B. Berk's comparison of prison camps which differed in milieu[43] and the comparative study of a group of training schools by David Street, Robert D. Vinter and Charles Perrow.[44]

The task of developing an adequate theoretical explication of the effects of correctional experiences on offenders is thus a heroic one, for a large number of interacting factors and variables would have to be considered in such a formulation.[45] Now, what data are currently available for constructing such a theory?

probation

A sizeable body of evidence indicates that probation agencies produce very high success rates in keeping persons out of further misbehavior. Over three-fourths of the adult offenders placed on probation remain free from further deviance. Why does probation produce these results? It is a highly selective disposition given mainly to petty offenders who are involved in transitory episodes of lawbreaking. Most of them are primary deviants who lack criminal self-concepts and are "self-correctors." Many of them have drifted into lawbreaking as a result of situational pressures.[46] The probation experience apparently involves a low degree of stigma that does not prevent these persons from withdrawing from misconduct.

juvenile training schools

At first glance, juvenile institutions appear to be dismal failures at the rehabilitation task. For example, studies in the California Youth Authority indicate that about three-fourths of the boys who serve time in state training schools ultimately break the law again,[47] although female training school wards are much less likely to become recidivists.[48]

Why do boys' training schools result in such a large number of failures? Is it because they operate in some fashion as "crime schools," do they encourage the development of "secondary deviation" on the part of boys, or do they function in some other direct, deleterious manner? Or, is it perhaps that the boys are already "bad risks" when they enter the institution? The available evidence on training schools indicates that these places have relatively slight effects upon boys who go through them. Apparently the factors which reinvolve youths in lawbreaking are ones which were set in motion *before* the boys were incarcerated. For example, a study by Thomas G. Eynon and Jon E. Simpson of several juvenile institutions in Ohio indicated that most of the delinquents showed no social-psychological changes over their period of incarceration, or if they did change, the movement was toward a more positive self-image and a more optimistic outlook on life.[49] Similar findings are reported for Fricot Ranch in the California Youth Authority system.[50] In short, it appears that training school wards have already become enmeshed in deviant careers before arriving at the institution. The training school neither rescues them from deviance nor drives them further into it.

adult prisons

Contrary to opinions that the majority of adult prisoners become recidivists after release from prison, Daniel Glaser has noted that "in the first two to five years after their release, only about a third of all the men released from an entire prison system are returned to prison."[51] He reviewed a number of studies from different penal systems throughout the United States and found that recidivism varied from about 20 to 40 percent of releasees in these investigations.[52] Glaser uncovered a large number of relationships between prison programs and success or failure of persons on parole in a massive study of the workings of the federal system. One of his most important observations was that "recidivism of adult male offenders varies inversely with their postrelease employment."[53] In turn, the relationship of success and employment was seen in the following terms: "Not training in vocational skills, but, rather, habituation of inmates to regularity in constructive and rewarding employment, and anti-criminal personal influences of work supervisors on inmates, are—at present—the major contributions of work in prison to inmate rehabilitation."[54] Glaser's work suggests that good behavior by offenders on parole is not directly due to positive effects of prisons; instead, the most successful parolee is one who is able to blend into a conventional social role outside the prison *in spite of* having been incarcerated.

Walter C. Bailey's review of 100 studies of correctional outcome also leads to a pessimistic evaluation of prison rehabilitation.[55] He reported that only a few of the studies published between 1940 and 1960 spelled out the behavioral and causal theory underlying the treatment. About two-thirds of the programs, however, were based on a view of the offender as "sick." Bailey's conclusion concerning these 100 studies was that: "it seems quite clear that, on the basis of the sample of outcome reports with all of its limitations, evidence supporting the efficacy of correctional treatment is slight, inconsistent, and of questionable reliability."[56]

Stanton Wheeler has provided an incisive analysis of prison effects, in which he claims that little or no resocialization occurs in these places.[57] He declares:

1. Persons do not enter prison motivated to seek a basically new and different vision of themselves.
2. To the extent that they do change, the change is produced as much by the reaction to being confined and separated from the free community as it is by the dynamics of life within the institution.
3. The values and attitudes expressed by prison inmates are shaped in important ways by the circumstances to which inmates have been exposed prior to their period of incarceration.
4. In addition to its impact on the values held by entering inmates, the external world influences the kind of culture and social organization that is formed within the prison, and which serves as the social context within which adaptation to imprisonment takes place.
5. As a result of these conditions, whatever impact the experience of imprisonment itself might have on inmates, either positive or negative, is sharply attenuated. *It is the social definition of the prison in society, rather than the social status of the inmate within the prison, that appears to be most relevant for the future life and career of prison inmates.* (emphasis in the original)
6. It follows from all of the above that a full understanding of processes of socialization and resocialization within the prison requires much greater attention than has heretofore been given to the relationship of both the prison and the prisoner to the external world.

It is clear from all these studies that different patterns of formal organization and structure may produce differences in inmate organization and in attitudes toward the prison experience. But these studies have not gone on to demonstrate the relationship between participation in inmate society and future behavior. Thus, as much as these studies tell us about the different patterns of organization within the prison and potentially different socialization processes, they have not yet shown whether changes occur that are deep and long lasting enough to produce real differences in rates of recidivism.

A number of other studies have examined the rates of recidivism for men housed in different types of institutions. This has been part of a long-term series of studies supported by the California Correctional System. And if there is one conclusion that appears to be safely drawn from these these studies, it is that differences in prison organization themselves apparently produce relatively little difference in recidivism rates. Once one takes account of the nature of the inmate population in the different prisons, the institutional differences in recidivism rates tend to disappear. Relatively small effects may be shown for one or another aspect of prison programs, but the overall sense one gets from such studies is that the differences attributable to institutions are small relative to the differences attributable to the prior backgrounds of individual inmates.[58]

A major theme in Wheeler's analysis is that prisons may deter some persons from continued criminality, but this effect depends more on the kinds of individuals who come into different penal institutions than on variations in correctional programs and social organization. Then too, the penitentiary apparently instills negative feelings about imprisonment, rather than positive social sentiments in the offenders.

John Irwin avers that many convicts come to entertain such negative views of prisons and resolve to avoid them.[59] According to Irwin, parole agents often force rigid Puritanical norms upon the parolee, exacerbating his difficulties of readjustment.[60] Speaking of post-prison failure, Irwin claims that:

From the standpoint of the felon a successful postprison life is more than merely staying out of prison. From the criminal ex-convict perspective it must contain other attributes, mainly it must be dignified. This is not generally understood by correctional people whose ideas on success are dominated by narrow and unrealistic conceptions of nonrecidivism and reformation. Importantly, because of their failure to recognize the felon's viewpoint, his aspirations, his conceptions of respect and dignity, or his foibles, they leave him to travel the difficult route away from the prison without guidance or assistance; in fact, with considerable hinderance, and with few avenues out of criminal life acceptable both to him and his former keepers.[61]

Many felons disentangle themselves from crime after release from prison, but a fair number drift back into deviance. As we have seen, neither the successes nor the failures can be attributed solely to the workings of the penal institution. Moreover, a majority of recent treatment experiments in penitentiaries have turned up negative results; that is, experiments involving innovative or expanded therapeutic intervention have not significantly reduced recidivism rates.

The Intensive Treatment program at San Quentin and Chino prisons in California was designed to increase the amount of psychotherapy received by prisoners. Parole evidence however, indicated that the intensively treated offenders fared no better after release than those who received only a conventional institutional experience. Also, the PICO (Pilot Intensive Counseling Unit) experiment in California administered intensive individual and group therapy to inmates classified either as amenable or nonamenable to treatment. In general, the treated amenables showed the most effect from the program, but the parole success of treated and control subjects was not markedly different.[62]

One quasi-experiment in the California system centers about the California Rehabilitation Center where drug addicts participate in intensive group treatment.[63] According to Troy Duster, this program fails to have much positive impact on the drug users involved.

The C-Unit experiment carried out in Deuel Vocational Institution in California indicates the formidable obstacles which treatment innovations in institutional settings must overcome.[64] This program attempted to develop a social community among inmates and staff, in which a shared moral code would regularize social interaction among members. This development was frustrated in a variety of ways, however, by the administration of the reformatory. According to the researchers, their project indicated it is theoretically possible to modify the nature of inmate-staff interaction and institutional social life in prisons; but, the C-Unit report is a chronicle of an experiment that failed due to the unwillingness and/or inability of the prison staff and the statewide correctional organization to engage in the reciprocal change required for successful innovation.

summary

On the whole, the materials in this section on correctional agencies and institutions present a fairly dismal picture. Even so, the evidence indicates that these organizations often operate in relatively neutral ways rather than as "crime schools." The data certainly present a challenge to anyone of a labeling persuasion who might offer an unequivocal and heated denunciation of correctional structures. In short, the real world stubbornly resists the labeler's efforts to characterize it in a few emphatic, plausible conjectures about negative career contingencies.

THE IMPACT OF SOCIETAL REACTIONS
ON THE MENTALLY ILL

The speculative commentary regarding labeling experiences and mental illness has been quite varied in character. Some argue that mental illness is entirely putative and that the publicly identified mentally ill are really no different from persons designated as normal. Other authorities assert that something unusual about a person's behavior causes him to be identified as mentally ill. In this view, people often are designated as "crazy" because they behave in aberrant ways.

Donald P. Jewell's report on "A Case of a 'Psychotic' Navajo Indian Male" indicates that the putative case does exist.[65] "Bill," as Jewell refers to the subject of his report, was hospitalized and classified as schizophrenic without having the usual psychiatric workup. He was institutionalized because he exhibited the classic signs of schizophrenia and, when mistaken for a Mexican, did not respond when questioned by a Spanish-speaking interviewer. Much of his behavior was consistent with traditional Navajo responses to stressful conditions, but unfortunately for Bill, this behavior conformed rather closely to the white American psychiatric definition of schizophrenia. For example, one of the symptoms of catatonic schizophrenia is *cerea flexibilitas,* or waxy flexibility. Bill exhibited this behavior pattern, but when interviewed by Jewell, who spoke the Navajo language, it turned out that Bill was holding the grotesque posture because he thought it was expected of him and not because of any underlying pathology. In short, he was simply confused by the hospital setting, retreated to the traditional Navajo response to threat and the learned deference for the white man, and wound up being hospitalized on a back ward.

The invalidity of Bill's label as mentally ill is readily apparent, but the issue here is not whether any such cases exist, but rather whether this is the most frequently encountered occurrence. Bill's unfortunate experiences surely do not prove that most of the publicly identified mentally ill are solely the product of putative processes.

The most explicit version of labeling theory applied to mental illness is found in the work of Thomas J. Scheff.[66] He contends that mental illness centers about residual rule breaking which consists of behavioral transgressions and conduct for which society lacks standard and explicit labels such as "second degree burglar," "involuntary homicide," and the like. He asserts that residual rule breaking is extremely widespread, and that great numbers of individuals are involved in some form of it at some time in their lives. Further, residual rule breaking is viewed as arising from diverse sources.

Scheff claims that stereotyped imagery of mental illness is widespread in the United States and that these citizen notions contain a view of the mentally ill as dangerous and bizarre persons. Individuals involved in residual rule breaking are sometimes able to disavow their illness, but many who engage in these violations are singled out as mentally disturbed and labeled accordingly. When this happens, they are likely to be treated as stereotypes. Finally, the public labeling of an individual as mentally ill is likely to stabilize his deviance, and the actor is then very prone to continue in this role. Also, once he is referred to mental health personnel, such as the psychiatrists and physicians in the emergency ward of county hospitals, involuntary commitment to a mental hospital is the almost inevitable result. According to Scheff, mental health workers are uniformly conservative, and they believe it is better to institutionalize and treat nearly everyone than it is to release an alleged mental case.

A detailed critique of the hypothesis that societal reactions produce mental illness has been provided by Walter B. Gove.[67] He concludes that those who view mental illness from the labeling perspective have overstated their case and that the disorientation of those labeled as mentally ill often exists quite apart from the reactions of social audiences. The data show that hospitalized persons, in particular, exhibit severe symptoms of stress, disorientation, and instability. These individuals are screened into the mental institution, while large numbers of less severely disturbed persons are screened *out of* the mental health treatment machinery. Then too, Gove notes much information to indicate that restitutive processes are often at work in the mental hospital; thus many patients gain mental stability there and are released with an improved prognosis for successful adjustment in free society. Gove's summary judgment about labeling theory is that: "Unfortunately, the societal reaction theorists have generally treated their framework as a sufficient explanatory system. In doing so they have underemphasized the importance of acts of primary deviance and overemphasized the importance of forces promoting secondary deviance."[68]

We agree that labeling arguments have often stressed the role of labeling experiences to the point of slurring over the role of other important factors in mental illness. But Gove's critique is a corrective to some of the exaggerated claims made by labeling theorists rather than an outright rejection of those propositions. Gove would agree, as we would, that labeling perspectives have directed attention to societal reaction influences which frequently are included among the factors crucial to understanding mental disorder. Let us examine some commentary which stresses the importance of labeling events.

The many writings of psychiatrist Thomas S. Szasz are relatively unique among persons of psychiatric persuasion, for he has argued with great vigor that the handing over of what is called mental illness to the psychiatric profession is a political or social control act wherein the persons whose behavior is perplexing or threatening to others are often categorized as mentally ill and then dealt with by a profession devoted to handling this so-called disorder. Szasz's *The Myth of Mental Illness*[69] and *Psychiatric Justice*[70] forcefully argue that psychiatry and the medical model in general are used to deal with troublemakers and nuisances for whom no other social control mechanism has been developed. If Szasz is correct, the labeling of persons as mentally ill is often a social control endeavor which has little relation to real illness or markedly serious psychological disorientation.[71]

Not all psychiatrists are as oblivious of the operation of societal responses in mental illness as Szasz's strident attacks imply. For example, R. D. Laing and A. Esterson in a suggestive study of only eleven cases argue that the perplexing activities of the schizophrenic become understandable when we examine at close range and in fine detail the dynamics of the family context within which the so-called schizophrenic operates outside the clinic hour.[72] Although these authors admit that their study is open to criticism because of the small number of cases examined, they believe that their argument has merit. As they explain, "those psychiatrists who are not prepared to get to know for themselves what goes on outside their clinics and hospitals simply do not know what goes on, and those sociologists who think that they can find out what goes on by analyzing medical records are merely trying to turn clinical sow's ears into statistical silk purses."[73]

One study showing that bizarre behavior does not automatically result in a label of mentally ill is that of Marian Radke Yarrow et al.[74] A wife threatened by the unusual behavior of her husband usually tries to defend herself from this threat, frequently by attempting to normalize her husband's peculiar behavior as somehow being no different from the actions of others. For example, one wife claimed that it is not strange to hear voices because she heard voices when experiencing menopause, while another argued, "a lot of normal people think there's something wrong when there isn't. I think men are that way; his father is that way."[75] Through such mechanisms the wife denies that there is anything wrong with the husband and postpones the time when outside forces may force a confrontation with him and apply the label of mentally ill to him.

Moreover, the probability of acquiring the official label of mentally ill is not solely determined by the behavior of individuals. According to Dennis L. Wegner and C. Richard Fletcher, one's prospects of being committed to a state mental hospital are affected by the presence or absence of legal counsel.[76] Regardless of the individual's condition as judged by nonpsychiatric observers, those persons represented by legal counsel are much less likely to be committed to the state mental hospital. "Lawyers, with their knowledge of the state legal statutes and its 'loopholes', appear to be fairly successful at influencing the commitment decision and securing the release of their clients."[77] Thus, not only does the individual's cultural milieu influence how he will behave and how others react to him as mentally ill; the social power that he can muster influences the disposition of his case and the diagnostic tag which will be hung on him.

The activities of mental health "experts" who label people as mentally ill also vary considerably. For example, Donald Conover has recently reviewed the approaches used by psychiatrists in making psychiatric distinctions and has attempted to provide a methodology whereby agreement between those who produce these diagnoses can be increased.[78] According to Conover, the degree of agreement between clinical judgments of independent psychiatrists is around 60 percent in research settings, while it is probably even lower in clinical settings.[79]

Professional opinions vary regarding the extent to which the experience of hospitalization aggravates the adjustment problems of the mental patient. According to Madeline Karmel, the lack of significant social structure including the absence of adequate leadership among chronic mental patients in an institution prevents the patients from developing a social role as a deviant.[80] According to her data, although the social identity which the person had in the outside world becomes attenuated in the institution, a hospital world social identity does not emerge around the role of chronic mental patient. These findings are in contrast to those presented by Benjamin M. Braginsky, Dorothea D. Braginsky, and Kenneth Ring, who see the mental hospital as a last resort.[81] They argue that the long-term schizophrenic patient in the mental institution adapts to the place and manipulates his self-presentation to remain in the hospital. Newcomers, by contrast, resist the label of schizophrenic, do not adapt to the institution as a way of life, and engage in other forms of manipulation to get out of the hospital.[82] The acceptance of the label of schizophrenic and adoption of a self-image centered about that identity appears to be a turning point; those who take this step are more likely to remain in the institution for an extended period of time.

Because the labeling perspective tends to concentrate on the drama of commitment to a mental hospital, researchers have been led to pay relatively little attention to out-patient, or clinical handling of persons with self-defined or other-defined mental problems. The treatment of the disturbed without hospitalization and with supportive chemotherapy is becoming much more common than in the past. Yet we know relatively little about the impact of such intervention on the self-concepts of patients or on their significant others.[83]

A fair summary of this material would be that social reactions and labeling directed at persons identified as mentally ill often affect the adjustment problems and life-chances of these individuals. The varied experiences summarized under the term *career contingencies* must be considered if we are to understand the phenomenon of mental illness in modern society. At the same time, the findings are drawn out of a richly varied world which defies simple description and we cannot analyze this diversity by insisting that labeling activities are the only significant factors in mental illness. Disagreements over the relative weight of each set of influences are thus bound to continue.[84]

SOCIETAL RESPONSES
TO MENTAL RETARDATION

A number of persons have argued that the responses of others are of more importance in mental retardation than is the measured intelligence level of the labeled retardate. For example, Jane R. Mercer has challenged the clinical definition of mental retardation as the measure of who is and who is not mentally retarded.[85] She has also examined the social settings in which labeling of mental retardation occurs and the ways in which these different settings lead to various effects from the labeling experience.

The clinical perspective holds that deviance is a personal attribute and assumes that professional diagnosticians do not err in their judgments on retardation. This approach then attempts to change the person so that he is not retarded or to remove him from society. In contrast, the labeling perspective according to Mercer "attempts to see the definition of an individual's behavior as a function of the values of the social system within which he is being evaluated."[86] In this view, both the persons who are labeled and other actors in the social system become equally appropriate objects for study.

By comparing matched samples of persons released from a facility for the mentally retarded with those retained in the institution, Mercer was able to identify some of the social factors involved in attaching the mentally retarded label to an individual and the impact of this experience on the life career of the person. Among her findings are the following: most of those who were released had been discharged as a result of family pressures on the authorities. The families who pressed for the release of family members were overly concentrated in the lower socioeconomic classes.[87] Further, the kin of wards who were released apparently resisted initial commitment of the person and protested against the initial labeling more than did the higher status parents.[88] Children from lower status families thus tended to be older when first tagged as mentally retarded and were more apt to have acquired the label through police and welfare agency intervention than from medical persons. Generally, Mercer concludes that the social system surrounding the lower status family minimizes the seriousness of behavior which would be perceived as a problem in upper status families. For example, not being able to perform tasks of mental agility is considered less of a problem in the lower status families than it is in those of higher social status. The retardate in the former case is likely to be viewed as "slow," rather than as mentally retarded, if indeed the lack of mental ability is seen as a problem at all.

The effects on family dynamics of a mentally retarded child have been studied by Arnold Birenbaum, who demonstrated how the reactions of others to the retarded child and the mother of the retardate affect the visiting patterns and the social interaction of the parents.[89] Of the 103 mothers interviewed, almost half felt that their friendship relationships had become curtailed after one of their children had been identified as retarded, but this did not mean that the family situation was a source of reported dissatisfaction. About three-fourths of the mothers reported that their family life was about the same or better than in families with only normal children.[90]

Finally, Robert B. Edgerton's *The Cloak of Competence* provides a fascinating account of how severely retarded persons cope with the problems of living in the world outside of an institution, including how they deal with the hostile or uncomprehending responses of other people.[91] Edgerton offers a rich body of details on the stratagems which the retarded employ to mask their stigmatizing labels and pass as normal.

SOCIETAL RESPONSE, PHYSICAL ILLNESS, AND PHYSICAL DISABILITY

The importance of societal responses to those identified as physically ill or disabled has also been examined by sociologists. Eliot Freidson has analyzed physical disability as social deviance, pointing to how the reactions of the social audience to a physical disability can lead to the adoption of a deviant role.[92] He notes Lemert's concept of secondary deviation, particularly that part which emphasizes the importance of imputations of deviance whether or not those judgments are supported by fact. He observes that some deviants are regarded by others as having caused their deviance by their own actions, while social audiences regard others as the victims of accident, inheritance, or other misfortunes over which they had no control. Similarly, some patterns of nonconformity are regarded as curable while others are seen as beyond alteration. Social group response to deviants depends rather heavily on which of these qualities are imputed to those persons.[93]

Regarding physical illness, Judith Lorber calls attention to how the individual who has been given or is trying to achieve a label as deviant may try to invalidate or validate that tag in the eyes of a social audience.[94] She points out that physical symptoms are not uniformly responded to by persons, and some attempt to become labelled as "sick" while others try to avoid that label. As she puts it, "Like other social situations, illness is a combination of physical reality and social evaluation and response. It is an interaction process with elements of conflict. The deviant struggles to achieve the kind of label he desires, using his physical state and his performing arts to build up an impression that will convince his social audience."[95]

A parallel examination of the positive benefits sometimes derived from assuming the sick role and persuading others that one is a legitimate occupant of that role is the work of Stephen Cole and Robert Lejune.[96] They argue that the sick role is one way to minimize one's deviant status and that "welfare recipients occupy a stigmatized status in America. A substantial proportion of welfare recipients themselves define being on welfare as a type of failure; yet many have given up hope of becoming independent. When people occupy self-defined illegitimate status and have little expectation of leaving this status they feel the need to legitimize their failure. We have shown that defining one's health as poor is one way that welfare mothers have of legitimizing their status."[97] In short, for many persons, being seen by others as sick rather than as a chronic welfare "bum" may be the less unattractive alternative.

Some commentators have pointed out that one of the problems in being a "cancer victim" is that there is no common understanding of the appropriate reaction to such a person. Although cancer is an emotionally charged term, as Morton Bard argues, the term is confusing because there are nearly 250 diseases subsumed under that rubric.[98] But whatever the form of cancer, the individual who has had cancer and his family are very apt to suffer permanent psychological invalidism. Radical mastectomy can result in the withdrawal of affection from the wife by the husband, or she may withdraw emotional support from him as a result of her feelings of inadequacy and generalized fear of cancer. The cancer is frequently interpreted, according to Bard, as retribution for past indiscretions, sins, or inadequacies.[99]

Although the career of a dying person is typically rather short, social responses are important here as well. For example, David Sudnow's examination of the process of dying in hospitals shows how the responses of others toward the dying patient vary depending on such attributes as age and perceived social utility of the person.[100] The physical condition of the individual is only one determinant of the treatment he receives. Among persons who arrive at the emergency room as possible "dead on arrival" cases, younger individuals are much more likely to be given emergency revival measures than are older ones.[101] Nor is age the only important factor. For example, patients who are perceived as alcoholics are not as likely to receive resuscitation measures as other people. Sudnow reports that in response to a question of whether or not an alcoholic with stomach ulcers should be given more blood the doctor replied, "I can't see any sense in pumping it into him because even if we can stop the bleeding he'll turn around and start drinking again and next week he'll be back needing more blood."[102]

THE IMPACT OF SOCIETAL RESPONSES
ON DRINKING BEHAVIOR AND ALCOHOLICS

Much social condemnation has focused on alcoholics and Skid Road drinkers. Laymen and social scientists alike often employ such terms as "homeless men" and "society's dregs" which reflect the general rejection of the Skid Road drunk. Some efforts have been made to specify how the responses of others lead the individual into alcoholism or push the drinker further into a deviant career.

A recent attempt to employ labeling notions in the analysis of deviant drinking careers is Steven R. Burkett's study of beer drinking among pledge classes of college fraternities.[103] His research contains a number of problems, however, including his argument that beer drinking is deviant behavior. It seems unlikely that the fraternity members either individually or collectively define getting drunk on beer as norm-violating behavior. Also, his investigation took place over only six months, a rather short period of time. Accordingly, his study can tell us little about the development of stable and continuing careers in drinking.

The societal response to problem drinking has been relatively ignored. Instead, most investigators focus on personality factors thought to predispose individuals to alcoholism[104] or upon social-psychological processes.[105] But, these latter works indicate that the social audience plays a part in the emergence of the career of the problem drinker. For example, Don Cahalan's discussion of changes in drinking behavior of persons over a three-year period indicates that alterations in such things as family or job situations are reasons often given by problem drinkers for shifting their drinking behavior.[106] These events imply changes in the social audiences and the social responses of others to the drinking behavior of the person.

Discordant responses to problem drinking probably compound the drinker's difficulties of adjusting to these social definitions. H. Paul

Chalfont and Richard A. Kurtz note that groups such as physicians, nurses, hospital personnel, and the general public hold ambiguous or ambivalent attitudes toward alcoholics, simultaneously seeing them both as sick and as morally or criminally blameworthy.[107] The social workers they queried viewed the alcoholic as sick along some dimensions but not on others. The labels hung on the heavy drinker and the reactions to him are thus often multiple and contradictory. If he is sick he deserves help but if he is volitionally deviant perhaps he needs punishment.

One report of the shifts in social responses to the developing alcoholic career is that of Joan K. Jackson.[108] She observes from her study of the wives of alcoholics that if attempts to ignore the husband's drinking fail, or if later, efforts to control the episodic drinking problems are unsuccessful, and if the children in the family begin to show the effects of family disruption, the wife usually abandons her attempts to control the deviant drinking, leaving the husband to his own devices.

As we have noted, labeling views often hold that the effects of labeling are almost irreversible; once secondary deviation becomes established return to nondeviance rarely occurs. But this is surely not always the case, for Harrison M. Trice and Paul Michael Roman suggest that Alcoholics Anonymous is an organization involved in group efforts to reverse the labeling process and help people out of alcoholism.[109] These authors identify three distinct ways in which problem drinkers could have their label of deviant removed: by changing community norms, by an official delabeling ceremony or procedure, or by developing mutual aid societies to help each other return to the conventional behavior patterns of the community.[110] It is the last of these strategies which Alcoholics Anonymous pursues, but because the public at large does not completely accept the AA definition of the "arrested alcoholic," success in delabeling is far from complete.

James P. Spradley offers a fairly pessimistic estimate of the chances of retreat from deviance in the case of the Skid Road alcoholic.[111] According to Spradley, once a person is processed on a public drunkenness charge, he becomes a drunk in the eyes of powerful others, regardless of his pattern of drinking and intoxication. Spradley declares that: "A man can even become a drunk by going to jail and requesting to be admitted!"[112] Similarly, Jacqueline P. Wiseman's analysis of the life styles of Skid Road alcoholics in San Francisco suggests that the social processing arrangements in which they become enmeshed ensures that these persons will remain permanently labeled and socially disvalued.[113]

To summarize the research on the alcoholic career, it is fair to say that societal reactions to heavy drinking appear to be uniformly negative and almost always to contribute to deeper involvement in deviant drinking patterns.

SOCIETAL RESPONSES TO HOMOSEXUALITY

Many popular media and psychiatric accounts of homosexuality claim that most homosexuals are tortured souls, filled with neurotic anxieties, suicidal tendencies, and self-hatred engendered in part by social condemnation which is heaped upon them in the United States.

From the research which has been produced to date, it is extremely difficult to generalize about the adjustment problems of homosexuals which are caused by negative social reactions. Most of the data on psychological and social adjustment problems come from inquiries in which the research subjects were undergoing psychiatric treatment.[114] Consider the study by Thomas Roesler and Robert W. Deisher dealing with sixty young male homosexuals.[115] They note that: "The institutions from which young people usually derive security—church, school, and family—are often nonsupportive when a youth reveals homosexual feelings and experiences. It is usually after such institutions have failed that a physician is called to answer the cry for help."[116] The authors report that about a third of their respondents had made suicide attempts and that many of them actively sought out others in such places as theaters and parks for the purpose of establishing sexual liaisons. All homosexuals, however, may *not* suffer the withdrawal of social support from the church, family, or school. Those who avoid this kind of rejection may also regard themselves in a favorable light, and they may not be suicidal or seek sex in public places. Stated differently, social rejection quite probably does have serious consequences for some homosexuals, but we are not yet in a position to estimate the number of homosexuals that experience social rejection. There surely is some reason to suppose that not all homosexuals encounter severe social condemnation.[117]

An account of the severe negative reaction generated by labeling of actual and putative homosexuals in one town is contained in John Gerassi's *The Boys of Boise*.[118] He documents the witch hunt which ensued in Boise, Idaho, inspired partly by political motivation, when homosexual activity in Boise became publicized. It is impossible to say with accuracy, of course, but it is probable that Boise had no more homosexual activity at the time of the scandal than any other town of comparable size. Yet the publicity growing out of the exposé ruined a number of lives, resulted in prison terms for others, and the loss of jobs for many. According to Gerassi, the repercussions of the "scandal" in Boise were visible and disruptive in the community a full decade later.

A documentation of the identity-defacing nature of the negative societal reaction to homosexuality and an account of the current attempts to counter this societal response is provided by Laud Humphries.[119] Drawing from his intensive involvement in the gay liberation movement, he documents how the push for civil rights has spread to homosexuals and has given impetus to the notion of gay power. The gay liberation movement is, of course, an example of the attempt, as identified by Trice and Roman, to change community norms and to be delabeled.

The problems of homosexuals in combating the negative attitudes of the larger society are clearly different from those of the blacks, but the hostility directed at them may be no less painful. Furthermore, Humphries shows that the gay liberation movement has many parallels with the civil rights movement. The male homosexual search for equality currently involves many clergymen, as did the early civil rights activities, and much of the terminology and tactics are taken from the civil rights experience. How successful the attempts at liberating the homosexual will be remains to be seen, but the consciousness-raising endeavors of the gay in America have been and will continue to be successful. It will probably not be possible to ignore homosexuals in America in the future, but the effect that this may have on their social acceptance is unclear.[120]

FINAL REMARKS

A discussion of the effects of labeling on careers would not be complete without some reference to the positive good which can accrue to the individual with a derisive label. One reward of being identified as a deviant would appeal only to those who are popularly called masochists for whom "stigma is not an object of dread but of greed."[121] But the masochistic craving for degradation is only one case of being rewarded for having been labeled. Many popular figures, entertainers, and the like, have had their careers enhanced by the publicity attendant upon being publicly labeled as a rule breaker or as one who has overcome the supposedly formidable handicap of having been processed through an official labeling agency.[122]

There are more direct financial benefits as well. Elliot A. Krause, in his review of illegal occupations (not all practitioners of which have been socially identified, by any means) concludes that many of these occupations are not only profitable, but barring certain marketplace shifts, they have a lucrative future.[123] More specifically one might point to the exnarcotic addicts referred to by Thomas S. Szasz who started working in a rehabilitation center in New York at an annual salary of $6,500 and in a short time were receiving $16,000 to $18,000.[124] Although few in number, these cases do suggest that there are opportunities to use the illegal structure as an entry point into the legal structure, and at very handsome fees.

SUMMARY

This chapter has reviewed much evidence on labeling experiences and some selected deviant careers. The data indicate that the effects of labeling processes on the development or avoidance of career involvement in deviance are far from uniform, and complete consensus on the importance of these factors is not likely in the near future.

We have concluded our review of the major conceptual and theoretical issues in the field of deviance analysis. In our final chapter, we turn to a difficult and challenging issue: the ethical limitations that ought to govern the work of researchers as they probe and poke into the behavior of real people in a real world.

NOTES

[1] Alexander Liazos, "The Poverty of the Sociology of Deviance: Nuts, Sluts, and Preverts," *Social Problems* 20 (Summer 1972): 103–20. Liazos maintains that the use of the term *deviant* itself constitutes a case of pejorative labeling and is a reflection of popular prejudices on the part of the sociologist. See our remarks in chapter one regarding Liazos's views.

[2] The extreme case in which identification of persons as deviants leads to severe societal reactions that in turn drive them unremittingly further into deviance is illustrated by Connor's study of the Soviet purge. See Walter D. Conner, "The Manufacture of Deviance: The Case of the Soviet Purge," *American Sociological Review* 37 (August 1972): 403–13. In this instance, the event of merely being arrested as a suspected political enemy resulted in severe consequences. Once arrested, it was virtually impossible for the individual to prove his innocence. Clearly, many of those who were arrested, convicted, and sent off to labor camps were persons who were falsely accused, but that made little difference in effects which the arrest and labeling had on the lives of those imprisoned during the purge.

³ Another possibility, not so frequently acknowledged in labeling arguments, is that some persons may assume a deviant identity in the absence of any official labeling experience directed at them. This possibility is discussed in Nanette J. Davis, "Labeling Theory in Deviance Research: A Critique and Reconsideration," *Sociological Quarterly* 13 (Autumn 1972): 460–62. Davis offers these possibilities as existing in the real world: first, official labeling may lead to a deviant identity, as in the case of prostitutes or psychiatric patients. But official labeling may also be accompanied by nondeviant identity, as illustrated by juvenile delinquents engaged in homosexual transactions with adult males. A third relationship is one in which an absence of official labeling is accompanied by a deviant identity, illustrated by middle-class "secret" homosexuals or physician- drug addicts. Finally, the absence of labeling may also result in nondeviant identity, as in such cases as illegal abortees or pool hustlers. Davis, p. 461.

⁴ Harold Garfinkel, "Conditions of Successful Degradation Ceremonies," *American Journal of Sociology* 61 (March 1956): 420–24.

⁵ There is an almost unlimited number of directions which the analysis of societal reactions might take. For example, the study of the social sources of sentiments about deviance is one important topic, but we have already addressed it in chapter five. Then, too, a number of questions might be posed regarding the limits of formal social control processes in coercing compliant behavior or the efficacy of formal sanctions as a means of repressing what are felt to be undesirable tendencies toward deviance in the general population. There is an extensive literature bearing upon the issue of the effectiveness of sanctions in controlling behavior. See, for example, Richard D. Schwartz and Sonya Orleans, "On Legal Sanctions," *The University of Chicago Law Review* 34 (Winter 1967): 472–300; William J. Bowers and Richard G. Salem, "Severity of Formal Sanctions as a Repressive Response to Deviant Behavior," *Law and Society Review* 6 (February 1972): 427–41; and Richard G. Salem and William J. Bowers, "Severity of Formal Sanctions as a Deterrent to Deviant Behavior," *Law and Society Review* 5 (August 1970): 21–40.

However, a large share of the commentary in the deviance literature has centered on the effects of particular labeling events on specific deviant individuals. Accordingly, we shall center most of our attention in this section on that aspect of labeling processes. Hence, our remarks will have little to say about such matters as the relative effectiveness of punitive sanctions as contrasted to other responses to deviants. Also, we will not devote much space to discussions of the role of sanctions in preventing the outbreak of deviant tendencies on the part of potential nonconformists.

Still another dimension of the societal reactions topic is the effects of labeling experiences on other individuals involved in social interaction with the labeled deviant, such as the consequences these events have for the spouses of convicted felons or incarcerated mental patients. For example, see Edwin M. Lemert, "The Occurrence and Sequence of Events in the Adjustment of Families to Alcoholism," *Quarterly Journal of Studies on Alcohol* 21 (December 1960):

679–97. But we have placed this matter outside the purview of this chapter in order to set some limits on our discussion.

[6] Erving Goffman, *Stigma* (Englewood Cliffs, N.J.: Prentice-Hall, 1963).

[7] Shlomo Shoham, *The Mark of Cain* (Jerusalem: Israel Universities Press, 1970).

[8] Bernard A. Thorsell and Lloyd W. Klemke, "The Labeling Process: Reinforcement or Deterrent?" *Law and Society Review* 6 (February 1972): 393–403.

[9] Ibid., pp. 401–2.

[10] John Lofland, *Deviance and Identity* (Englewood Cliffs, N.J.: Prentice-Hall, 1969).

[11] Ibid., p. 146.

[12] Ibid., p. 79.

[13] Ibid., p. 81.

[14] Edwin M. Schur, *Labeling Deviant Behavior: Its Sociological Implications* (New York: Harper and Row, Publishers, 1971).

[15] Ibid., pp. 153–54.

[16] Daniel Glaser, *Social Deviance* (Chicago: Markham Publishing Co., 1971). Glaser essentially agrees with Schur's comments cited previously, for in his review of the relationship between labeling phenomena and the development of deviant careers, Glaser asserts: "to summarize, deviant careers generally develop in a non-linear and not easily predictable manner. Like all other behavior, deviance that is gratifying tends to be continued and that which is not gratifying is extinguished." Ibid., p. 50.

[17] This point is discussed in Don C. Gibbons, *Society, Crime, and Criminal Careers,* 2d ed. (Englewood Cliffs, N.J.: Prentice-Hall, 1973), p. 223; see also Milton Mankoff, "Societal Reaction and Career Deviance," *Sociological Quarterly* 12 (Spring 1971): 204–18.

[18] Edwin Lemert, *Social Pathology* (New York: McGraw-Hill Book Co., 1951).

[19] Ibid., pp. 75–79 ff.

[20] It might also be noted that Lemert is not always careful to distinguish actual deviation from putative deviation. For example, he describes narrowing of major role choices for the female college student who was living with her paroled convict father who was frequently intoxicated; males either stopped dating her or assumed that she was sexually available. In this case, it was the father and not the daughter who was deviant. Ibid., pp. 77–78.

[21] Mankoff, "Societal Reaction and Career Deviance."

[22] We are not in agreement with Mankoff's assertion that this claim about labeling constitutes a theory, nor do we agree that it is a profound argument. We disagree with Mankoff's use of an omnibus conception of deviance. That choice leads him to set up a typology of rule breaking in which he attempts to separate ascriptive rule breaking from achieved rule breaking. By the former he

means stigmatized individuals such as dwarfs, the extremely ugly, women, or blacks. As examples of achieved rule breaking, he lists such cases as dance musicians, taxi dancers, and strippers. The question arises: what important rules are broken if one is short, black, or a taxi dancer going about her business? Further, Mankoff's analysis seems detached from reality when he argues that learning to be a marijuana smoker is an example of learning a deviant career. Those who smoke marijuana quite regularly can hardly be said to be involved in a pervasive career pattern, in that the use of "grass" does not constitute a major social role nor does it ramify to other major social roles of the person. Finally and most important, Mankoff renders the labeling argument almost tautological when he claims that ascribed deviation best fits the labeling model. After all, the definition of ascribed deviation is that it is the product of social labeling of characteristics of the individual over which he has no control. Then too, Mankoff changes the character of the labeling argument by applying it to dwarfs, the ugly, etc., in that most labeling theorists have been arguing for the career effects of social reactions upon achieved rule breakers.

One positive comment about Mankoff's essay is that he points out that (1) persons sometimes engage in career deviance in the absence of social reactions, (2) others desist from norm violations after having been subjected to a social response, and (3) some individuals persist in deviant careers even when they have the opportunity to withdraw from them. Examples are criminals who persist in lawbreaking because they enjoy the excitement of a criminal career, political extremists who are positively motivated to flaunt conventional rules, and other types who choose to continue along deviant pathways. See fn.17. Also, for some evidence on this point dealing with career criminals, see Peter Letkemann, *Crime as Work* (Englewood Cliffs, N.J.: Prentice-Hall, 1973).

[23] Jack D. Douglas, "Deviance and Order in a Pluralistic Society," in John D. McKinney and Edward A. Tiryakian, eds., *Theoretical Sociology* (New York: Appleton-Century-Crofts, 1970), pp. 367–401.

[24] Ibid., p. 392.

[25] David Matza, *Becoming Deviant* (Englewood Cliffs, N.J.: Prentice-Hall, 1969).

[26] Note that the analysis of the labeling process by Thorsell and Klemke, "The Labeling Process," draws very heavily on examples from criminality. See also David Downes and Paul Rock, "Social Reaction to Deviance and its Effects on Crime and Criminal Careers,'. *British Journal of Sociology* 22 (December 1971): 351–64.

[27] Documentation of this claim can be found in Gibbons, *Society, Crime, and Criminal Careers*, pp. 472–73.

[28] Erving Goffman, *Asylums* (Garden City, N.Y.: Doubleday and Co., 1961), pp. 321–86. Although Goffman is principally concerned with mental health tinkering and tinkerers in mental hospitals, his observations hold with equal force for correctional treatment workers.

[29] Extended discussions of the problems of correctional treatment, along with evidence on the efficacy of correctional programs, can be found in Gibbons, *Society, Crime, and Criminal Careers,* pp. 501–43; Gibbons, *Delinquent Behavior* (Englewood Cliffs, N.J.: Prentice-Hall, 1970), pp. 221–61.

[30] Frank Tannenbaum, *Crime and the Community* (New York: Ginn and Co., 1938), pp. 19–21.

[31] A more comprehensive review of the evidence and articulation of major problems for future deterrence research is Charles R. Tittle and Charles H. Logan,, "Sanctions and Deviance: Evidence and Remaining Questions," *Law and Society Review* 7 (Spring 1973): 371–92; Tittle, "Punishment and Deterrence of Deviance," in Simon Rottenberg, ed., *The Economics of Crime and Punishment* (Washington, D.C.: American Enterprise Institute for Public Policy Research, 1973), pp. 85–102; Franklin Zimring and Gordon J. Hawkins, *Deterrence: The Legal Threat in Crime Control* (Chicago: University of Chicago Press, 1973).

[32] Although our concern in this essay is principally with the effects of social reactions on specific offenders, it is difficult to discuss penal sanctions without giving some attention to general deterrence. This is because penal sanctions are intended by those who apply them to have both specific and general effects.

[33] Daniel Glaser, *The Effectiveness of a Prison and Parole System* (Indianapolis: Bobbs-Merrill Co., 1964), pp. 13–35. Observers have sometimes concluded that most inmates become recidivists or repeaters from observing an offender population in prison at one point in time. On any particular day the prison population does contain a large portion of inmates who have been imprisoned a number of times previously. At the same time, a large number of individuals proceed through the institution over time and do not subsequently return. Unless we take some kind of census outside of the prison, or unless we follow a cohort of newly admitted prisoners for an extended period of time, we are likely to overlook the prisoners who do not return to the institution for a second time. Nonetheless, the successes are at least as frequent as are the cases of those who keep coming back through the "revolving door" of the penitentiary.

[34] Franklin E. Zimring, *Perspectives on Deterrence* (Washington, D.C.: National Institute of Mental Health, 1971); see also Paul W. Tappan, *Crime, Justice and Correction* (New York: McGraw-Hill Book Co., 1960), pp. 241–61.

[35] William J. Chambliss, "The Deterrent Influence of Punishment," *Crime and Delinquency* 12 (January 1966): 70–75.

[36] Jack P. Gibbs, "Crime, Punishment, and Deterrence," *Southwestern Social Science Quarterly* 28 (March 1968): 515–30.

[37] Charles R. Tittle, "Crime Rates and Legal Sanctions," *Social Problems* 16 (Spring 1969): 409–23.

[38] Theodore G. Chiricos and Gordon P. Waldo, "Punishment and Crime: An Examination of Some Empirical Evidence," *Social Problems* 18 (Fall 1970): 200–17; Waldo and Chiricos, "Perceived Penal Sanction and Self-Reported Criminality: A Neglected Approach to Deterrence Research," *Social Problems* 19

(Spring 1972): 522–40. In this latter study, Waldo and Chiricos quizzed a sample of college students about theft behavior and marijuana use. Certainty of punishment appeared to have the greatest effect in deterring these persons from involvement or continuation in these activities.

[39] Donald T. Campbell and H. Laurence Ross, "The Connecticut Crackdown on Speeding: Time-Series Data in a Quasi-Experimental Analysis," *Law and Society Review* 3 (August 1968): 33–53.

[40] Goffman, *Asylums.*

[41] Richard D. Schwartz and Jerome H. Skolnick, "Two Studies of Legal Stigma," in Howard S. Becker, ed., *The Other Side* (New York: Free Press of Glencoe, 1964), pp. 103–17. See also: H. Laurence Ross, "Legal Stigma," and Schwartz and Skolnick, "Rejoinder to Ross" (Communications and Opinions), *Social Problems* 10 (Spring 1963): 390–92.

[42] Mary Owen Cameron, *The Booster and the Snitch* (New York: Free Press of Glencoe, 1964).

[43] Bernard B. Berk, "Organizational Goals and Inmate Organization," *American Journal of Sociology* 71 (March 1966): 522–34.

[44] David Street, Robert D. Vinter, and Charles Perrow, *Organization for Treatment* (New York: Free Press of Glencoe, 1966).

[45] The study of correctional effects is actually even more complicated than we have suggested. There are other variables, additional to those noted here, which would have to be taken into account in the analysis of correctional effects. For example, the average sentence length served by inmates in state prisons varies markedly from one state to another. In 1964, the median time served by first releasees (men being released for the first time after serving the sentence for their current offense) ranged from 9.0 months in New Hampshire to 39.0 months in Hawaii, with the national average of time served being 21.0 months. See Assembly Committee on Criminal Procedure, *Deterrent Effects of Criminal Sanctions* (Sacramento: California State Assembly, 1968), p. 44. One might also point out that these figures suggest that "rehabilitation" may turn out to be a cruel joke perpetrated upon criminals. That is, California has been widely identified as the most progressive, "treatment-oriented" state in the nation as far as correctional handling of offenders is concerned. But, offenders now undergo nearly three years of "treatment" in that state, compared to shorter sentences in other, less treatment-oriented states. There is no evidence to suggest that an individual's chances of succeeding on parole are increased through serving a long sentence; on the contrary, the best guess is that long sentences operate to reduce the offender's prospects for successful rehabilitation. In the instance of California, the incarcerated offender would seem to "lose" twice. First, he is pressured into participation in therapy involving assaults upon his sense of dignity and self-worth, as he undergoes pressure to define himself as "sick" and in need of therapy, rather than as a "bad ass" or "bad man." But in addition, having engaged in therapy, the offender then finds that he is to be kept in prison longer than prisoners in many other states.

[46] Situational causation of criminality is discussed at length in Don C. Gibbons, "Observations on the Study of Crime Causation," *American Journal of Sociology* 77 (September 1971): 262–78.

[47] Data on the success rates of training schools can be found in Gibbons, *Delinquent Behavior*, pp. 249–60.

[48] Girls' training schools have received little research attention. One study which suggests some of the factors which are involved in low recidivism rates for these places is Raymond J. Adamek and Edward Z. Dager, "Social Structure, Identification and Change in a Treatment-Oriented Institution," *American Sociological Review* 33 (December 1968): 931–44.

[49] Thomas G. Eynon and Jon E. Simpson, "The Boy's Perception of Himself in a State Training School for Delinquents," *Social Service Review* 39 (March 1965): 31–37; one indication that official intervention at earlier points in the juvenile correctional process does not produce stigmatizing effects can be found in Jack Donald Foster, Simon Dinitz, and Walter C. Reckless, "Perceptions of Stigma Following Public Intervention for Delinquent Behavior," *Social Problems* 20 (Fall 1972): 202–9.

[50] Carl F. Jesness, *The Fricot Ranch Study* (Sacramento: State of California, Department of the Youth Authority, 1965).

[51] Glaser, *The Effectiveness of a Prison and Parole System*, p. 24.

[52] Ibid., pp. 13–35; see also Assembly Committee on Criminal Procedure, *Deterrent Effects of Criminal Sanctions*, p. 50.

[53] Glaser, *The Effectiveness of a Prison and Parole System*, p. 509.

[54] Ibid., p. 508.

[55] Walter C. Bailey, "An Evaluation of 100 Studies of Correctional Outcome," in Norman A. Johnston, Leonard Savitz, and Marvin E. Wolfgang, eds., *The Sociology of Punishment and Correction*, 2d ed. (New York: John Wiley and Sons, 1970), pp. 733–42.

[56] Ibid., p. 738.

[57] Stanton Wheeler, "Socialization in Correctional Institutions," in David A. Goslin, ed., *Handbook of Socialization Theory and Research* (Chicago: Rand McNally and Co., 1969), pp. 1005–23.

[58] Ibid., pp. 1019–20.

[59] John Irwin, *The Felon* (Englewood Cliffs, N.J.: Prentice-Hall, 1970).

[60] Ibid., pp. 152–73.

[61] Ibid., p. 204.

[62] These projects are discussed in Gibbons, *Society, Crime, and Criminal Careers*, pp. 533–43; parallel results for group counseling at California Men's Colony, San Luis Obispo are reported in Gene Kassebaum, David A. Ward, and Daniel Wilner, *Prison Treatment and Parole Survival* (New York: John Wiley and Sons, 1971).

[63] Troy Duster, *The Legislation of Morality* (New York: Free Press of Glencoe, 1970), pp. 133–213.

[64] Elliot Studt, Sheldon L. Messinger, and Thomas P. Wilson, *C-Unit: Search for Community in Prison* (New York: Russell Sage Foundation, 1968).

[65] Donald P. Jewell, "A Case of a 'Psychotic' Navaho Indian Male," *Human Organization* 11 (Spring 1962): 32–36. The reader should note that we are using the concept of putative deviant here in a somewhat different fashion than in chapter five. There, we spoke principally of erroneous beliefs that become attached to actual deviants, while *putative* in the present context has to do with false imputations of mental illness.

[66] Thomas J. Scheff, *Being Mentally Ill* (Chicago: Aldine Publishing Co., 1966).

[67] Walter B. Gove, "Societal Reaction as an Explanation of Mental Illness: An Evaluation," *American Sociological Review* 35 (October 1970): 873–84; see also H. Warren Dunham, "Comment on Gove's Evaluation of Societal Reaction Theory as an Explanation for Mental Illness," *American Sociological Review* 36 (April 1971): 313–14; David Mechanic, "Comment on 'Mental Illness,' " *American Sociological Review* 36 (April 1971): 314; Gove, "Reply to Dunham and Mechanic," *American Sociological Review* 36 (April 1971): 314–16; Ronald L. Akers, "Comment on Gove's Evaluation of Societal Reaction as an Explanation of Mental Illness," *American Sociological Review* 37 (August 1972): 487; Gove, "Reply to Akers," *American Sociological Review* 37 (August 1972): 488–90.

[68] Gove, "Societal Reaction as an Explanation of Mental Illness": 882–83.

[69] Thomas S. Szasz, *The Myth of Mental Illness* (New York: Hoeber-Harper, 1961).

[70] Szasz, *Psychiatric Justice* (New York: The Macmillan Company, 1965).

[71] A fascinating account of the development of the insane asylum as a social control device in the United States is contained in David J. Rothman, *The Discovery of the Asylum* (Boston: Little, Brown & Co., 1971). He shows how the development of institutions for deviants—the penitentiary, the workhouse, and the insane asylum—developed apace with the general philosophies of those in power, along with the medical models available to practitioners.

Although the originators of institutionalization as a social policy supposed that custodial programs would rehabilitate their wards, Rothman indicates that: "By 1870 both the reality of institutional care and the rhetoric of psychiatrists made clear that the optimism of reformers had been unfounded, that the expectation of eradicating insanity from the New World had been illusory" (p. 265). Even so, incarceration as a mode of dealing with the non-understandable, who typically had been the foreign-born and the immigrant, was established in the national life and continues to be so to this day. While the treatment in institutions of persons judged to be mentally aberrant has improved in humanitarian terms, it remains an open question whether or not the efficacy of these places has been increased through the humanitarian changes in institutional milieu.

[72] R. D. Laing and A. Esterson, *Sanity, Madness, and the Family,* 2d ed. (Baltimore: Penguin Books, 1970).

[73] Ibid., p. 13.

[74] Marian Radke Yarrow, Charlotte Green Schwartz, Harriet S. Murphy, and Leila Calhoun Deasy, "The Psychological Meaning of Mental Illness in the Family," in Dorrian Apple, ed., *Sociological Studies of Health and Sickness* (New York: McGraw-Hill Book Co., 1960).

[75] Ibid., pp. 66–67.

[76] Dennis L. Wegner and C. Richard Fletcher, "The Effect of Legal Counsel on Admissions to a State Mental Hospital," *Journal of Health and Social Behavior* 10 (March 1969): 66–72.

[77] Ibid., p. 71.

[78] Donald Conover, "Psychiatric Distinctions: New and Old Approaches," *Journal of Health and Social Behavior* 13 (June 1972): 167–80.

[79] Ibid., p. 168.

[80] Madeline Karmel, "The Internalization of Social Roles in Institutionalized Chronic Mental Patients," *Journal of Health and Social Behavior* 11 (September 1970): 231–35.

[81] Benjamin M. Braginsky, Dorothea D. Braginsky and Kenneth Ring, *Methods of Madness: The Mental Hospital as a Last Resort* (New York: Holt, Rinehart and Winston, 1969).

[82] Ibid., chapter 2. "Experimental Studies of the Manipulative Tactics of Mental Patients."

[83] For one study of the route to seeking help for mental illness that does not involve hospitalization, see Charles Kadushin, *Why People Go to Psychiatrists* (New York: Atherton Press, 1969). Kadushin's work does not fall within the labeling perspective, but at one point (p. 248), he reports that" even among applicants to a sophisticated psychoanalytic clinic . . . 90 per cent said *yes* to our question, 'Do you think there is something wrong with a person who goes to a psychiatrist?' " Surely the "self involvement and shame" of which Kadushin speaks involves labeling and stigmatizing quite independent of the effects of being hospitalized as mentally ill.

[84] The lack of agreement over how much difference societal reactions to the label *mental illness* makes becomes clear when we look at the review of the literature by Clarizio, the reanalysis of these data by Scheff and Sundstrom, and the comment on both of these by Black. See H. Clarizio, "Stability of Deviant Behavior Over Time," *Mental Hygiene* 52 (April 1968): 288–93; Thomas J. Scheff and Eric Sundstrom, "The Stability of Deviant Behavior Over Time: A Comment," *Journal of Health and Social Behavior* 12 (March 1971): 37–43. Stephen Black, "Deviant Behavior Over Time: A Comment," *Journal of Health and Social Behavior* 12 (March 1971): 81–83.

Clarizio reviewed a number of studies, both retrospective and longitudinal, and concluded that there is variability in the stability of a deviant role depending upon, most importantly, the kind of deviation involved. Scheff and Sundstrom, in their reevaluation of Clarizio's work, suggest that this variability in stability can better be accounted for by the labeling perspective than by the medical model. Black, in his comment, suggests that Scheff and Sundstrom have confused the issue through their lack of understanding of what is involved in the medical model, for the medical model itself allows for self-limiting diseases. He also charges them with the mistake of aggregating different kinds of behavioral problems such that childhood reading problems and the like are lumped with all other types of mental illness and with assuming that only the labeling perspective can account for mental illness when, according to Black, anomie theory has much to offer as an explanation. Thus, using essentially the same pool of studies, the three different sets of commentary come to widely differing views on the importance of societal reaction and, therefore, the importance of the labeling perspective in generating long-term involvement in the career of mental illness.

[85] Jane R. Mercer, "Career Patterns of Persons Labeled as Mentally Retarded," *Social Problems* 13 (Summer 1965): 18–34; see also Mercer, *Labelling the Mentally Retarded* (Berkeley: University of California Press, 1973).

[86] Ibid., p. 20.

[87] Ibid., pp. 24–26.

[88] Ibid., pp. 29–30.

[89] Arnold Birenbaum, "On Managing a Courtesy Stigma," *Journal of Health and Social Behavior* 11 (September 1970): 196–201.

[90] Ibid.

[91] Robert B. Edgerton, *The Cloak of Competence* (Berkeley: University of California Press, 1967).

[92] Eliot Freidson, "Disability as Social Deviance," in Marvin B. Sussman, ed., *Sociology and Rehabilitation* (Washington, D.C.: American Sociological Association, 1966), pp. 71–99. One study of these matters as they have to do with blindness is Robert A. Scott, *The Making of Blind Men* (New York: Russell Sage Foundation, 1969).

[93] Haber and Smith have recently tried to reconceptualize the relationship between physical disability and social deviance. According to these authors, a major distinguishing feature between the two is the element of willfulness in the enactment of deviant behavior. That is, the physically disabled are not appropriately thought of as having engaged in a deliberate attempt to be physically disabled in the same way as the deviant actor. See Lawrence D. Haber and Richard T. Smith, "Disability and Deviance," *American Sociological Review* 36 (February 1971): 87–97.

[94] Judith Lorber, "Deviance as Performance: The Case of Illness," *Social Problems* 14 (Winter 1967): 302–10.

[95] Ibid., p. 309.

[96] Stephen Cole and Robert Lejune, "Illness and the Legitimation of Failure,'" *American Sociological Review* 37 (June 1972): 344–56.

[97] Ibid., pp. 355–56.

⁹⁸ Morton Bard, "The Price of Survival Among Cancer Victims," in Anselm L. Strauss, ed., *Where Medicine Fails* (Chicago: Aldine Publishing Co., 1970), pp. 99–110.

⁹⁹ Ibid., pp. 102–3.

¹⁰⁰ David Sudnow, *Passing On* (Englewood Cliffs, N.J.: Prentice-Hall, 1967).

¹⁰¹ Ibid., pp. 100–4.

¹⁰² Ibid., pp. 105.

¹⁰³ Steven R. Burkett, "Self-Other Systems and Deviant Career Patterns," *Pacific Sociological Review* 15 (April 1972): 169–83.

¹⁰⁴ A recent example is the intensive work by McClelland et al., relating alcohol consumption to "power needs." David C. McClelland, William N. Davis, Rudolf Kalin and Eric Wanner, *The Drinking Man* (New York: The Free Press, 1972).

¹⁰⁵ A good example of this approach is Don Cahalan, *Problem Drinkers* (San Francisco: Jossey-Bass, 1970).

¹⁰⁶ Ibid., p. 132.

¹⁰⁷ H. Paul Chalfont and Richard A. Kurtz, "Alcoholics and the Sick Role," *Journal of Health and Social Behavior* 12 (March 1971): 66–72.

¹⁰⁸ Joan K. Jackson, "The Adjustment of the Family to the Crisis of Alcoholism," *Quarterly Journal of Studies in Alcohol* 15 (December 1954): 562–86.

¹⁰⁹ Harrison M. Trice and Paul Michael Roman, "Delabeling, Relabeling, and Alcoholics Anonymous," *Social Problems* 17 (Spring 1970): 538–46.

¹¹⁰ Ibid., p. 539.

¹¹¹ James P. Spradley, *You Owe Yourself a Drunk* (Boston: Little, Brown and Company, 1970).

¹¹² Ibid., p. 83.

¹¹³ Jacqueline P. Wiseman, *Stations of the Lost* (Englewood Cliffs, N.J.: Prentice-Hall, 1970).

¹¹⁴ A case in point is Irving Bieber, Harvey J. Dain, Paul R. Dince, Marvin G. Grellich, Henry G. Grand, Ralph M. Gundlach, Malvina W. Kremer, Alfred H. Rifkin, Cornelia B. Wilbur, and Tony B. Bieber, *Homosexuality* (New York: Basic Books, 1962).

¹¹⁵ Thomas Roesler and Robert W. Deisher, "Youthful Male Homosexuality," *Journal of the American Medical Association* 219 (February 21, 1972): 1018–23.

¹¹⁶ Ibid., p. 1023.

¹¹⁷ The observations of Simon and Gagnon regarding variations in adjustment patterns of homosexuals are germane to this point. See William Simon and John H. Gagnon, "Homosexuality: The Formulation of a Sociological Perspective," *Journal of Health and Social Behavior* 8 (September 1967): 117–35; see also Colin J. Williams and Martin S. Weinberg, *Homosexuals and the Military* (New York: Harper and Row, Publishers, 1971). This research suggests that persons

who receive less than honorable discharges from military service because of homosexuality suffer no more stigma than do those homosexuals who receive honorable discharges.

[118] John Gerassi, *The Boys of Boise* (New York: The Macmillan Co., 1967).

[119] Laud Humphries, *Out of the Closets* (Englewood Cliffs, N.J.: Prentice-Hall, 1972).

[120] For a sampling of statements from gay liberation spokesmen, see Joseph A. McCaffrey, ed., *The Homosexual Dialectic* (Englewood Cliffs, N.J.: Prentice-Hall, 1972).

[121] Shoham, *The Mark of Cain*, p. 53.

[122] Shoham uses the life of Jean Genet to illustrate the individual's progress through a career in deviance, starting with Genet's early self-recognition as a bastard. We would point out that the same biography can be used to illustrate the value of being labeled as different. Ibid., chapter 10. We could also direct attention at cases such as a prominent contemporary criminologist who served a prison sentence in California. That scholar's career has prospered, in part, out of the notoriety he has achieved as "one who has been there."

[123] Elliot A. Krause, *The Sociology of Occupations* (Boston: Little, Brown and Co., 1971), Chapter 11, "Illegal Occupations."

[124] Thomas S. Szasz, "The Ethics of Addiction," *Harper's* (April 1972): 74–79. The "New Careers" program in corrections which employs ex-offenders in correctional treatment roles is another example of deviant status ultimately providing occupational rewards for the person. For a brief discussion of opportunities available for exploiting the ex-addict identity, see Dan Waldorf, *Careers in Dope* (Englewood Cliffs, N.J.: Prentice-Hall, 1973), pp. 25–27.

ethical issues
in the
study of deviance

M ost of this book has focused almost single mindedly on various conceptual issues and empirical questions that need to be addressed in the study of deviance. We have been almost exclusively concerned with *what* to study rather than with *how* to go about inquiry. We do not intend to conclude this text with an extended discussion of research methodology, for another entire book could deal with that subject.[1] But, a few brief comments about investigative strategies are in order.[2]

First, almost the full range of research methods and procedures employed in social science has been used by investigators of norm violations and violators. We saw in chapter five that survey research techniques have often been employed in order to gather data on public conceptions of deviance. Chapter three noted epidemiological studies which usually deal with secondary data, that is, statistics gathered by some social control agency. The *Uniform Crime Reports* compiled by the Federal Bureau of Investigation, for example, are frequently used to gauge the parameters of the crime problem in the United States. These reports present statistics on crimes known to the police and arrests that are assembled by the federal agency.

Some investigators have attempted to uncover etiological processes in specific forms of deviance by examining social agency case records of identified norm violators, while other researchers have conducted their own interviews with samples of deviants. A few instances can be found in which experimental techniques have been employed to examine some particular hypotheses about norm-violating behavior. Finally, various nonparticipant or participant observer tactics have been used by many who probe into deviance.

Although methodological diversity has characterized the study of deviance in recent years, a number of persons have begun to argue that only through direct observation of deviants can valid generalizations about their behavior be developed. For example, John I. Kitsuse and Aaron V. Cicourel have contended that official statistics and reports regarding criminals and delinquents are of little value as accurate descriptions of these persons; agency-gathered statistics and files tell us principally about the workings of official agencies and how they process and label individuals.[3] A similar point has been made by Jack D. Douglas concerning official data on suicides.[4] He argues that some cases officially recorded as suicides are probably misclassified. Along the same line, Ned Polsky has argued that we must engage in studying criminals in their natural settings if we are to understand these persons.[5]

Then too, as a number of critics of contemporary perspectives on deviance have remarked, this area of inquiry has concentrated on various exotic or bizarre forms of deviant conduct, such that the literature abounds with comments on strippers, pool hustlers, mate swappers and "swingers," teen-age prostitutes, con men, patrons of "gay bars" and "tea rooms" (public restrooms), and kindred souls. Incumbents of these roles infrequently turn up in statistics gathered by people-processing agencies, hence the researcher is obliged to assemble his own facts. But most of these individuals are understandably reticent about presenting themselves to social researchers for scrutiny through questionnaires or subjecting themselves to focused interviews. As a result, various unobtrusive and sometimes disguised forms of nonparticipant or participant observer research methodology have been advocated.[6] Techniques of "soft methodology" in which the researcher infiltrates deviant groups have frequently been described as the methodology *par excellence* for the study of deviance.

Techniques of direct observation involve problems of objectivity, matters about which standard methodology textbooks have much to say. These procedures raise a number of ethical questions as well, particularly when they are used in unobtrusive and secretive ways to study deviance and relatively powerless individuals who are involved in these activities. Thus far, methodology texts have been relatively quiet on these issues.

What responsibilities do social researchers have toward research subjects? In particular, what are the rights of deviants? Should they be free to refuse to be observed and scrutinized in the name of science? Are we obliged to inform deviants that we are monitoring and recording their behavior? Or, is it permissible for investigators to infiltrate deviant groups and to conduct observations of the members without their knowledge?

Queries of this form have rarely been entertained by social scientists until relatively recently. But in the past decade or so, sociologists and other social scientists have begun paying increased attention to ethical problems and related concerns.[7] When sociologists write about ethics they refer variously to one of three rather distinct and different issues: the relationship of sociology and sociologists to the formation and implementation of public policy; the morality or moral position of sociology or of individual sociologists, and, finally, strictures on the behavior of individual sociologists in their research activities.[8]

This third matter will be given major attention in this chapter. We shall examine how the sociologist conducts his research and attempt to pinpoint ethical problems surrounding inquiries into deviance. Then too, we shall identify some specific questions which must be faced in the development of an ethical stance. A brief discussion of the issues of public policy and morality will set the stage for the commentary on ethics which follows.

SOCIOLOGY AND PUBLIC POLICY[9]

A recent celebrated instance of the debate over the proper role of sociology in public policy making involved Project Camelot. That project, funded by the United States Army through the Special Operations Research Office, was intended to expend approximately $6,000,000 for "measuring and forecasting the causes of revolution and insurgency in underdeveloped areas."[10] Chile was selected as the area of investigation, but before the field work began the project was vigorously attacked by Johan Galtung, a Norwegian sociologist, and members of the Chilean political left.

The governments of Chile and the United States became embroiled in controversy, leading to the cancellation of the project before it had gotten fully underway. Part of the issue involved here was the rivalry between Department of State and the Department of Defense, but a large part centered around the general question of the acceptability of governmental agency sponsorship of the research of sociologists.

Jessie Bernard,[11] Gideon Sjoberg,[12] and Irving Louis Horowitz,[13] among others, have reviewed the development of the project. They have all raised questions about the propriety of research by sociologists which is sponsored by the military or other governmental agencies.[14] For example, Bernard identified several crucial issues including the ethics of funding, the responsibilities of social scientists for the uses of their findings, and the problem of censorship.[15]

According to Sjoberg: "the major problem social scientists faced in Project Camelot, and encounter in many other research projects as well, is the inability to achieve a sufficient degree of autonomy vis-a-vis the administrative-control sector of the social system that supports these research efforts."[16] Thus, Sjoberg feels that the major difficulties experienced in Project Camelot, as well as in the Michigan State University involvement in research in Vietnam under CIA funding, centered primarily around the inability of the investigators to maintain independence from their funding source and to preserve freedom of inquiry.

In his analysis, Horowitz contends that: "The question of who sponsors research is not nearly so decisive as the question of ultimate use of such information."[17] For him, the most important issue turns upon the "Knowledge for What?" question. Is it proper and appropriate for social researchers to conduct investigations which may provide authorities representing the status quo with tools for suppressing some sorts of social change and facilitating other sorts?

In summary, the debate inspired by Project Camelot was primarily about questions of appropriate sponsorship, public policy, and the relations between these two facts of social life and the conduct of social science inquiry. It is instructive in this connection to examine Sjoberg's *Ethics, Politics, and Social Research.*[18] Although the title of this volume speaks of ethics, only two of the fourteen essays, those by Richard A. Brymer and Buford Farris[19] and by Richard Colvard,[20] directly focus on the rights of research subjects in social science research. Most of the selections in that work deal with policy and sponsorship questions and are silent regarding our obligations to those we study.

In their study of a housing project, Lee Rainwater and David J. Pittman[21] indicate that they became involved in issues of ethics and sponsorship. They comment: "While many ethical issues cut across the question of sponsorship and one's charter for conducting the research, some of the most difficult ones stem from the effort to reconcile the legitimate demands of professional standards, the sponsor's needs, and the elusive public interest."[22] Although these authors do deal with subjects' rights, particularly with regard to assurances of confidentiality, the consideration of those rights is accorded secondary attention.

Peter Berger has addressed some of the issues he sees involved in the ethics of the sociologist in this book, *Invitation to Sociology,*[23] particularly in chapter 7, "Excursis: Sociological Machiavellianism and Ethics (or: How to Acquire Scruples and Keep on Cheating)." As Berger puts it: "Only he who understands the rules of the game is in a position to cheat" and "in this sense, every sociologist is a potential saboteur or swindler, as well as a putative helpmate of oppression."[24] In other words, Berger sees the ethical issues as involving a choice between adhering to or opposing the existing social order, not a question of how individual sociologists act towards individual research subjects. The heaviest emphasis is thus on the ways in which the sociologist's knowledge can be used to influence social policy or be used by individuals to alter their relationship to social policy and the administration of that policy. For Berger the question of ethics revolves around how the knowledge generated by the sociologist may be put to use, rather than how the sociologist ought to generate that knowledge from empirical observation of real living human beings.

MORALS, VALUES, AND SOCIAL PROBLEMS

A number of authors have applied the term ethics to topics that are also frequently identified as matters of morality or values. One of the clearest examples of this usage is that of Harold Orlans,[25] who identifies his discussion of the more common ethical dilemmas as a commentary on: "some of the problems commonly cast in moral terms by one or the other party to a research grant,"[26] by which he means: "simply conduct deemed proper and principled, good, honest, right, and equitable."[27] For example, he discusses the propriety of diverting allocated research funds to purposes or persons other than those stated in grant applications.

In a similar vein, John R. Seeley argues that sociologists ought to pay more attention to major social issues of society and to how the profession might help deal with these issues and problems.[28] He concludes that sociology would be of greater value and better rewarded if a profession related to society in moral and intellectual responsibility should come into being and if the profession discharged that responsibility by providing real guidance and aid to society.[29] In short, he regards an ethical sociology as one which is forcefully involved in social problem solving.

A more recent and ambitious effort in this same direction is that of Richard L. Means. In *The Ethical Imperative: The Crisis in American Values*[30] he attempts to explicate a value basis for the definition and study of social problems and social deviance. In particular he is opposed to the "subjective" definitions of such persons as Howard S. Becker. According to Means, if deviance is only that which is so labeled, then it would be incorrect and improper to designate the killing of Jews in Nazi Germany as deviant. But Means argues: "I do not think the deviant-behavior definition as expressed by Becker gives us the intellectual grounds to delineate the true nature of problems of this kind."[31] It seems dubious however, that there is sufficient consensus in American society on acceptable behavior to generate a value-based definition of deviance that would allow a "true" description of what is problematic to which all would agree.[32]

A very different approach to the problems of value orientation and ideologies is found in the writings of such students of deviance as Howard S. Becker[33] and Ned Polsky.[34] Becker has argued that all researchers of deviance have biases. Some sympathize with certain nonconformists while others are hostile to various patterns of deviance, and these biases essentially reflect value positions. He concludes by recommending that: "we take sides as our personal and political commitments dictate."[35] In other words, we ought to expose our value biases rather than pretending to an impossible value-free posture.

The necessity of recognizing one's own values and ideologies and of communicating them to respondents in participant observation is also stressed by Polsky. He argues that if this is not done, one is apt to wind up "going native" when studying criminals in their "native setting" and to become a criminal accomplice by being drawn into involvement in the behavior that one is ostensibly studying.[36]

ETHICS, THE RIGHT TO PRIVACY, AND THE STUDY OF DEVIANCE

Sociology has a long history of investigation of both public and private social behavior, and research on private social activity perhaps accounts most heavily for the current popularity of sociology as well as for its historical influence. In all of this, however, relatively short shrift has been given to the rights of the objects of investigation.

From LePlay's persistent prying into the secrets of the family budget among European workers to Kinsey's intimate inquiries into the secrets of sexual behavior among American females, social science has continually ignored, evaded, or assailed conventional limits and taboos by asserting its right to know everything that seems worth knowing about the behavior of human beings. If this poses a threat to privacy, the risk must be weighted against the gain. We now know more about human behavior than has ever been known by any society recorded in history. The question: Is this gain worth the risk?[37]

The *aristocratic contention* is Sidney Wilhelm's term for the "knowledge for knowledge's sake" argument which contends that sociologists should be unfettered in their search for data. This argument, holding that "We do because we are," allows those who invoke it to evade any ethical responsibility for their actions.[38] Wilhelm would not say that the gain is always worth the risk. Instead, he would compel us to honor the rights of humans while we pursue knowledge. The plain and unpleasant fact, however, is that the aristocratic contention is often used to justify the invasion of the privacy of individuals to study deviant behavior.

We might begin by noting that the legal doctrine of the right to privacy is not a constitutional one but has entered Common Law only within the past century, starting with an article entitled "The Right to Privacy," which appeared in the *Harvard Law Review* in December, 1890.[39] In the development of this doctrine,

> Privacy has been defined as the right of an individual to be free from undesired or unwarranted revelation to the public of matters regarding which the public is not concerned, and also as "the right of a person to be left alone," in a word the right of "inviolate personality."[40]

But it is not the legal doctrine by itself which is our major concern here. Rather, we wish to draw attention to the dilemma that arises when that doctrine is transferred to the study of deviance. How can we reconcile societal concern for solutions to problems and the necessity of public knowledge with the individual's right to be left alone and to have control over what information about himself becomes public knowledge?

If one grants, as we do, that the individual ought to be able to control what is divulged about him or about his ways of behaving, then simply to assert in research reports that subjects are protected by anonymity does not go far enough in protecting them. (Other issues involving anonymity will be discussed below.)

Herbert Kelman has stated the issue of the protection of privacy succinctly:

> In social research, protection of the subject's privacy depends directly on the manner in which his consent is secured and the confidentiality of his data is respected, since the essence of the right to privacy is that the individual himself controls what information about himself he is to disclose, to whom, at what time, and for what purposes. To the extent to which the subject is coerced into participation, or deceived about the purposes of the research, or observed without his knowledge, the principle of consent and thus his right to privacy are violated.[41]

There are several reasons why the ethics involved in the study of deviance will be examined more closely than they have in the past. The methodologies and interests of sociologists are changing: with the rise of such approaches in sociology as ethnomethodology, phenomenology, and the labeling approach, the objects of study are changing.[42] No longer is sociological scrutiny centered so exclusively on the socially disvalued and powerless. Notice the difference, for example, between the human subjects in James P. Spradley's *You Owe Yourself a Drunk*[43] (Skid Roaders) and Sherri Cavan's *Liquor License* (middle-class citizens).[44] Skid Road alcoholics are socially powerless persons with a low degree of perceived social utility whose rights can be violated with impunity. After all, why worry about the human rights of "drunken bums?" (This is explicitly *not* intended as a comment on the ethical nature of Spradley's research, but only as an observation about his research population.) However, when one studies the range of public drinking places as did Cavan in her urban ethnography, middle-or upper-class citizens who frequent public drinking places are as liable to be subjects of investigation as are the Skid Road denizens. While we may decry the fact that as sociologists we tend to be more concerned with protection of persons like ourselves than we are with the human rights of the "bad guys," it is nevertheless fairly easy to document such biased concern. Thus, when powerless and influential citizens are equally likely to be subjects of study, the sociologists and the "good guys" both begin to be bothered about the ethical implications of the methodologies of those studies.

A second development, not to be dismissed lightly, is the growing organization and militancy of the powerless themselves. The militant articulation of the grievances found in the black communities, the coalitions and unions form by welfare clients, and the organization of Chicanos and American Indians are all indications of the resistance of those who have been traditionally defined as deviants or as fair game for sociological probing to a continuation of that definition, and to continued exploitation in any form, including being infringed upon for research purposes by the academician—social snooper.[45]

Other social trends will also compel us to pay more attention to the rights of individuals. Certainly the Supreme Court decisions granting fuller legal rights to the criminally accused and directing juvenile courts to observe the civil rights of youths being processed in such tribunals reflect this concern about assaults on privacy and individual rights in a mass society. Complete freedom to pry into the lives of relatively powerless deviant groups will probably not continue as such prying may be restricted by legal restraints.

The concern expressed in the popular press over invasion of privacy has also helped to raise the level of public concern about various kinds of investigators. Works such as Vance Packard's *The Naked Society*[46] and Myron Brenton's *The Privacy Invaders*[47] have sounded the alarm over such matters as prying on people without their knowledge for credit investigations, fund-raising campaigns, and the like.

A more scholarly documentation of how information about citizens is collected and maintained is found in *On Record: Files and Dossiers in American Life,*[48] edited by Stanton Wheeler. The fourteen essays in that work survey a wide gamut of organizations ranging from schools through consumer credit, insurance, and governmental agencies to mental hospitals. These reports suggest that not only does the citizen not have control over information about himself, he is frequently quite unaware that it has even been collected. Dossier making is a pervasive feature of modern society.

As important as these broad forces have been, however, the most important pressure on us to protect the rights of human subjects has been the Public Health Service mandate for the protection of human subjects in research.[49] That edict grew out of the experiences of medical experimentation and experimentation with various drugs, given impetus by Henry K. Beecher's documentation of numerous cases in which hazadous experimentation was conducted on human beings without their consent.[50] Two important features of this mandate are: (1) the demand that the right of privacy of individuals be protected; and (2) the requirement that research subjects give their consent before participation in research and experimentation. As a mechanism for enforcing these requirements, the Department of Health, Education and Welfare requires a series of reviews of research proposals, including scrutiny by an institutionally designated committee on the rights of human subjects.

To add strength to this demand, a requirement is that all research, whether funded or unfunded, must be reviewed by the institutional Committee on Rights of Human Subjects prior to its initiation, and ongoing inquiry must be monitored to assess the degree to which the investigatory practices match the guarantees stipulated in the research program.

However, there is a major difficulty in these requirements. It is relatively easy to ascertain whether or not a research proposal has been reviewed by the Human Subjects Committee if that research program has been submitted for federal financing. In this case, the proposal for funding must have written stipulation that the proposal has been so reviewed. But it is much harder to ensure that monitoring of ongoing inquiry has been carried out. It is even more difficult to guarantee that unfunded research has been reviewed by anyone other than the researcher himself. In short, we have yet to develop any viable structure for policing the research activities of the unfunded or free-lance investigator. At the same time, there is no reason to assume that the researcher not supported by a grant will always manage to avoid infringing upon the rights of human subjects.[51]

Indeed, how is one to decide when a sociologist is engaged in research or nonresearch? As the sociologist reflects on his past experiences, he may well use recollections of the actions and behaviors of others which he observed with no research intent involved. For example, Reece McGee reports that it was only years later that he could put a sociological analysis frame around a behavioral segment he observed in the segregated South,[52] and Sherri Cavan reports that she lived in the Haight-Ashbury district of San Francisco for some time before she decided to systematize her observations, some of which she made before she embarked on a deliberate study of hippies.[53]

The sociologist usually embarks upon a research protocol, however, with the intent of doing research. Particularly in investigations of social deviance, accidental or unplanned investigation is unlikely, because relatively few sociologists interact on a sustained basis with burglars, "queers," "crazies," political radicals, "hookers," and the like. Instead, sociologists are usually from the square world, only occasionally making forays into the social environments of the outsiders in our society. (It might be added that some sociologists never seem in contact with the real world!) The researcher simply does not encounter deviant folks by accident, at least not with the frequency necessary to sustain a research program. Thus, we usually find ourselves doing studies such as the one by Charles A. Varni of swingers, which he describes as a "form and degree of participant observation" but which actually was based on interviews with persons who asserted that they had engaged in swinging.[54] In any event, Varni had to go out and drum up study subjects.

Those few terse statements that have appeared in the sociological literature regarding the rights of subjects have typically placed too much trust in the good will and good intentions of the investigator. For example, in their discussion of grounded theory, Barney G. Glaser and Anselm Strauss say that in order to apply theory, the individual practitioner must have control over the situation. They dismiss the issue of the ethics of such control with the statement: "we shall not consider here the ethical problems involved in controlling situations."[55] They enter the caveat that they refer only to "benign controls" and not to "absolute diabolic control over man." But who is to say what is benign control and what is diabolic control? If the individual is unaware that he is being controlled, is this fact alone not sufficient to merit calling the control diabolic? How are we to assess the intent or motive of the controller accurately enough so that all would agree that the motivation is benign or diabolic?

This reference to ethics in the Glaser and Strauss work appears in the discussion of the *application* of grounded theory. There is no analysis of ethics in the larger part of the volume devoted to the *generation* of grounded theory and to *strategies* for qualitative research.

A striking example of placing faith in the researcher and then ignoring the ethical problem as if it will simply go away is the following. The National Academy of Sciences, through its Committee on Science in Public Policy, and the Social Science Research Council, through its Committee on Problems and Policy, cooperatively sponsored the volume *The Behavioral and Social Sciences: Outlook and Needs.*[56] Although this book includes statements on values and ethics, one finds nothing more than optimistic public relations statements and empty shibboleths when seeking guidance for evaluating the ethical nature of the research enterprise. For example, speaking of the social scientist, the committees state: "there are times, however, when the scientist becomes an advocate of some procedure on the basis of his evidence and the probability that adopting the procedure will help to meet a desired end. Here his roles as scientist and citizen become difficult to distinguish, and it is out of such situations that the more serious ethical conflicts arise. Social scientists are aware of these problems."[57] Or, the committees refer to several propositions such as: "participation in behavioral investigation should be voluntary and based on informed consent to the extent that this is consistent with the objectives of the research." A second proposition asserts: "it is fully consistent with the protection of privacy that, in the absence of full information, consent be based on trust in the qualified investigator and the integrity of the institution under whose auspices the research is conducted. Professional organizations of behavioral and social scientists accept these propositions and bring effective force to bear to assure that they are observed. There are borderline cases however, and the ethical questions in such cases are settled, in part, by a give-and-take process in which accommodation between protection of privacy and obtaining necessary information is gradually achieved."[58] These surely are not very useful guides to how these differences are to be resolved or the direction that resolution is to take.

The committees note that: "there are many threats to privacy, of course, that are unrelated to behavioral and social science research. Surveillance by private agents, credit organizations, and mere curiosity seekers is insidious, in sharp contrast to organized scientific efforts, which have ethical controls built into them."[59] The committee ends its considerations of ethics by noting that various organizations of social scientists, including the American Sociological Association, have developed codes of ethics. According to their evaluation of these codes: "The primary purpose of the codes is to protect the public and the demands made upon it and in services received, and thus, indirectly, to enhance confidence in and respect for the profession. Because new ethical problems are always arising, if the codes are to be made more than pious statements they will require frequent revision to keep them abreast of specific new issues that behavioral and social scientists will be facing in the future."[60] We might respond, "You can say that again!"

The National Academy of Science and Social Science Research Council report does not come to grips with the issues involved in the ethical responsibilities of social science investigators toward human subjects. Instead, it is primarily concerned with the policy implications of social science research and new social science knowledge, and with how the profession best ought to relate to society as a whole, or perhaps more accurately to the policy-makers and decision-makers of the larger society. It does not scrutinize the meaning of the right to privacy as far as the individual citizen is concerned, nor does it explore in any detail the notion of informed consent; on the contrary, it endorses the proposition that in many cases informed consent is a luxury which the social scientist in his role as investigator simply cannot afford. Implicit faith is placed in the good sense of the social science investigator to do "what's right."

This attitude will not do. Possession of the Ph.D. signifies a number of things, but it is exceedingly doubtful that conferral of that degree automatically produces in the recipient sound judgment, wisdom, and a deep-seated respect for the autonomous individuality of one's fellow man. Indeed, as Edward A. Shils has pointed out, the process of acquiring that degree may well serve to alienate one from his fellow man.[61]

Furthermore, we would point out that the code of ethics of the American Sociological Association is, like other codes of ethics, designed primarily to do two things either independently or simultaneously. First, it is intended to provide the trappings of professionalization for a fairly large number of people working at a common occupation.[62] Secondly, it is supposed to protect individual members of that occupation from infringement or harrassment by other members of that or another occupation. Upon finishing his term as chairman of the American Sociological Association's Committee on Professional Ethics, Lewis A. Coser opined that the future work of the committee would largely be devoted to settling disputes between professional sociologists on charges of plagiarism, and between professors and graduate students on charges of exploitation.[63] In both cases, the primary intent of the code is to protect the members of the occupation, not the public. And what is more important for the purposes of this discussion, the code is virtually silent on the individual rights of the subjects or of the clients of the profession of sociology.[64]

As one outgrowth of their study of the impact of modern society and technology upon privacy, Oscar M. Ruebhausen, a lawyer, and Orville G. Brim, Jr., a sociologist, enunciated seven principles for inclusion in a general code of ethics for behavioral research, following a review of what they saw as the fundamental problems in the relationship between science, technology, and the right to privacy.[65] But there are problems with their statement as well. For one, Ruebhausen and Brim leave too much leeway for the investigator by including such equivocations as: *"whenever possible,* both consent and anonymity should be sought in behavioral research." (emphasis added)[66] Similarly, they aver: "the minimal requirements of privacy seem to call for the retention of the private data in a manner that assures its maximum confidentiality *consistent with the integrity of the research.*" (emphasis added)[67] It strikes us that these escape clauses leave the door open to the aristocratic contention and allow the researcher the luxury of saying: "I'll do all I can to protect the rights of subjects as long as it doesn't inconvenience me or my research."

A second major problem with these suggestions is that they over-rely on the integrity of the researcher and his administrative superiors. For example, Ruebhausen and Brim declare that "needing no more than a passing mention, is the integrity of the behavioral research scientist, which, along with his interest in science, must be assumed as a basic prerequisite."[68] They argue that this integrity will protect the rights of subjects. But if that is so, why do we need a code of ethics and control machinery?

A final problem with this formulation is that it calls for a review board to be composed of the responsible officials of the institutions financing, administering and sponsoring the research, all of whom may be assumed to have vested interests in maintaining the research program of the institution.[69] We hold that what is called for is an autonomous review board that includes outsiders without such vested interests.

The work of Eugene J. Webb and his associates is one more example of dodging the ethical issue.[70] In the preface to the volume *Unobtrusive Measures: Nonreactive Research in the Social Sciences,* the authors state that "in presenting these novel methods, we have purposely avoided consideration of the ethical issues which they raise."[71] Webb and his collaborators do discuss the question of ethics on the two following pages, indicating that the secret recording of jury deliberations or of conversations of individuals in bed together have lead to moral revulsion of many social scientists and that the arousal of anxiety or aggression may well have permanent psychological effects on subjects. However, they report that there are currently no guidelines which would aid the researcher attempting to select an ethical approach to his research. Moreover, they propose no guidelines. Instead, one finds mention in their volume of the techniques of wearing rubber heels to sneak up and eavesdrop on conversations and acknowledgment that hiding microphones to collect data is a controversial tactic when employed in certain settings, and illegal in many.[72] They offer the suggestion that the best way to hide a microphone is to rig it in a fake hearing device so that the unsuspecting subject will tend to lean over directly into what he perceives to be a hearing aid, thereby giving a better recording.[73]

An additional anecdote in *Unobtrusive Measures* relating to the ethical issue deals with a political campaign manager who, unable to interview his opponent's campaign manager, contrived to search through his opponent's wastebasket daily, thus allowing him to "ingeniously (although perhaps not ethically)" obtain data bearing upon the plans, strategies, and activities of his opponent.[74] Would this episode have been seen as unethical if the rummaging through the wastebasket had been done by a social scientist rather than by a campaign manager? Should the search for data be unrestrained, or must we consider the methods by which these observations of witting or unwitting subjects are gathered?

In addition to the violations of the basic rights of others—and we reiterate that subjects do indeed have such rights, even if they happen to be people of low social value—there are risks to the field of sociology which are incurred when the rights of subjects are not respected. Others have pointed to some potential harmful consequences to sociology which result through failure to respect the human dignity of research subjects. One line of commentary can be found in observations by Theodore M. Mills who observes that the use of laboratory manipulation or of deception, can simply be a process of creating the findings which one wishes to discover.[75] This is scarcely a process which will lead to a cumulative social science, a point also made by Erikson and discussed more fully below.[76]

It should be noted that Mill's biting diatribe against observers and experimenters inflicting themselves upon subjects frequently deals more with matters of private sensibilities than with matters of ethics. A situation in which one is discomfited by observing "an attractive young lady [who] moves over to the mirror, fluffs her hair, strokes her eyebrows, then with her little finger probes deeply into her nose"[77] is more a matter of the private sensibilities of the observer than it is a matter of ethics. We would argue that the ethical concern should not be concentrated on the reaction of the researcher to this bit of private behavior when he only intended to watch a contrived laboratory exercise, but on the whole arrangement whereby the observer watches the young woman without her knowledge or voluntary acquiescence to that observation.

The study by John F. Lofland and Robert A. Lejune directly involves the matter of ethics and prompted an incisive exchange of opinions.[78] In this research the investigators arranged for students to disguise themselves, go to Alcoholics Anonymous meetings, and record the frequencies and types of interactions which took place. One negative response to this study was offered by Fred Davis, who raised some fundamental questions having to do with the propriety of deceiving subjects as to the intent of one's research, the lack of consideration of the rights of respondents to control the release of information about themselves, and the dangers of closing off an important area of research when other AA chapters learned about how one New York chapter had been used to serve academic purposes.[79] Lofland's reply, it seems to us, conforms fairly closely to the aristocratic contention referred to above.[80] He argues that the approach was the only one which would have worked, and besides, no harm was done to the respondents or to Alcoholics Anonymous as an association.

A more comprehensive analysis of the problems of disguised observation is that of Kai T. Erikson.[81] He lists four ethical objections to the practice of participant observation being conducted by a disguised observer. According to Erikson "disguised observation constitutes an ugly invasion of privacy and is, on that ground alone, objectionable."[82] Disguised observation also runs the risk of destroying the public faith in sociology and closing off any future research with those whose privacy has been invaded. Then too, the disguised participant observer is most frequently a graduate student who is forced into a role which contains some very real dangers of psychological and moral discomforture. Finally, the adoption of a disguise and the impersonation of a group member means that the data gathered by surreptitious participant observation tactics are tainted by the presence of the observer in ways which make a meaningful analysis of those data almost impossible.

Erikson recognizes the difficulty of drawing a clear-cut line between ethical and unethical investigative activity. However, he proposes some recommendations which might deal with at least one end point of the continuum from highly ethical to highly unethical. He maintains that "first it is unethical for a sociologist to *deliberately misrepresent* his identity for the purpose of entering a private domain *to which he is not otherwise eligible;* and second, that it is unethical for a sociologist to *deliberately misrepresent* the character of the research in which he is engaged." (emphasis in the original)[83]

The position statement by Erikson is a fairly strong one with which we are in agreement, although it may not be emphatic enough. In the first place, he suggests that "in point of sheer volume, of course, the problem is relatively small, for disguised participant observation is probably one of the rarest research techniques in use amongst sociologists."[84] This claim may be open to challenge in the contemporary scene, given the growing popularity of new interests in such things as labeling theory, ethnomethodology, "the sociology of the absurd," and the social construction of reality. These perspectives often imply the use of unobtrusive, disguised observation. Secondly Erikson intended his statement to apply only to the role of the disguised participant observer, not to some other more general issues such as disguised observations in non-participatory research or to the disguised purposes of inquiry which can be hidden even in such apparently open methodologies as survey research.[85]

A recent research endeavor by Laud Humphreys has generated considerable discussion of the ethics involved in the study of deviance. His investigation, culminating in his *Tearoom Trade*,[86] involved his acting as a participant in the public rest rooms ("tearooms") used by male homosexuals for fleeting impersonal sex acts. He served as a "watchqueen" or lookout in various tearooms, observing the transitory social encounters of fellatio. Then, in order to determine the social characteristics of those involved in public sex, he noted license numbers of the cars driven by some of the participants. Later, by use of vehicle registration lists, he included these persons as part of a larger survey research program and hence gained social demographic data about them. Thus, the survey research led respondents to reveal data about themselves that was used for purposes other than those which were presented to them. Portions of Humphreys's research report were published in *Trans-action*,[87] which led to the "Sociological Snoopers and Journalistic Moralizers" exchange between Nicholas von Hoffman, a journalist, and Irving Louis Horowitz and Lee Rainwater, sociologists and editors of *Trans-action*.[88]

The essence of von Hoffman's criticism is: "No information is valuable enough to obtain by nipping away at personal liberty."[89] The Horowitz and Rainwater reply deserves reading in its entirety. They assert that such research is necessary, that it serves the valuable purpose of providing knowledge on which to base public policy, and that: "Humphreys' follow-up had to be performed with tact and with skill precisely because he discovered that so many of the people in his survey were married men and family men."[90] But this later assertion rings false, for by Humphreys's own report the social characteristics of those men he had observed became clear only in the household interview conducted a considerable time *after* the observations were made.[91]

The references to anonymity of respondents also raise interesting questions. Typically, in research dealing with deviants, the problem of preserving anonymity can be sloughed off by an unconcerned researcher (unless the police or other regulatory agents come to believe that he has important inside information that might be useful to them).[92] As mentioned previously, garden-variety deviants are typically the powerless of society; thus the researcher is under much less pressure to maintain the anonymity of respondents in a survey of Skid Road dwellers in a given city than in an investigation of the power structure of that same community. After all, there is only one mayor of a city, and politicians are more apt to read sociological treatises than are "winos." Furthermore, one's audience is much more apt to identify from various clues which city commissioner is being discussed, and to care about it, than to be able to identify, or care about, some drunk.

We often face a difficult choice in the publication of sociological research reports. If the locale and participants are not disguised, then anonymity is not assured; but if it is disguised, then replication becomes more difficult. In the past this dilemma probably applied less to studies of deviance and to deviant populations than to other areas of sociological endeavor. At least, the researcher who was unconcerned about the privacy of others could violate that privacy without incurring the wrath of his subjects or his sociological peers. However, we would assert that if sociologists ever begin to study the more powerful deviants, including large-scale criminals such as "white collar offenders," then the problems of anonymity in the publication of research results will be forced on the student of deviance as well.

A case in point is William J. Chambliss's report of the vice power structure in a city he calls "Rainfall West."[93] The use of this name for the city, as well as thinly disguised alterations of persons' names, lead us to believe that this is surely a report of Seattle, Washington, and that if anyone cared to do so, it would be a relatively easy task to identify the major figures such as "Sheriff McAllister" about whom Chambliss speaks. If the city is not Seattle, then the problem remains, for surely others as well will believe it is Seattle.

It appears that there are two ways to resolve the dilemma between anonymity and the need to know. One is for the researcher who conducts studies of important persons who have transgressed the law to be as forthright as the journalist about identifying the persons being discussed. In this role the sociologist is a moral reformer and journalist, and he runs the strong risk of reaction by those written about. The alternative is not to discuss the setting or the persons and to maintain complete anonymity in reporting. This solution makes replication more difficult, perhaps, but does allow the researcher to remain honest in his writings.[94]

Finally, let us emphasize that we hold that sociologists ought to be concerned about maximizing the rights of research subjects even in the absence of any pressure to do so from the subjects or the larger public. Sociologists have no business treating "bums," "crooks," or other outsiders as second-class citizens. At the very least, we are convinced that the continued lack of attention to the ethical strictures on the study of deviance could endanger the only natural resource of sociology: the cooperation of the people being studied.

NOTES

[1] The reader should consult Travis Hirschi, "Procedural Rules and the Study of Deviant Behavior," *Social Problems* 21 (Fall 1973): 159–73, for a broad, incisive critique both of theoretical and methodological assumptions in the study of deviance. Hirschi notes a number of assumptions and procedural rules that have hindered the development of sound empirical propositions in this area of inquiry.

[2] Some issues raised here were previously discussed in Joseph F. Jones, "Unethical Experimentation is Unnecessary," paper presented at the Pacific Sociological Association annual meetings, April 1972, Portland, Oregon.

[3] John I. Kitsuse and Aaron V. Cicourel, "A Note on the Use of Official Statistics," *Social Problems* 11(Fall 1963): 131–39; see also Cicourel, *The Social Organization of Juvenile Justice* (New York: John Wiley and Sons, 1968).

[4] Jack D. Douglas, *The Social Meanings of Suicide* (Princeton, N.J.: Princeton University Press, 1967).

[5] Ned Polsky, *Hustlers, Beats, and Others* (Chicago: Aldine Publishing Co., 1967), pp. 117–49.

[6] For example, see Jack D. Douglas, ed., *Observations on Deviance* (New York: Random House, 1970); Douglas, ed., *Research on Deviance* (New York: Random House, 1972).

[7] Earlier discussions had, of course, taken place. See, for example, Joseph H. Fichter and William L. Kolb, "Ethical Limitations on Sociological Reporting," *American Sociological Review* 18 (October 1953): 544–50; see also the statement "Participant Observation and the Military: An Exchange" by Lewis A. Coser, Julius A. Roth, Mortimer A. Sullivan, Jr., and Stuart A. Queen, *American Sociological Review* 24 (June 1959): 397–400.

[8] A notable exception is Glazer's recent volume, *The Research Adventure,* in which all three of these topics are touched upon. This work is also notable for the amount of previously unpublished commentary by other field researchers it contains. Myron Glazer, *The Research Adventure* (New York: Random House, 1972). Peterson includes the issue of protection of human subjects in a wide-ranging commentary on social research which includes a defense of the United States Census Bureau and a defense of academic freedom. See William Peterson, "Forbidden Knowledge," in Saad Z. Nagi and Ronald G. Corwin, eds., *The Social Context of Research* (New York: John Wiley and Sons, 1972).

[9] Much of the literature dealing with ethical issues in research will be omitted in this essay because it, like the literature dealing with Project Camelot used here for illustrative purposes, does not deal with the study of deviancy.

A classic in the field of social science ethics is the so-called jury-bugging case, wherein arrangements were made to secretly tape-record jury deliberations. For an account of this research and the responses it evoked, see Ted R. Vaughn, "Governmental Intervention in Social Research: Political and Ethical Dimensions in the Wichita Jury Recordings," in Gideon Sjoberg, ed., *Ethics, Politics, and Social Research* (Cambridge, Mass.: Schenkman Publishing Company, 1967), pp. 50–77.

Waldo W. Burchard studied the reactions of lawyers, political scientists and sociologists to the issues involved in this case. He concluded that all three types of respondents favored this kind of study, although the lawyers favored it less strongly than the other two professions. See: Waldo W. Burchard, "A Study of Attitudes Toward the Use of Concealed Devices in Social Science Research," *Social Forces* 36 (October 1957): 111–16.

Another celebrated case is: Stanley Milgram, "Obedience and Disobedience to Authority," *Human Relations* 18 (February 1965): 57–75. Milgram deceived subjects into applying what they thought were electrical shocks up to and beyond the point where these shocks would be life threatening. Some of the deceived subjects reacted rather markedly to their own behavior. Also see Diana Baumrind, "Some Thoughts on Ethics of Research: After Reading Milgram's Study of Obedience," *American Psychologist* 19 (June 1964): 421–23.

More recently Milgram has described the obedience experiment more fully and has offered a summary of his responses to criticisms of the ethical nature of the experiment, including Baumrind's criticisms: Milgram, *Obedience to Authority* (New York: Harper and Row, 1974). See especially Appendix I "Problems of Ethics in Research" where Milgram defends the ethical nature of the research on the basis that it leads to moral development for the subjects.

A number of studies have been aborted as a result of the researcher's discovering that the manipulations were having unexpected, and frightening effects. See Phillip G. Zimbardo, "The Pathology of Imprisonment," in Elliot Aronson and Robert Helmeich, eds., *Social Psychology in the World Today* (New York: Van Nostrand Reinhold Co., 1973).

[10] Irving Louis Horowitz, "The Life and Death of Project Camelot," *Transaction* 3 (November-December 1965): 3–7, 44–47.

[11] Jesse Bernard, "Letter to the Editor," *The American Sociologist* 1 (November 1965): 24–25.

[12] Gideon Sjoberg, *Ethics, Politics, and Social Research,* pp. 141–61.

[13] Horowitz, "The Life and Death of Project Camelot." Also see Horowitz, ed., *The Rise and Fall of Project Camelot: Studies in the Relationship of Social Science and Practical Politics* (Cambridge, Mass.: MIT Press, 1967).

[14] This is a point which has received considerable attention in the field of anthropology. See the exchange "Toward an Ethics for Anthropologists," *Current Anthropology* 12 (June 1971): 321–56.

[15] Bernard, "Letter to the Editor."

[16] Sjoberg, *Ethics, Politics, and Social Research,* p. 152.

[17] Horowitz, *The Rise and Fall of Project Camelot,* p. 517.

[18] Sjoberg, *Ethics, Politics, and Social Research.*

[19] Richard A. Brymer and Buford Farris, "Ethical and Political Dilemmas in the Investigation of Deviance: A Study of Juvenile Delinquency," in Sjoberg, *Ethics, Politics, and Social Research,* pp. 297–318. It is interesting that the editor of this volume, Sjoberg, is listed (p. 303) as advocating a secret research role even if this might require countenancing delinquent acts. The secret role was not, however, adopted.

[20] Richard Colvard, "Interaction and Identification in Reporting Field Research: A Critical Reconsideration of Protective Procedures," in Sjoberg, *Ethics, Politics, and Social Research,* pp. 319–58.

[21] Lee Rainwater and David J. Pittman, "Ethical Problems in Studying a Politically Sensitive and Deviant Community," *Social Problems* 14 (Summer 1966): 357–66.

[22] Ibid., p. 354.

[23] Peter Berger, *Invitation to Sociology* (New York: Doubleday & Co., 1963).

[24] Ibid., p. 152.

[25] Harold Orlans, "Ethical Problems in the Relations of Research Sponsors and Investigators," in Sjoberg, *Ethics, Politics, and Social Research,* pp. 3–24. An example of concentrating on the "morality" of specific research behaviors is provided in Richard A. Berk and Joseph M. Adams, "Establishing Rapport with Deviant Groups," *Social Problems* 18 (Summer 1970): 102–17. Berk and Adams deal with the "morality" issue (pp. 115–16) in the context of the obligation of the researcher to inform the police of illegal activities performed or planned by the subjects. They note that it is incumbent on the researcher to inform the subjects that such reporting might take place, thereby implying some consideration of the notion of informed consent, but this issue is not squarely faced.

[26] Ibid., p. 3.

[27] Ibid.

[28] John R. Seeley, "The Making and Taking of Problems: Toward an Ethical Stance," *Social Problems* 14 (Summer 1966): 382–89.

[29] Ibid., p. 389.

[30] Richard L. Means, *The Ethical Imperative: Crisis in American Values* (New York: Doubleday & Co., 1969).

[31] Ibid., p. 16.

[32] On this point see, *inter alia,* Don C. Gibbons and Joseph F. Jones, "Some Critical Notes on Current Definitions of Deviance," *Pacific Sociological Review* 14 (January 1971): 20–37 and adapted in this volume, chapter four.

[33] Howard S. Becker, "Whose Side Are We On?" *Social Problems* 14 (Winter 1967): 239–347.

[34] Polsky, *Hustlers, Beats, and Others.*

³⁵ Becker, "Whose Side Are We On?" See also our discussion in chapter one.

³⁶ Polsky, *Hustlers, Beats and Others,* pp. 131–32.

³⁷ Daniel Lerner, ed., *The Human Meaning of the Social Sciences* (New York: Meridan Books, 1959), p. 7.

³⁸ Sidney Wilhelm, "Scientific Unaccountability and Moral Accountability," in Irving Louis Horowitz, ed., *The New Sociology* (New York: Oxford University Press, 1964), pp. 181–87; a recent example of invoking the aristocratic contention is Galliher's analysis of the code of ethics of the American Sociological Association. Among other things, Galliher (p. 98) suggests that the code be changed from "All research should avoid causing personal harm to subjects used in research" to "All research should avoid causing personal harm to subjects used in research unless it is evident that the gain by society and/or science is such that it offsets the probable magnitude of individual discomfort." Galliher would further have it that professional judgments of what is probable harm would be adequate. But who is to say that "science" can be benefited by causing personal harm? Presumably other scientists, who may well place the advancement of answers to their curiosity above the rights of subjects. See John F. Galliher, "The Protection of Human Subjects: A Reexamination of the Professional Code of Ethics," *The American Sociologist* 8 (August 1973): 93–100.

³⁹ Samuel D. Warren and Louis D. Brandeis, "The Right to Privacy," *Harvard Law Review.* 4 (December 15, 1890): 193–221.

⁴⁰ Samuel H. Hofstadter and George Horowitz, *The Right of Privacy* (New York: Central Book Co., 1964), pp. 2–3.

⁴¹ Herbert Kelman, *A Time to Speak* (San Francisco: Jossey-Bass, 1968), p. 204.

⁴² The revival of interest in qualitative methodology and the development of ethnomethodology has resulted in methodology texts dealing with these procedures. A sampling of the diverse discussions of ethical issues in them includes the following: William J. Filstead's *Qualitative Methodology* contains a collection of six articles under the heading of "Ethical Problems in Field Studies" (although the essay by J. A. Barnes, "Some Ethical Problems in Modern Field-work" comes closer to what we have identified as issues of public policy and morality). See William J. Filstead, ed., *Qualitative Methodology: Firsthand Involvement with the Social World* (Chicago: Markham Publishing Co., 1970).

Leonard Bickman and Thomas Henchy frequently refer to the need for a concern with ethical issues in the introductory chapter of their edited volume, but the selections which are included do not address those issues. Leonard Bickman and Thomas Henchy, eds., *Beyond the Laboratory: Field Research in Social Psychology* (New York: McGraw Hill Book Co., 1972).

Finally, Matthew Speier has authored what purports to be an introduction to "doing" ethnomethodology which is completely silent on the rights of the subjects to be protected from being unobtrusively observed, secretly filmed and/or tape recorded by students, techniques which he recommends. Matthew Speier, *How to Observe Face-to-Face Communication: A Sociological Introduction* (Pacific Palisades, Calif.: Goodyear Publishing Co., 1973).

[43] James P. Spradley, *You Owe Yourself a Drunk* (Boston: Little, Brown and Co., 1970).

[44] Sherri Cavan, *Liquor License* (Chicago: Aldine Publishing Co., 1966).

[45] Becker makes a similar point concerning the study of populations in general. Becker, "Whose Side Are We On?", p. 243. For an account of a social survey which met with organized resistance from persons traditionally defined as powerless (poor blacks), see Eric Josephson, "Resistance to Community Surveys," *Social Problems* 18 (Summer 1970): 117–29. Ethel Sawyer has attempted, not very successfully in our opinion, to raise some of these issues as they relate to the black researcher in the black community. Ethel Sawyer, "Methodological Problems in Studying So-Called 'Deviant' Communities," in Joyce Ladner, ed., *The Death of White Sociology* (New York: Vintage Press, 1973).

[46] Vance Packard, *The Naked Society* (New York: David McKay, 1964).

[47] Myron Brenton, *The Privacy Invaders* (New York: Coward-McCann, 1964).

[48] Stanton Wheeler, ed., *On Record: Files and Dossiers in American Life* (New York: Russell Sage Foundation, 1969); See also Malcolm Warner and Michael Stone, *The Data Bank Society* (London: George Allen and Unwin Ltd., 1970). James B. Rule, *Private Lives and Public Surveillance: Social Control in the Computer Age* (New York: Schocken Books, 1974).

[49] U.S. Department of Health, Education and Welfare, "Protection of the Individual as a Research Subject" (Washington, D.C.: U.S. Government Printing Office, 1969). Also see "Protection of Human Subjects," Chapters 1–40 in *Grants Administration Manual* (Washington, D.C.: U.S. Government Printing Office, 1971). A sociologically oriented research report of the ethical practices and beliefs of research physicians is provided by Barber *et al.,* who conducted both an extensive survey of hospitals and an intensive study of two hospitals. See Bernard Barber, John J. Lally, Julia Loughlin Makarushka and Daniel Sullivan, *Research on Human Subjects: Problems of Social Control in Medical Experimentation* (New York: Russell Sage Foundation, 1973).

The entire Spring, 1969, issue of *Daedalus* is devoted to "Ethical Aspects of Experimentation with Human Subjects." Note that most of this discussion deals with medical and/or pharmacological research.

A recent comprehensive (1159 pages) case book on the subject of experimentation is Jay Katz, ed., *Experimentation with Human Beings* (New York: Russell Sage Foundation, 1972). The thrust of this volume is not to provide answers but to provoke discussion and study, and it is primarily devoted to disciplines other than sociology. Also see Richard W. Wertz, ed., *Readings on Ethical and Social Issues in Biomedicine* (Englewood Cliffs, N.J.: Prentice-Hall, 1973); Preston

Williams, ed., *Ethical Issues in Biology and Medicine* (Cambridge, Mass.: Schenkman Publishing Co., 1973).

[50] Henry K. Beecher, "Ethics and Clinical Research," *The New England Journal of Medicine* 274 (June 16, 1966): 1354–60.

[51] This is a seldom discussed implication of the so-called publish or perish syndrome in universities. As pressure mounts for research publications, the aspiring scholar is tempted to put his future before the rights of subjects. cf. Ibid., pp. 1359–60. Beecher's view is that data which have been improperly obtained should not be published for "failure to obtain publication would discourage unethical experimentation." The data presented by Barber *et al.,* documents the effects of the pressure to publish on the young physician researcher, and upon those who do not feel adequately rewarded, leading to a lack of concern for the ethics of their research. See Barber, *Research on Human Subjects,* chapter 6 and *passim.*

[52] Reece McGee, *Points of Departure* (Hinsdale, Ill.: The Dryden Press, 1972), pp. 151–53.

[53] Sherri Cavan, *Hippies of the Haight* (St. Louis, Mo.: New Critics Press, 1972), pp. 32–33. An additional problem with this work is that after making the decision to conduct a study, Cavan did not tell her acquaintances and informants that she was collecting data from them, thus she failed to obtain their consent to be studied.

[54] Charles A. Varni, "An Exploratory Study of Spouse Swapping," *Pacific Sociological Review* 15 (October 1972): 507–22. Varni reports that he placed advertisements in newspapers to attract persons to be interviewed, but that he never informed them of his research interest. Why not? Although Kelman speaks of the training of social psychologists, his statement appears to have a more general application: "What concerns me is not so much that deception is used, but precisely that it is used without question. . . . I sometimes feel that we are training a generation of students who do not know that there is any other way of doing experiments in our field, who feel that deception is as much *de riguer* as significance at the .05 level. Too often deception is used not as a last resort, but as a matter of course. Our attitude seems to be that if you can deceive, why tell the truth?" Kelman, *A Time to Speak,* p. 211.

[55] Barney G. Glaser and Anselm L. Strauss, *The Discovery of Grounded Theory* (Chicago: Aldine Publishing Co., 1967), p. 245.

[56] The Behavioral and Social Sciences Survey Committee, *The Behavioral and Social Sciences: Outlook and Needs* (Englewood Cliffs, N.J.: Prentice-Hall, 1969). See the "Review Symposium," *American Sociological Review* 35 (April 1970): 329–41 for generally laudatory comments on this book, especially the statement by Charles P. Loomis (p. 336) that the book contains "a praise worthy chapter on ethics for practitioners."

[57] The Behavioral and Social Survey Committee, *The Behavioral and Social Sciences,* p. 129.

[58] Ibid., p. 37.

⁵⁹ Ibid., pp. 131–32. Implicit in this is a reference to the field of medicine, with its code of ethics and peer review. That these don't work to protect the subject is attested to by Beecher's article referred to previously. The work of Barber *et al.,* is germane: "Our data show that socialization into scientific values does occur in medical school but socialization into humane treatment of human subjects has yet to be brought into its proper place in medical education." Barber, *Research on Human Subjects,* p. 8.

A recent case is that of the so-called Tuskegee Study. This study, originally established by the United States Public Health Service to evaluate the efficacy of the heavy metals and arsenic treatment for syphilis used experimental and control (untreated) groups. Several aspects of this study are worth noting. One is that the reporting of this experiment was begun in 1936, but a public furor did not develop until 1972. (All of the subjects were black; see our comments above on the powerless.) Another is that members of the control group were left untreated even after penicillin became the proven, effective cure for syphilis. See "The 40-Year Death Watch," *Medical World News* 13 (August 18, 1972): 15–17.

⁶⁰ The Behavioral and Social Science Survey Committee, *The Behavioral and Social Sciences,* p. 133. For a discussion of the ways in which changes in technique force ethical issues on the medical profession see "Ethical Questions Hippocrates Did Not Have to Face," *Medical World News* 13 (July 14, 1972): 37–50.

⁶¹ Edward A. Shils, "Social Inquiry and the Autonomy of the Individual," in Lerner, *The Human Meaning of the Social Sciences,* pp. 149–51. On this point, see Richard T. Morris and Bodel J. Sherlock, "Decline of Ethics and the Rise of Cynicism in Dental School," *Journal of Health and Social Behavior* 12 (December 1971): 290–99 and Howard S. Becker and Blanche Geer, "The Fate of Idealism in Medical School," *American Sociological Review* 23 (February 1958): 50–56.

In a more recent, and somewhat puzzling essay, Shils appears to take the position that the various disciplines in the social sciences can be trusted, however, to pursue important truth. Shils feels that the imposition of the federally required controls, as these have been interpreted at the University of California at Berkeley, will serve to silence social scientists on their attempts to portray accurately the activities of the groups which they study. Our feeling is that the protection of the rights of human subjects must be taken into account while they are being studied, but that this does not *ipso facto* prevent research. See Edward Shils, "Muting the Social Sciences at Berkeley," *Minerva* 11 (July 1973): 290–95.

⁶² Galliher makes this point explicit: "A Code of Ethics for sociology is useful, if for no other reason than furtherance of public relations, since (sic) it keeps sociology professionally abreast of other social sciences including psychology and anthropology, which have such bodies of rules." Galliher, "The Protection of Human Subjects," p. 98, fn. 3. See also Eliot Freidson, "Political Organization and Professional Autonomy," in his *Profession of Medicine* (New York: Dodd, Mead and Co., 1970), pp. 23–46.

⁶³ Lewis A. Coser, personal interview with Joseph F. Jones.

[64] It might be noted in passing that among the other distinctions between the profession of medicine and the profession of sociology is that, within the former there is a much greater probability that the subject of the practitioner's ministrations will also be the client. In sociology, it is rare indeed that the client, that is, the individual who is paying the bill, will be the same person as the subject, that is, the individual who is being subjected to sociological scrutiny. Some might also take the view that sociology differs from medicine in that sociology does little of lasting importance. That is, medical experiments frequently involve the danger of undesirable side effects, including death, whereas sociological experimentation is not this serious.

But the issue of the long-term effects of sociological experimentation may be open to empirical question. Consider, for example, the line of research represented by James Walters, Ruth Connor and Michael Zunich, "Interaction of Mothers and Children from Lower-Class Families," *Child Development* 35 (June 1964): 433–40. These researchers misled lower-class mothers about their child's constructiveness, imagination, and maturity so that they could see how the knowledge that the child did not do well in a test of these items would affect the mother's interaction with the child. One of their conclusions was that mothers are indeed sensitive to the criticism of experts. (p. 439) Now it is true that the research could not have been done if the mothers had been told that the interest was in the behavior of the mother, not in the performance of the child. Yet nowhere in the report is there any indication that the mothers were later informed of the true purpose of the research, and there is increasing evidence that expectations of authority figures are a crucial element in the performance of children, at least in school. (See, *inter alia,* Ray C. Rist, "Student Social Class and Teacher Expectations: The Self-Fulfilling Prophecy in Ghetto Education," *Harvard Educational Review* 40 (August 1970): 411–51.) How can we know that there is no long-term effect from the laboratory setting?

Another example of research in which disclosure is not reported, but which seems to us to have had the potential of long-term effects is the research by Garfinkel, in which college students were misled into thinking that they were getting counseling on matters of importance to them such as interfaith dating, when in fact the "counseling" was a random series of yes and no responses to questions. Harold Garfinkel, "Common-Sense Knowledge of Social Structures: The Documentary Method of Interpretation" in Jordan M. Scher, ed., *Theories of the Mind* (New York: Free Press of Glencoe, 1963), pp. 689–712. Contrast these with the report of Milgram, *Obedience to Authority,* of disclosure of the nature of research and of a year long follow-up with counseling to ensure that the subjects were not suffering long-term effects from the experimental task.

[65] Oscar M. Ruebhausen and Orville G. Brim, Jr., "Privacy and Behavioral Research," *Columbia Law Review* 65 (November 1965): 1184–1211.

[66] Ibid., p. 1201.

[67] Ibid., p. 1204.

[68] Ibid., p. 1205.

[69] Ibid., p. 1210. Note that the inclusion of outsiders on such a review board is advocated by Barber *et al., Research on Human Subjects,* pp. 194–96. The Governing Council of the American Public Health Association adopted in 1972 a policy resolution calling not only for outsiders to sit on review committees in prisons and other institutions with captive populations, but also for the inclusion of members of the captive populations.

[70] Eugene J. Webb, Donald T. Campbell, Richard D. Schwartz, and Lee Sechrest, *Unobtrusive Measures: Nonreactive Research in the Social Sciences* (Chicago: Rand McNally & Co., 1966).

[71] Ibid., p. v.

[72] Ibid., p. 130.

[73] Ibid., p. 150.

[74] Ibid., pp. 177–78. The authors label this anecdote "amusing." We wonder if they would find the Watergate affair equally amusing.

[75] Theodore M. Mills, "The Observer, the Experimenter and the Group," *Social Problems* 14 (Summer 1966): 373–81. For an example of intended beneficial intervention, consider Dumont's distributing vitamin pills to "down-and-outers" after he had studied them from a disguised role. Matthew P. Dumont, "Tavern Culture: Sustenance of Homeless Men," *American Journal of Orthopsychiatry* 37 (October 1967): 638–45.

[76] Kai T. Erikson, "A Comment on Disguised Observation in Sociology," *Social Problems* 14 (Spring 1967): 366–73. Erikson also distinguishes between "personal morality" and "professional ethics" and restricts himself to the latter.

[77] Mills, "The Observer, the Experimenter and the Group," p. 375.

[78] John F. Lofland and Robert A. Lejune, "Initial Interaction of Newcomers in Alcoholics Anonymous: A Field Experiment in Class Symbols and Socialization," *Social Problems* 7 (Fall 1960): 102–11

[79] Fred Davis, "Comment on 'Initial Interactions of Newcomers in Alcoholics Anonymous,'" *Social Problems* 7 (Spring 1961): 364–65. Another example of research posing similar problems is Donald J. Black, "Production of Crime Rates," *American Sociological Review* 35 (August 1970): 733–48. Black stationed observers in police cars in Washington, D.C., Chicago, and Boston, telling the policemen that the observers were to note instances in which citizens engage in abusive responses to officers. But the observers actually accumulated evidence on abusive actions of policemen toward citizens. Black reports quite matter of factly: (p. 736) "In fact the officers were told that our research was not concerned with police behavior but only with citizen behavior toward the police and the kinds of problems citizens make for the police. Thus the study partially used systematic deception." Indeed, here is a case of sociologists practicing "entrapment" upon the police!

We do not take the hard line that deception of research subjects is never warranted, for there are some instances in which significant research topics could not be investigated without deceiving research subjects. But, we submit that the decision to practice deception should be taken only after careful thought and deliberation. Further, research subjects should have the matter of deception reported to them after the conclusion of the research, along with a full explanation of the need for such deception. Further, the subject ought to be given some opportunity to have data about him returned to him in the event that the researcher cannot convince him that he should cooperate in the research even after the program is finished. A final comment on the Black case is that not only is deception questionable in this case, it also would seem unnecessary. That is, other investigators have been able to gather data about misconduct among policemen, even when those persons were aware that their activities were being monitored by observers. See "Interrogation in New Haven," *Yale Law Journal* 76 (July 1967): 1521–1648.

[80] John Lofland, "Reply to Davis," *Social Problems* 7 (Spring 1961): 365–67.

[81] Erikson, "A Comment on Disguised Observation in Sociology."

[82] Ibid., p. 366.

[83] Ibid., p. 373.

[84] Ibid., p. 366.

[85] A classic example of manipulation through ostensible survey research is the research on income tax reporting done by Schwartz and Orleans. These investigators used two types of instruments, one containing "sanction" (read "punishment") oriented questions and one containing "conscience" questions to determine the effects of asking these kinds of questions on income tax reporting. The respondents, naturally, only knew that they had been interviewed. Richard D. Schwartz and Sonya Orleans, "On Legal Sanction," *University of Chicago Law Review* 34 (Winter 1967): 274–300.

[86] Laud Humphreys, *Tearoom Trade* (Chicago: Aldine Publishing Company, 1970).

[87] Laud Humphreys, "Impersonal Sex in Public Places," *Trans-action* 7 (January 1970): 8–25.

[88] Nicholas von Hoffman and Irving Louis Horowitz and Lee Rainwater, "Sociological Snoopers and Journalistic Moralizers," *Trans-action* 7 (May 1970): 4–8.

[89] von Hoffman, "Sociological Snoopers and Journalistic Moralizers," p. 6. While not completely endorsing von Hoffman's view, we would raise an additional question. "Is the information obtained necessary for advancing our understanding of public sex?" Some of the materials in *Tearoom Trade* seem of doubtful utility on this count.

[90] Horowitz and Rainwater, "Sociological Snoopers and Journalistic Moralizers," p. 7.

[91] Humphreys, *Tearoom Trade*, pp. 37–38. See Humphreys's postscript. "A Question of Ethics," Ibid., pp. 167–73, in which he attempts to deal with the points made by Erikson referred to *supra*. For one editor's view that these points

are successfully dealt with see George Ritzer, *Issues, Debates, and Controversies* (Boston: Allyn and Bacon, 1972), pp. 25–26.

Sanders approves Humphreys's observation of private behavior because: "Humphreys was not invading a private space, and that criterion alone justified his presence without announcing that he was a sociologist engaged in research" and "no one needs special permission to enter a public toilet as one would need for entering a private home." William B. Sanders, *The Sociologist as Detective: An Introduction to Research Methods* (New York: Praeger, 1974), pp. 10–11. This evaluation overlooks the fact that Humphreys did gain access to some of the persons whom he had observed by entering their homes in the guise of a survey researcher dealing with other matters.

[92] For a report by a concerned group of researchers who went to great lengths to protect their respondents (and who report a 92% completion rate on questionnaires and interviews dealing with such topics as drug use, radical politics and private sex lives) see Dean I. Manheimer, Glen D. Mellinger, Robert H. Somers and Marianne T. Klemon, "Technical and Ethical Considerations in Data Collection," *Drug Forum* 1 (July 1972): 323–33.

[93] William J. Chambliss, "Vice, Corruption, Bureaucracy, and Power," *Wisconsin Law Review* (1971): 1150–73.

[94] Still another course would be to allow the social science researcher a privileged status with his respondents, on the order of the relationship which is allowed attorneys and their clients. We do not believe that this alternative will be taken in the very near future, nor are we necessarily convinced that this is the best one. For a discussion of the issue see Samuel Hendel and Robert Bard, "Should There be a Researcher's Privilege?" *American Association of University Professors Bulletin* 59 (Winter 1973): 398–401. For a general discussion of the problems involved in disguising the identities of research sites, see Don C. Gibbons, "Unidentified Research Sites and Fictitious Names," *The American Sociologist,* in press.

index

NAME INDEX

Sundstrom, Eric, 178, 179
Sussman, Marvin B., 59, 137, 179
Sutherland, Edwin H., 21, 22, 26, 33, 38, 98, 99, 107, 123, 134, 137
Sykes, Gresham M., 107, 122, 136
Szasz, Thomas S., 160, 161, 170, 177, 181
Szymanski, Albert, 11

Tannenbaum, Frank, 139, 150, 174
Tappan, Paul W., 174
Taylor, Ian, 10, 99, 108, 109, 138, 140
Thio, Alex, 7, 8, 9, 10, 97, 105, 107
Thornberry, Terence P., 63
Thorsell, Bernard A., 146, 172, 173
Tiryakian, Edward A., 24, 107, 110, 137, 173
Tittle, Charles R., 152, 174
Toffler, Alvin, 104
Trice, Harrison M., 167, 169, 180
Turk, Austin, 99, 108
Turner, Roy, 73, 106
Tyroler, Herman A., 38

Van Arsdol, Maurice D., Jr., 17, 25
Varni, Charles A., 193, 206
Vaughn, Ted R., 202

Veroff, Joseph, 70, 79
Vinter, Robert D., 154, 175
Vold, George B., 99, 108, 119, 135
Volks, Holger, 78
von Hoffman, Nicholas, 199, 210

Waldo, Gordon P., 152, 174, 175
Waldorf, Dan, 181
Walker, Darlene, 78
Walters, James, 208
Walton, Paul, 10, 99, 108, 109, 138, 140
Wanner, Eric, 180
Ward, David A., 176
Ward, Sally K., 77
Warner, Malcolm, 205
Warren, Samuel D., 204
Weaver, James, 109
Webb, Eugene J., 196, 209
Weber, Max, 93
Wegner, Dennis L., 161, 178
Weil, Robert J., 19, 26
Weinberg, Martin S., 138, 180
Weinberg, S. Kirson, 25
Werle, Raymund, 78
Wertz, Richard W., 205
Westley, William A., 139

Wheeler, Stanton, 39, 46, 55, 60, 63, 156, 157, 176, 191, 205
Whitehead, P. C., 78
Wilbur, Cornelia B., 180
Willhelm, Sidney, 189, 204
Williams, Colin J., 180
Williams, Oliver, 78
Williams, Preston, 206
Williams, Robin M., Jr., 58, 59, 63
Wilner, Daniel, 176
Wilson, Thomas P., 177
Winograd, Barry, 140
Winslow, Robert W., 141
Winslow, Virginia, 141
Wiseman, Jacqueline P., 167, 180
Witmer, Helen L., 105
Wolfgang, Marvin E., 176
Woodward, Julian L., 70, 79

Yablonsky, Lewis, 140
Yarrow, Marian Radke, 161, 178
Young, Jock, 10, 99, 108, 109, 138, 140

Zimbardo, Phillip G., 202
Zimring, Franklin E., 151, 174
Zuckerman, Harriet, 105
Zunich, Michael, 208